PRINCIPLES AND PRACTICE OF MANAGEMENT

Dr. Akansha Deshmuksh

TANEESHA PUBLISHING

ISBN : 9788169244527
Edition : First, June 2026
Title : Principles and Practice of Management
Author : Dr. Akansha Deshmukh

Published by

TANEESHA PUBLISHING

An Imprint of **Taneesha and Prachi NextGen Publication**

Plot No. 48, Khasra No. 646, Road No. 2,
Suman Nagar, Haridwar - 249402, Uttarakhand (India)
Website : www.taneeshapublishing.com
E-mail : support@tpnextpub.com
Phone : 01334-388862

Printed by :
Techshresta Solutions Private Limited
Hebbal Kempapura, Bangalore, Karnataka - 560024, India

PREFACE

Management is a discipline that touches every part of modern life. From the smallest kirana shop to the largest multinational company, from the village panchayat to the Government of India, from a single-doctor clinic to a thousand-bed hospital, the principles of management are at work everywhere. Whoever wishes to play a meaningful role in the economic and social life of the country—as a businessman, a professional, a government servant, a teacher or a social worker—cannot afford to be ignorant of the subject.

No book of this size can be the work of one person alone. I have drawn freely from the writings of the great teachers of management—F.W. Taylor, Henri Fayol, Elton Mayo, Peter Drucker, Abraham Maslow, Frederick Herzberg, Douglas McGregor, Henry Mintzberg, Michael Porter, Philip Kotler and many others.

I have learnt much from the well-known Indian textbooks of L.M. Prasad, P.C. Tripathi, R.D. Agrawal, T.N. Chhabra, Y.K. Bhushan, V.S.P. Rao, C.B. Gupta and others, whose works have shaped the teaching of management in our country for several decades. Wherever a particular idea has been drawn from a specific source, the source has been acknowledged in the text. My debt to the larger community of management writers, however, goes far beyond what can be acknowledged in any list.

I am only too aware that even after all the care that has gone into its preparation, this book is likely to contain errors, both of fact and of judgement, and that there will be many places where the explanation could be made clearer or the example more apt. Suggestions and corrections from readers—students, teachers and managers alike—will be most welcome and will be taken into account in any future edition. The book has been written with affection for the subject and with respect for the readers; if it succeeds in lighting even a small lamp of understanding in the minds of those who use it, the labour of writing it will have been amply rewarded.

Dr. Akansha Deshmuksh

Indore
2026

PREFACE

Management is a discipline that touches every part of modern life. From the smallest kirana shop to the largest multinational company, from the village panchayat to the Government of India, from a single-doctor clinic to a thousand-bed hospital, the principles of management are at work everywhere. Whoever wishes to play a meaningful role in the economic and social life of the country—as a businessman, a professional, a government servant, a teacher or a social worker—cannot afford to be ignorant of the subject.

No book of this size can be the work of one person alone. I have drawn freely from the writings of the great teachers of management—F.W. Taylor, Henri Fayol, Elton Mayo, Peter Drucker, Abraham Maslow, Frederick Herzberg, Douglas McGregor, Henry Mintzberg, Michael Porter, Philip Kotler and many others.

I have learnt much from the well-known Indian textbooks of L.M. Prasad, P.C. Tripathi, R.D. Agrawal, T.N. Chhabra, Y.K. Bhushan, V.S.P. Rao, C.B. Gupta and others, whose works have shaped the teaching of management in our country for several decades. Wherever a particular idea has been drawn from a specific source, the source has been acknowledged in the text. My debt to the larger community of management writers, however, goes far beyond what can be acknowledged in any list.

I am only too aware that even after all the care that has gone into its preparation, this book is likely to contain errors, both of fact and of judgement, and that there will be many places where the explanation could be made clearer or the example more apt. Suggestions and corrections from readers—students, teachers and managers alike—will be most welcome and will be taken into account in any future edition. The book has been written with affection for the subject and with respect for the readers; if it succeeds in lighting even a small lamp of understanding in the minds of those who use it, the labour of writing it will have been amply rewarded.

Dr. Akansha Deshmuksh

Indore
2026

CONTENTS

CHAPTER 1

INTRODUCTION TO MANAGEMENT

Learning Objectives

After studying this chapter, the reader should be able to:

- understand the meaning and definition of management;
- explain the nature and characteristics of management;
- discuss whether management is a science, an art or a profession;
- differentiate between management and administration;
- identify the levels of management and the functions performed at each level; and
- appreciate the importance and scope of management in modern business.

Introduction

Management is as old as human civilization. From the construction of the Pyramids of Egypt and the Great Wall of China to the planning of the Indus Valley cities of Harappa and Mohenjo-daro, every collective human effort has required some form of management. In the family, in the village panchayat, in religious institutions and in the running of ancient kingdoms, the principles of management have always been at work, even though they were not called by that name.

In the modern industrial age, however, management has emerged as a distinct discipline and as a recognised field of study. With the growth of large business houses, the complexity of business operations has increased manifold. A small shopkeeper may manage his shop with the help of his family members, but running a company like Tata Steel, Reliance Industries or Infosys requires the coordinated effort of thousands of employees spread across the country and even across continents. Such large-scale activity is not possible without systematic management.

Management is the lifeblood of every organisation. Whether it is a business firm, a government department, a hospital, a school, a cooperative society or a non-profit organisation, the efficiency and success of the organisation depend largely upon the quality of its management. It is rightly said that there are no underdeveloped countries, only undermanaged ones. The progress of nations like Japan, South Korea, Germany and Singapore is, to a great extent, the result of the effective management of their resources.

This chapter introduces the reader to the basic concept of management. It explains the meaning, nature and characteristics of management, examines whether management is a science or an art, distinguishes management from administration, describes the various levels of management, and finally throws light on the importance and scope of this important discipline.

1.1 Meaning and Definition of Management

The word "management" has been derived from the Italian word "maneggiare", which means "to handle", particularly the handling of horses. It is also said to have come from the Latin word "manus", meaning "hand". In the French language, the word "ménagement" was used to convey the art of directing and guiding. Over time, the meaning of the word has widened. Today, management refers to the process of getting things done through and with the people of an organisation in an effective and efficient manner.

In simple words, management may be defined as the process of planning, organising, staffing, directing and controlling the human and other resources of an enterprise for the purpose of achieving the predetermined objectives.

Different scholars have defined management in different ways. Some of the leading definitions are given below:

1. Henri Fayol— "To manage is to forecast and plan, to organise, to command, to coordinate and to control."

2. F.W. Taylor— "Management is the art of knowing what you want to do and then seeing that it is done in the best and the cheapest way."

3. Peter F. Drucker— "Management is a multipurpose organ that manages a business and manages managers, and manages workers and work."

4. Harold Koontz— "Management is the art of getting things done through and with people in formally organised groups."

5. Mary Parker Follett— "Management is the art of getting things done through people."

6. George R. Terry— "Management is a distinct process consisting of planning, organising, actuating and controlling, performed to determine and accomplish stated objectives by the use of human beings and other resources."

7. Louis A. Allen— "Management is what a manager does."

A careful study of these definitions reveals that management is a goal-oriented process which involves the use of human and material resources, requires the application of certain functions, and aims at the achievement of organisational objectives in the most effective and efficient manner.

Two terms occur repeatedly in the study of management and must be clearly understood. Effectiveness refers to doing the right things, that is, achieving the desired results. Efficiency, on the other hand, refers to doing things in the right manner, that is, achieving the maximum output with the minimum input. A good manager strives for both effectiveness and efficiency in his work.

1.2 Characteristics and Nature of Management

The nature of management can be understood from the following characteristics:

1. Goal-Oriented Process. Management is always aimed at the achievement of certain pre-determined goals. Without a goal, the management process becomes meaningless. For example, in a manufacturing company like Maruti Suzuki, every department works towards the common goal of producing quality cars at a reasonable price.

2. Pervasive Activity. Management is required in every type of organisation, whether it is small or big, profit-seeking or non-profit, business or non-business. From a small kirana shop to a multinational company, from a primary school to a university, from a temple committee to a hospital, management is present everywhere. It is needed at all levels and in all functional areas.

3. Continuous Process. Management is not a one-time activity. It is a never-ending process. So long as the organisation continues to exist, the process of planning, organising, staffing, directing and controlling goes on without interruption. The cycle keeps repeating itself.

4. Multi-dimensional in Nature. Management does not deal only with people or only with work. It is concerned with the management of work, the management of people and the management of operations together. All three dimensions are equally important.

5. Group Activity. Management is a social process which is performed in a group situation. A single individual working in isolation cannot be said to be performing management. It involves the co-ordinated efforts of a number of persons working together towards a common purpose.

6. Dynamic Function. Management is not static. It must change with the changing environment. New technologies, changing customer preferences, government policies, competition and global trends all require management to adapt itself constantly. For example, the rise of e-commerce has forced traditional retailers in India to rethink their business strategies altogether.

7. Intangible Force. Management cannot be seen with the naked eye, but its presence is felt through the results it produces. A well-managed organisation runs smoothly, achieves its targets and earns the goodwill of customers and employees. A poorly managed organisation, on the other hand, faces losses, disputes and decline.

8. Both Science and Art. Management has the features of both a science and an art. It is based on certain principles and theories, and at the same time it requires personal skill and creativity in their application.

9. Universal Application. The basic principles of management are applicable to all types of organisations and at all levels. The principles laid down by Henri Fayol nearly a hundred years ago are still relevant today, though their application may differ from situation to situation.

10. Distinct Activity. Management is a separate and distinct activity. It is different from the operative work of the organisation. A foreman who himself works at the lathe is not performing management; but a foreman who plans the work, assigns it to others, supervises and controls them is performing management.

1.3 Management as Science, Art and Profession

1.3.1 Is Management a Science?

A science is an organised body of knowledge which is based on observation, experiment and verification. It contains principles which have been tested and proved. Let us examine whether management possesses these features.

Management has a systematic body of knowledge. Books, journals and research studies have built up a vast literature on the subject. There are well-developed principles, theories and concepts in the areas of planning, organising, motivation, leadership and control. The principles of management can be taught and learnt, and they are also based on observation and experience.

However, management is not an exact science like physics, chemistry or mathematics. In the physical sciences, if water is heated to 100 degrees Celsius at sea level, it will always boil. But in management, the same principle does not always give the same result. The reason is that management deals with human beings, whose behaviour cannot be predicted with absolute certainty. The same motivational technique that works on one employee may not work on another.

For this reason, management is described as a social science or a behavioural science. It is also called an "inexact science" or a "soft science."

1.3.2 Is Management an Art?

An art is the personal skill of applying knowledge to achieve desired results. It is based on practice and personal experience. The greater the practice, the greater is the skill.

Management is certainly an art. It involves the application of theoretical knowledge to practical situations. Two managers may have the same degree from the same business school, but their performance in the field may differ widely. This difference arises out of their personal skills, creativity, judgement and experience. The famous industrialists of India such as J.R.D. Tata, Dhirubhai Ambani, Narayana Murthy and

Azim Premji are admired not only for what they knew but for how they applied their knowledge in practice.

Thus, management is both a science and an art. It is a science because it has an organised body of knowledge, and it is an art because that knowledge has to be applied with personal skill. The science part can be taught in the classroom; the art part is developed only through practice in real situations.

1.3.3 Is Management a Profession?

A profession is an occupation which is based on specialised knowledge, requires formal education and training, follows a code of conduct, has a recognised professional body, and renders service to society.

In modern times, management has acquired most of the features of a profession. The following points support this view:

- It has a well-developed body of knowledge.
- Formal education in management is imparted by institutions such as the Indian Institutes of Management (IIMs), XLRI, FMS, NMIMS and many universities all over the country.
- Professional bodies such as the All India Management Association (AIMA) have been established at the national level.
- A code of conduct for managers is gradually taking shape.
- Management exists to serve society by providing goods and services, generating employment and contributing to economic growth.

However, unlike doctors and chartered accountants, it is not compulsory for a manager to possess a formal management degree. Many successful businessmen in India have built large enterprises without any formal management qualification. Therefore, management cannot yet be called a fully developed profession in the strict sense, but it is moving steadily in that direction.

1.4 Management versus Administration

Therc has been a long-standing debate among scholars about the relationship between management and administration. The various views may be grouped into three categories.

1.4.1 Administration is Higher than Management

This view was put forward by Oliver Sheldon, William Spriegel, Milward and others. According to them, administration is a higher-level activity which determines the broad policies and objectives of the enterprise, while management is concerned with the actual execution of these policies. In this sense, administration is a thinking function and management is a doing function. The owners and the Board of Directors perform administration, whereas the executives and managers perform management.

1.4.2 Management is Higher than Administration

This view is supported by Kimball and Kimball, Richman and others. According to them, management is the wider term and administration is a part of management. Administration is concerned mainly with routine office work, record-keeping and clerical activities, which are done under the overall direction of management.

1.4.3 Management and Administration are the Same

This view, supported by Henri Fayol, William Newman, Peter Drucker, George R. Terry and others, treats management and administration as one and the same thing. According to them, there is no real distinction between the two. The functions of planning, organising, directing and controlling are the same whether they are performed in a business enterprise or in a government department. Only the names differ. In business, we call it management; in government, we call it administration.

In actual practice, the modern tendency is to use the two terms interchangeably. The functions performed are the same; only the context may differ. The traditional distinction between the two, however, may be presented as follows:

Basis of Difference	Administration	Management
Nature of Work	It is a thinking function. It decides what is to be done and	It is a doing function. It puts the plans into action and gets the work

Basis of Difference	Administration	Management
	when.	done.
Scope	Takes major decisions affecting the entire enterprise.	Takes decisions within the framework laid down by administration.
Level	Top-level activity.	Middle and lower-level activity.
Skills Required	Conceptual and human skills.	Technical and human skills.
Influencing Factors	Influenced mainly by external factors such as public opinion, government policy, etc.	Influenced mainly by internal factors such as the values and policies of administrators.
Usage	Generally used in government, military and educational institutions.	Generally used in business enterprises.

1.5 Levels of Management

In every organisation, except the very small ones, the work of management is divided among different levels. The number of levels depends upon the size of the organisation, but generally three levels are recognised—top management, middle management, and lower or supervisory management. These three levels together form what is known as the managerial hierarchy or the management pyramid.

1.5.1 Top-Level Management

The top level consists of the Board of Directors, the Chairman, the Managing Director, the Chief Executive Officer (CEO), the General Manager and other top executives. It is the highest level of management and is responsible for the overall functioning of the enterprise.

The main functions of top management are as follows:

- to determine the objectives, policies and broad plans of the organisation;
- to organise the activities and resources of the enterprise;
- to appoint the executives for middle-level positions;
- to provide overall direction and leadership;
- to maintain contact with the outside world, including the government, shareholders and the general public; and
- to be responsible for the welfare and survival of the organisation as a whole.

The top management requires conceptual skills more than technical skills, because it has to take long-term and policy decisions affecting the entire organisation.

1.5.2 Middle-Level Management

This level lies between the top management and the lower management. It includes departmental heads such as the Production Manager, Sales Manager, Finance Manager, Personnel Manager and so on. In large organisations, there may be more than one layer of middle management.

The main functions of middle management are as follows:

- to interpret and implement the policies framed by the top management;
- to prepare departmental plans and targets within the broad framework of organisational goals;
- to assign duties and responsibilities to the subordinates;
- to co-ordinate the activities of different sections of the department;
- to motivate the employees for better performance; and
- to act as a bridge between the top and the lower management.

The middle managers require a balance of conceptual, human and technical skills.

1.5.3 Lower or Supervisory Management

This is the lowest level of management. It consists of foremen, supervisors, section officers, superintendents, inspectors and similar persons. They are in direct contact with the workers and are responsible for getting the actual work done.

The main functions of the supervisory management are as follows:

- to plan the day-to-day activities at the operational level;
- to assign jobs to the workers;
- to supervise and guide them in their work;
- to maintain discipline and good working conditions;
- to check the quality and quantity of output;
- to send regular reports to the middle management; and
- to redress the grievances of the workers.

The supervisory management requires more of technical and human skills than conceptual skills. The three levels of management together resemble a pyramid, with the top management at the apex, the middle management in the middle, and the supervisory management at the base. As we move from the bottom to the top, the number of personnel decreases but the responsibility goes on increasing.

1.6 Importance and Scope of Management

1.6.1 Importance of Management

Management plays a key role in the success and growth of every organisation, as well as in the development of a nation. Its importance can be appreciated from the following points:

1. Achievement of Goals. Management helps the organisation to achieve its objectives by making the best use of its resources. It directs the efforts of the individuals towards a common purpose.

2. Optimum Utilisation of Resources. Resources such as men, money, materials, machines and information are limited. Management ensures that these scarce resources are used in the most efficient manner so that there is the minimum wastage and the maximum output.

3. Effective Leadership and Motivation. Management provides leadership to the workers and motivates them to give their best. A motivated and well-led workforce is the greatest asset of any organisation.

4. Sound Industrial Relations. Good management establishes a healthy relationship between the employer and the employees. It reduces industrial disputes and creates a peaceful work atmosphere.

5. Adaptation to Change. The business environment is constantly changing. Management equips the organisation to face changes in technology, market conditions, government policies and consumer preferences.

6. Reduction in Cost. Through proper planning and control, management helps to reduce the cost of production and increase the profitability of the firm.

7. Expansion and Growth. Successful management makes possible the expansion and diversification of business. The growth of companies like Reliance Industries, the Tata Group, the Aditya Birla Group and Infosys is the direct result of good management.

8. Development of Society. Management does not benefit only the owners of the business. It benefits the workers through better wages and working conditions, the customers through better goods and services, the government through taxes, and the society through employment and economic progress.

9. National Development. It has been rightly observed by Peter Drucker that management is the crucial factor in economic and social development. The progress of any country depends largely on the quality of management of its industries, agriculture and public services.

1.6.2 Scope of Management

The scope of management is very wide. It covers all the activities that are necessary for the running of an enterprise. The major functional areas under the scope of management are as follows:

1. Production Management. It deals with the planning, organising and control of production activities, including selection of plant location, plant layout, quality control, inventory control and production scheduling.

2. Marketing Management. It is concerned with the identification of customer needs and the activities of product development, pricing, promotion and distribution.

3. Financial Management. It deals with the planning, raising and utilisation of funds, capital budgeting, dividend policy and financial control.

4. Personnel or Human Resource Management. It is concerned with the management of people in the organisation—manpower planning, recruitment, training, performance appraisal, wage administration and industrial relations.

5. Office Management. It deals with planning, organising and controlling the office work, including record-keeping, correspondence and office communication.

6. Other Areas. In modern organisations, the scope of management has further extended to areas such as research and development management, information technology management, materials management, project management and environmental management.

Thus, management is not confined to any one area. It is a multi-dimensional activity covering all aspects of organisational life.

Summary

Management is the process of planning, organising, staffing, directing and controlling the resources of an enterprise for the achievement of its objectives. It is a goal-oriented, continuous, pervasive and dynamic activity, performed in a group situation through human and material resources. Management has the features of both a science and an art, and is gradually emerging as a profession.

The terms management and administration are sometimes used in different senses, but in modern practice they are treated as interchangeable. The work of management is performed at three levels—top, middle and lower—each having its own set of functions and responsibilities.

The importance of management lies in the fact that it helps in achieving organisational goals, ensures the optimum use of resources, provides effective leadership, maintains good industrial relations and contributes to the development of society and the nation. The scope of management is very wide and covers all the functional areas of an enterprise such as production, marketing, finance and personnel.

Key Terms

Management, Administration, Effectiveness, Efficiency, Top Management, Middle Management, Supervisory Management, Levels of

Management, Science, Art, Profession, Henri Fayol, F.W. Taylor, Peter Drucker, All India Management Association (AIMA).

Review Questions

A. Short Answer Questions (2 marks each)

1. Define management in your own words.
2. State any four characteristics of management.
3. What is meant by efficiency and effectiveness?
4. Name the three levels of management.
5. Give two arguments to show that management is an art.

B. Long Answer Questions (10 marks each)

6. Discuss the meaning, nature and characteristics of management.
7. "Management is both a science and an art." Examine this statement.
8. Distinguish between management and administration.
9. Describe the various levels of management along with their functions.
10. Explain the importance and scope of management in modern business.

C. Practical / Case-Based Questions

11. Visit any small or medium business in your locality. Identify the levels of management present in it and the activities performed at each level. Prepare a short report.
12. Take the example of any successful Indian company (such as Tata Motors, Infosys, ITC or Hindustan Unilever) and discuss how good management has contributed to its growth.

CHAPTER 2

EVOLUTION OF MANAGEMENT THOUGHT

Learning Objectives

After studying this chapter, the reader should be able to:

- trace the historical development of management thought;
- explain the contributions of the early pioneers of management;
- understand the principles and techniques of scientific management given by F.W. Taylor;
- discuss the fourteen principles of management laid down by Henri Fayol;
- describe the Hawthorne experiments and the human relations approach;
- outline the modern approaches to management; and
- appreciate the contributions of Peter Drucker and Indian management thinkers.

Introduction

Management, as a subject of study and as a recognised discipline, has a comparatively short history. The systematic thinking on management began only towards the end of the nineteenth century, when the Industrial Revolution had brought about a great change in the methods of production. However, the practice of management is as old as human society itself. The Egyptian Pyramids, the Roman Empire, the Great Wall of China and the temple cities of ancient India bear witness to the fact that even our ancestors knew how to plan, organise and control large-scale activities.

The Industrial Revolution, which began in England around the middle of the eighteenth century, marked a turning point. The use of steam power, the introduction of machinery and the rise of the factory system completely changed the way in which goods were produced. Small workshops and cottage industries gave way to large factories employing hundreds and thousands of workers. The problems of managing such large units could not be solved by tradition and common sense alone. There arose a need for a systematic approach to management, and it is out of this need that the modern theory of management has grown.

The growth of management thought may be studied under five broad phases—the pre-scientific management era, the scientific management movement led by F.W. Taylor, the administrative management theory of Henri Fayol, the human relations and behavioural approach, and finally the modern approaches such as the systems, contingency and quantitative approaches. The present chapter discusses each of these phases in turn and also throws light on the contribution of Peter Drucker and of some of the leading thinkers from India.

2.1 Pre-Scientific Management Era

The period before the writings of F.W. Taylor is generally known as the pre-scientific management era. During this period, the factory owners had to find their own ways of dealing with the new problems thrown up by the Industrial Revolution. There was no formal body of management knowledge, and the methods used were largely based on trial and error. However, some thinkers of this period did try to put down their ideas in writing and thus prepared the ground for the scientific management movement that was to follow. The most important of these pioneers were the following:

1. Robert Owen (1771–1858). A Welsh textile manufacturer, Robert Owen is often regarded as the father of personnel management. At his New Lanark mills in Scotland, he provided better working conditions, reduced the working hours, refused to employ children below the age of ten and even started a school for the children of his workers. He believed that money spent on the welfare of the workers was the best investment a businessman could make. His ideas were far ahead of his time.

2. Charles Babbage (1792–1871). An English mathematician and the inventor of the early mechanical computer, Charles Babbage wrote a book titled On the Economy of Machinery and Manufactures in 1832. He emphasised the use of science and mathematics in the factory, advocated the division of labour and stressed the need for cost reduction through the careful study of operations.

3. Henry Robinson Towne (1844–1924). An American engineer, he read a famous paper titled "The Engineer as Economist" before the American Society of Mechanical Engineers in 1886. In this paper he argued that the engineer must also be an economist and that management should be treated as a separate field of study. His paper greatly influenced F.W. Taylor.

4. Henry Metcalfe (1847–1917). A captain in the United States Army, Metcalfe wrote a book entitled The Cost of Manufactures in 1885. He developed a system of cost accounting and of shop control and is regarded as one of the pioneers of management accounting.

5. James Watt Jr. and Mathew Robinson Boulton. These two industrialists, who took charge of the Soho Engineering Foundry near Birmingham in the early nineteenth century, introduced a number of management practices that were far ahead of their times. These included production planning, standardisation of components, a system of cost accounts and welfare schemes for the workers.

The work of these early thinkers was not very systematic, but it brought to light certain important problems of factory management. The need for a more organised and scientific approach was felt strongly, and this need was fulfilled by the writings of F.W. Taylor.

2.2 F.W. Taylor and Scientific Management

Frederick Winslow Taylor (1856–1915), an American mechanical engineer, is rightly called the "Father of Scientific Management." He began his career as a labourer in the Midvale Steel Company in the United States and rose, by his hard work and intelligence, to the position of Chief Engineer. Later he worked at the Bethlehem Steel Company. His direct experience on the shop floor convinced him that there was tremendous wastage of effort and money in the factories of his time, mainly because the work was being done by rule of thumb rather than by a scientific method.

Taylor put forward his ideas in two well-known books—Shop Management (1903) and The Principles of Scientific Management

(1911). According to him, "Scientific management is knowing exactly what you want men to do and seeing that they do it in the best and the cheapest way."

2.2.1 Principles of Scientific Management

Taylor laid down the following principles of scientific management:

1. Science, Not Rule of Thumb. Every job in the factory should be performed by scientific methods rather than by guesswork or tradition. Each task should be studied carefully and the best method of doing it should be worked out.

2. Harmony, Not Discord. There should be complete harmony between the workers and the management. Both should realise that their interests are the same and that they cannot prosper without the other.

3. Co-operation, Not Individualism. The workers and the management should work together as a team for the welfare of the enterprise. Each should help the other, and both should share the gains of increased production.

4. Maximum, Not Restricted Output. Both the workers and the management should aim at the maximum possible output. Restricted output, whether due to soldiering by workers or short-sightedness of management, is harmful to all.

5. Development of Each Person to Greatest Efficiency. Every worker should be scientifically selected, trained and developed so that he may give the best of which he is capable. This will benefit both the workers and the enterprise.

2.2.2 Techniques of Scientific Management

To put his principles into practice, Taylor suggested a number of techniques. The important ones among these are as follows:

1. Functional Foremanship. Taylor proposed that each worker should receive directions from eight different foremen, four for planning and four for execution—route clerk, instruction card clerk, time and cost clerk, disciplinarian, gang boss, speed boss, repair boss and inspector. Each foreman would be a specialist in his own area.

2. Standardisation and Simplification. The materials, tools, methods, working conditions and quality of work should all be standardised. The variety of products should be reduced so that production may be simplified.

3. Work Study. Each job should be studied scientifically to discover the best method of doing it. Work study includes time study (the time required for each operation), motion study (the movements of the worker), fatigue study (the rest pauses required) and method study (the procedure to be followed).

4. Differential Piece-Rate System. Taylor suggested two rates of wages—a higher rate for those who completed or exceeded the standard, and a lower rate for those who failed to do so. This was meant to encourage the efficient workers and to penalise the inefficient ones.

5. Scientific Selection and Training. Workers should be selected on the basis of their physical and mental fitness for the job and should then be trained scientifically.

6. Mental Revolution. Taylor laid the greatest emphasis on what he called "mental revolution"—a complete change of attitude on the part of both the workers and the management. They must give up the old feeling of conflict and adopt the new spirit of co-operation.

2.2.3 Other Contributors to Scientific Management

Several other thinkers contributed to the scientific management movement. Henry Lawrence Gantt (1861–1919), a close associate of Taylor, developed the well-known Gantt chart for production scheduling and introduced the task and bonus system of wage payment. Frank Bunker Gilbreth (1868–1924) and his wife Lillian Moller Gilbreth (1878–1972) carried out pioneering work on motion study and developed the concept of "therbligs" (basic units of motion). Harrington Emerson (1853–1931) is remembered for his Twelve Principles of Efficiency.

2.2.4 Criticism of Scientific Management

In spite of its great contribution, scientific management has been criticised on several grounds. It treats the worker as a machine and ignores the human side of work. The over-specialisation that it brings about makes the job monotonous and dull. The differential wage system is considered unfair by the workers. The trade unions in many countries strongly opposed the introduction of scientific management because they feared that it would lead to retrenchment, speeding up of work and weakening of their bargaining power. In spite of these criticisms, however, the contribution of Taylor and his followers cannot be denied. They laid the foundation of modern management.

2.3 Henri Fayol and Administrative Theory

While F.W. Taylor was working on the problems of factory management in the United States, Henri Fayol (1841–1925), a French mining engineer, was developing his ideas on management in Europe. Fayol joined the Commentry-Fourchambault mining company at the age of nineteen and rose to become its Managing Director. He saved the company from financial ruin and, on his retirement in 1918, left it in a sound condition. His long experience as a top executive gave him a deep insight into the problems of management.

Fayol set down his ideas in a book titled Administration Industrielle et Générale, published in French in 1916. It was translated into English much later, in 1949, under the title General and Industrial Management. Because his approach to management was from the top downwards, Fayol is often called the "Father of Modern Management" or the "Father of Administrative Management."

2.3.1 Six Activities of an Industrial Undertaking

Fayol observed that the activities of an industrial undertaking could be divided into six groups, namely:

- Technical activities, including production and manufacture;
- Commercial activities, such as buying, selling and exchange;
- Financial activities, that is, the search for and the optimum use of capital;
- Security activities, relating to the protection of property and persons;
- Accounting activities, including stocktaking, balance sheet, cost and statistics; and
- Managerial activities, consisting of planning, organising, commanding, coordinating and controlling.

Of these six groups, Fayol considered the managerial activities to be the most important and devoted his book mainly to them.

2.3.2 The Fourteen Principles of Management

The most outstanding contribution of Henri Fayol is his statement of the fourteen principles of management. These principles, in his own words, are "flexible and capable of adaptation to every need." They are briefly explained below:

1. Division of Work. Work should be divided among the workers and the managers according to their specialisation. Division of work increases efficiency and skill.

2. Authority and Responsibility. Authority is the right to give orders and responsibility is the duty to perform. The two must always go together.

3. Discipline. Discipline means obedience, respect for authority and observance of established rules. Without discipline, no enterprise can prosper.

4. Unity of Command. Each employee should receive orders from one superior only. If one employee receives orders from two or more superiors, confusion and conflict are bound to arise.

5. Unity of Direction. All activities having the same objective should be directed by one manager using one plan. This ensures unity of action.

6. Subordination of Individual Interest to General Interest. The interest of the organisation as a whole should always come before the interest of any individual or group of individuals.

7. Remuneration. The wages and other payments to the employees should be fair and reasonable. They should give satisfaction both to the employees and to the employer.

8. Centralisation. The degree of centralisation or decentralisation of authority depends upon the circumstances of each case. The aim should be the best use of all the personnel.

9. Scalar Chain. There should be a clear line of authority from the top to the bottom of the organisation. All communication should normally pass through this chain. However, in cases of urgency, two persons at the same level may communicate directly with each other by what Fayol called the "gang plank."

10. Order. There should be a place for everything and everything should be in its place. This applies both to materials (material order) and to people (social order).

11. Equity. The managers should deal with the subordinates in a kind and just manner. Equity is a combination of justice and kindness.

12. Stability of Tenure of Personnel. Frequent change of employees is harmful to the organisation. The employees should be given a reasonable period to settle down and to learn their work.

13. Initiative. The subordinates should be encouraged to take initiative in their work. A manager who is able to draw out the initiative of his subordinates is far superior to one who does not.

14. Esprit de Corps. This French phrase means team spirit. The manager should promote a feeling of belongingness and unity among his employees. "Union is strength," as Fayol himself put it.

2.3.3 Taylor and Fayol—A Comparison

Both Taylor and Fayol are regarded as the pioneers of modern management thought. However, there are some important differences between their approaches. The main points of difference are given in the following table:

Basis	**F.W. Taylor**	**Henri Fayol**
Approach	Bottom-upwards; starting from the shop floor.	Top-downwards; starting from the top management.
Focus	Increasing the efficiency of the workers.	Improving the efficiency of the managers.
Name of Theory	Scientific Management.	Administrative or Process Management.
Major Contribution	Techniques such as work study, standardisation and differential piece rate.	Fourteen principles and the five functions of management.

Basis	F.W. Taylor	Henri Fayol
Title	Father of Scientific Management.	Father of Modern (or Administrative) Management.

2.4 Hawthorne Experiments and the Human Relations Approach

In the years between 1924 and 1932, a series of experiments was carried out at the Hawthorne plant of the Western Electric Company at Cicero, near Chicago. These experiments are known as the Hawthorne studies. They were led by Professor Elton Mayo (1880–1949) of the Harvard Business School, along with his colleagues F.J. Roethlisberger and W.J. Dickson. The studies were originally meant to find out the effect of physical working conditions on the productivity of the workers, but they ended in opening up a new line of thinking on management. The Hawthorne studies are generally regarded as the starting point of the human relations approach to management.

The Hawthorne studies were conducted in four main phases:

1. The Illumination Experiments (1924–1927). The researchers tried to study the effect of changes in lighting on the productivity of the workers. To their surprise, productivity went up not only when the lighting was improved but also when it was reduced. This showed that something other than physical conditions was at work.

2. The Relay Assembly Test Room Experiments (1927–1928). A small group of women workers was placed in a separate test room. Changes were made in the working hours, rest pauses and methods of payment. The output of the group went on increasing irrespective of the changes. It was concluded that the workers responded mainly to the special attention given to them and to the feeling of being part of an important experiment.

3. The Mass Interviewing Programme (1928–1930). About twenty-one thousand employees were interviewed to find out their feelings about their supervisors and working conditions. The interviews showed that the workers had many problems and grievances which had nothing to do with the physical conditions of work.

4. The Bank Wiring Observation Room Experiment (1931–1932). A group of fourteen male workers engaged in wiring telephone equipment was observed for several months. It was found that the group had developed its own informal norms of output and that workers who produced more or less than the group norm were punished by the others. This brought to light the importance of informal groups at the workplace.

2.4.1 Main Findings of the Hawthorne Studies

The Hawthorne studies established the following important truths about industrial life:

- The worker is not merely an economic being; he is a social being with feelings, sentiments and emotions.
- Productivity is influenced not only by physical and economic factors but also by social and psychological factors.
- Informal groups exist in every workplace and they have a powerful influence on the behaviour of their members.
- The attitude of the supervisor and the style of supervision have a great impact on the morale and the output of the workers.
- Effective communication and worker participation are essential for high productivity.
- Non-monetary incentives, such as recognition and a sense of belonging, are often more powerful than monetary incentives.

These conclusions led to the development of the human relations approach to management. Other notable contributors to this school of thought were Mary Parker Follett (1868–1933), who emphasised the dynamic nature of administration and the idea of "power with" rather than "power over" others, and Chester I. Barnard (1886–1961), who in his book The Functions of the Executive (1938) developed the acceptance theory of authority.

2.5 Modern Approaches to Management

After the Second World War, a number of new approaches to management came into being. The most important of these are discussed below.

2.5.1 The Behavioural Science Approach

The behavioural science approach is an extension of the human relations approach. It draws upon the findings of psychology, sociology and anthropology to study human behaviour in organisations. The leading writers of this school include Abraham Maslow (hierarchy of needs), Frederick Herzberg (two-factor theory), Douglas McGregor (Theory X and Theory Y), Rensis Likert (system 4 management) and Chris Argyris (maturity-immaturity theory). These thinkers placed great emphasis on the motivation, leadership and group behaviour of employees.

2.5.2 The Systems Approach

The systems approach, developed mainly during the 1950s and 1960s, looks upon an organisation as a system composed of a number of interrelated and interdependent parts. The leading contributors to this approach were Ludwig von Bertalanffy, Kenneth Boulding, Chester Barnard and Daniel Katz. The organisation is treated as an open system which takes inputs from the environment (materials, manpower, capital, information), transforms them into outputs (goods and services) and supplies the outputs back to the environment. Feedback from the environment helps the organisation in adjusting its working. The systems approach has helped managers in viewing the organisation as a whole rather than in isolated parts.

2.5.3 The Contingency or Situational Approach

The contingency approach, developed during the 1970s, rejects the idea that there is one best way of managing in all situations. Its central thesis is that the appropriate course of managerial action depends upon the situation. What works well in one situation may not work well in another. The leading writers of this school are Joan Woodward, Paul Lawrence, Jay Lorsch, Tom Burns and G.M. Stalker. The manager, according to this approach, must analyse each situation carefully and then choose the course of action best suited to it.

2.5.4 The Quantitative or Management Science Approach

This approach, also known as the operations research approach, makes use of mathematical models, statistical techniques and computers in solving managerial problems. It was developed during the Second

World War to deal with military problems and was later extended to industry and business. Techniques such as linear programming, queuing theory, decision theory, network analysis (PERT and CPM), inventory models and simulation are now widely used in areas such as production planning, inventory control, transportation and capital budgeting.

2.6 Peter Drucker and Indian Management Thinkers

2.6.1 Peter F. Drucker (1909–2005)

Peter Ferdinand Drucker, an Austrian-born American thinker, is widely regarded as the "Father of Modern Management." In a writing career spanning more than sixty years, he wrote about thirty-nine books on management, economics and society. His important works include The Practice of Management (1954), Managing for Results (1964), The Effective Executive (1966), Management: Tasks, Responsibilities, Practices (1973) and Innovation and Entrepreneurship (1985).

The main contributions of Peter Drucker to management thought are as follows:

- He gave the concept of Management by Objectives (MBO), under which the superior and the subordinate jointly set the goals and review the performance.
- He emphasised that management is a discipline and a practice and that it should be studied seriously.
- He brought into focus the role of the knowledge worker in the modern economy.
- He highlighted the importance of marketing and innovation as the two basic functions of a business.
- He was an early advocate of decentralisation and of the federal form of organisation.
- He stressed that a business has a responsibility to society and not merely to its shareholders.

2.6.2 Indian Management Thinkers and the Indian Tradition

India has a rich tradition of thinking on administration and management. Ancient Indian texts contain a vast amount of wisdom on the conduct of affairs of the state and of business. The Arthashastra of Kautilya (also known as Chanakya), written in the fourth century B.C., is one of the earliest works on public administration, finance and statecraft anywhere in the world. The Bhagavad Gita offers valuable lessons on leadership, decision-making, duty (karma) and self-control. The Tirukkural of Thiruvalluvar gives guidance on ethics in administration.

In modern times, India has produced a number of great industrialists and thinkers who have made valuable contributions to management practice. A few of them are briefly mentioned below:

- Jamsetji N. Tata (1839–1904) and J.R.D. Tata (1904–1993), who built the House of Tata on the principles of trusteeship and service to society.
- Sir M. Visvesvaraya (1861–1962), the great engineer-administrator who advocated planned industrial development for India.
- Verghese Kurien (1921–2012), the architect of Operation Flood and the father of the cooperative dairy movement in India through Amul.
- C.K. Prahalad (1941–2010), who gave the world the concepts of "core competence" and "the fortune at the bottom of the pyramid."
- N.R. Narayana Murthy (born 1946), the founder of Infosys, known for his emphasis on corporate governance and value-based leadership.
- Azim H. Premji (born 1945), the chairman of Wipro, known for his simplicity, ethics and philanthropic work.

These industrialists and thinkers have shown that the principles of modern management can be successfully blended with the Indian values of ethics, trusteeship and concern for society. This blend has come to be known as the Indian Ethos in Management and is being increasingly studied in business schools across the country.

Summary

The growth of management thought may be traced through several phases. The pre-scientific management era saw the early efforts of thinkers like Robert Owen, Charles Babbage, Henry Towne and Henry Metcalfe. F.W. Taylor, the Father of Scientific Management, gave a systematic theory based on the scientific study of work, with principles such as "science, not rule of thumb" and "harmony, not discord." Henri Fayol, working from the top management point of view, gave the five functions of management and the fourteen principles which still guide managers all over the world.

The Hawthorne experiments brought out the human side of work and gave rise to the human relations approach. The modern phase has seen the development of the behavioural, systems, contingency and quantitative approaches, each of which throws light on a different aspect of management. Peter Drucker, with his concept of Management by Objectives and his emphasis on the social responsibility of business, has greatly enriched modern management thought. India too has made important contributions, both through its ancient texts and through the work of its industrialists and thinkers in modern times.

Key Terms

Scientific Management, Administrative Management, Functional Foremanship, Differential Piece-Rate System, Mental Revolution, Fourteen Principles of Management, Scalar Chain, Esprit de Corps, Hawthorne Effect, Human Relations Approach, Informal Groups, Systems Approach, Contingency Approach, Management by Objectives (MBO), Arthashastra, Indian Ethos in Management.

Review Questions

A. Short Answer Questions (2 marks each)

1. Name any three pioneers of the pre-scientific management era.
2. Who is known as the Father of Scientific Management? Mention any two of his books.
3. What is meant by functional foremanship?
4. State the six activities of an industrial undertaking as given by Henri Fayol.
5. What is the Hawthorne effect?
6. Give any two contributions of Peter Drucker to management thought.

B. Long Answer Questions (10 marks each)

7. Discuss the principles and techniques of scientific management as given by F.W. Taylor.

8. Explain the fourteen principles of management laid down by Henri Fayol.

9. Compare and contrast the contributions of F.W. Taylor and Henri Fayol to management thought.

10. Describe the Hawthorne experiments and explain how they led to the human relations approach to management.

11. Write a brief note on the modern approaches to management.

12. Discuss the contribution of Indian thinkers, both ancient and modern, to the field of management.

C. Practical / Case-Based Questions

13. Identify any Indian company which, in your opinion, follows the principles given by Henri Fayol. Justify your answer with examples.

14. Visit a small factory or workshop in your locality and observe whether any techniques of scientific management are being used. Prepare a short report on your observations.

CHAPTER 3

FUNCTIONS AND ROLES OF A MANAGER

Learning Objectives

After studying this chapter, the reader should be able to:

- explain the various functions of management with special reference to POSDCORB;
- describe the ten managerial roles given by Henry Mintzberg;
- understand the three types of managerial skills suggested by Robert L. Katz;
- list the essential qualities of an effective manager; and
- identify the major challenges faced by managers in the present-day business environment.

Introduction

In the previous two chapters, we discussed the meaning, nature and evolution of management as a discipline. The work of management, however, is actually performed by living human beings called managers. A manager is the person who plans, organises, directs and controls the activities of others in order to achieve the goals of the organisation. He is, in a sense, the conductor of the orchestra; without him, the various players cannot produce harmonious music.

In a small enterprise, the owner himself may perform the work of a manager. In a large organisation, however, there are many managers placed at different levels and in different departments. From the Managing Director at the top to the supervisor on the shop floor, all of them carry out the work of management, though the nature and the extent of their work differ. A study of the functions, roles, skills and qualities of a manager is, therefore, essential for every student of management.

This chapter discusses the various functions performed by managers, the different roles they play in modern organisations as identified by

Henry Mintzberg, the skills required for managerial effectiveness as suggested by Robert L. Katz, the qualities that make a manager truly successful, and the new challenges that the managers of today have to face.

3.1 Functions of Management

Different writers have given different lists of the functions of management. The lack of agreement on a single list is partly due to the fact that the work of a manager is a continuous process in which one function flows into another. The various functions cannot be sharply separated from one another. They are like the colours of a rainbow which shade into one another without clear boundaries.

Henri Fayol, as we have already seen in Chapter 2, gave the following five functions: planning, organising, commanding, coordinating and controlling. Luther Gulick, an American writer, coined the well-known word "POSDCORB" to describe the work of a Chief Executive. The letters of this word stand for the following seven functions:

- P—Planning;
- O—Organising;
- S—Staffing;
- D—Directing;
- Co—Coordinating;
- R—Reporting; and
- B—Budgeting.

Koontz and O'Donnell, two leading writers on management, have given a slightly different list: planning, organising, staffing, directing and controlling. This list is the most widely accepted today. The functions of coordinating, reporting and budgeting are usually treated as parts of these five main functions. The five functions are discussed below in some detail.

3.1.1 Planning

Planning is the first and the most basic function of management. It is the process of deciding, in advance, what is to be done, how it is to be done, when it is to be done, where it is to be done and by whom it is to be done. In simple words, planning means looking ahead. It bridges the gap between where we are today and where we wish to be in the future.

Planning involves the setting of objectives, the gathering of information, the forecasting of future conditions, the development of alternative courses of action, the selection of the best course, and the laying down of policies, procedures, rules and budgets. A railway timetable, the annual budget of a company, the marketing plan for a new product, and even the daily schedule of a college teacher are all examples of plans.

Planning is necessary because the future is uncertain and the resources of the enterprise are limited. Without planning, the work of the organisation would proceed in a haphazard manner and the desired results would not be achieved. As the saying goes, "if you fail to plan, you plan to fail."

3.1.2 Organising

After the plans have been prepared, the next step is to organise the resources for their execution. Organising is the process of identifying the activities required for the attainment of the goals, grouping these activities into departments, assigning them to different positions, delegating the necessary authority, and establishing the relationships among the various positions.

In other words, organising is concerned with building the structure within which the work of the enterprise is to be carried out. The result of organising is the organisation—a system of well-defined positions and relationships, each having a clear set of duties and authority. The organisation chart of a company, showing the various departments and the levels of authority, is the visible form of this structure.

3.1.3 Staffing

Staffing is the function of filling the various positions in the organisation with suitable persons and keeping them filled. It is the human resource function of management. Staffing includes the following sub-activities:

- estimating the requirement of personnel for various jobs (manpower planning);
- recruitment, that is, attracting suitable candidates;

- selection of the right person for the right job;
- placement and induction of new employees;
- training and development of the personnel;
- performance appraisal;
- promotion, transfer and other career-related decisions; and
- fixation of wages and salaries.

Staffing has come to occupy a very important place in modern management because the people who work in the organisation are now recognised as its most valuable resource. A famous saying among personnel managers is that "machines do not make a company—people do."

3.1.4 Directing

Once the plans have been drawn up, the structure has been built and the people have been put in their places, the next step is to set them to work. This is the function of directing. Directing means guiding, supervising, motivating, communicating with and leading the employees so that they put in their best effort in achieving the goals of the organisation.

Directing has four important elements:

- Supervision, that is, overseeing the work of the subordinates;
- Motivation, that is, inspiring the employees to work willingly and enthusiastically;
- Leadership, that is, influencing the employees to follow the manager; and
- Communication, that is, sharing information, ideas and feelings with the employees.

Directing is sometimes called the "heart of management," for it is through directing that all the other functions are put into action. Without effective directing, the most carefully prepared plans and the most elaborately built organisation would remain only on paper.

3.1.5 Controlling

Controlling is the function of ensuring that the actual performance is in conformity with the planned performance. It involves the setting of standards, the measurement of actual performance, the comparison of the two, and the taking of corrective action wherever the actual performance falls short of the standard. Controlling thus completes the management cycle. The information obtained through control becomes the basis for fresh planning, and the cycle starts again.

It is for this reason that controlling is described as a continuous and forward-looking activity. It is closely linked with planning. As Koontz and O'Donnell have put it, "Planning and controlling are the Siamese twins of management."

3.1.6 Coordination—The Essence of Management

Apart from the five functions described above, coordination is sometimes treated as a separate function of management. Coordination means the orderly arrangement of group effort so that the various activities of different departments and individuals work together towards the common goal. However, the modern view is that coordination is not a separate function; it is the very essence of management. Every function of the manager, from planning to controlling, has coordination at its core. As Mary Parker Follett observed, coordination is the "first test of the validity of management."

3.2 Mintzberg's Managerial Roles

Henry Mintzberg, a Canadian writer on management, made a careful observation of the actual work of five chief executives in his classic study, The Nature of Managerial Work, published in 1973. He found that the work of a manager could not be described adequately in terms of the traditional functions alone. The manager, according to him, performs ten different roles, which fall into three broad groups—interpersonal roles, informational roles and decisional roles.

3.2.1 Interpersonal Roles

These roles arise out of the manager's formal authority and his contact with people both inside and outside the organisation. There are three interpersonal roles:

1. Figurehead. Every manager is required to perform certain ceremonial and symbolic duties. He greets visitors, attends social functions, signs legal documents, and takes part in the formal events of the organisation. For example, the Managing Director who inaugurates a new branch or presides over the annual general meeting is performing the figurehead role.

2. Leader. The manager is also a leader. He hires, trains, motivates and guides his subordinates. He is responsible for the overall performance of his team and for the morale of his employees.

3. Liaison. The manager maintains contacts with persons outside his unit—customers, suppliers, government officials, bankers, fellow managers and others. These contacts help him in collecting information and in influencing others on behalf of his organisation.

3.2.2 Informational Roles

As a result of his interpersonal contacts, the manager becomes the nerve centre of his unit. He receives a great deal of information and passes it on to others. The three informational roles are as follows:

4. Monitor. The manager constantly gathers information about the working of his unit and about the environment. He reads reports, listens to people, observes operations and keeps himself well-informed.

5. Disseminator. He passes on the relevant information to his subordinates and colleagues. Thus he transmits both factual data and value based judgements to the members of his unit.

6. Spokesperson. The manager also speaks on behalf of his unit to people outside. He addresses the press, the shareholders, the government and the public regarding the activities of the organisation.

3.2.3 Decisional Roles

The information collected and shared by the manager forms the basis of important decisions. The four decisional roles are as follows:

7. Entrepreneur. The manager acts as an entrepreneur within his organisation. He initiates new projects, brings about improvements, introduces new methods of work and exploits new opportunities.

8. Disturbance Handler. Every manager is, from time to time, faced with unexpected problems—a strike by workers, a quarrel between two officers, the sudden cancellation of an order, the breakdown of a machine, and so on. He must take quick decisions to handle these disturbances.

9. Resource Allocator. The manager decides how the limited resources of his unit—money, manpower, materials and time—are to be distributed among various activities. He approves the budgets, the schedules and the targets for his subordinates.

10. Negotiator. The manager has to negotiate with many persons, both inside and outside the organisation. He negotiates with the trade unions over wages, with the suppliers over prices, with the customers over terms of sale, and with his own subordinates over targets and rewards.

Mintzberg's study has been very useful in giving us a more realistic picture of what managers actually do. It tells us that the work of a manager is not as orderly and as well-organised as the textbooks sometimes make out. The manager has to play many roles, often simultaneously, and switch from one role to another in a matter of minutes.

3.3 Katz's Managerial Skills

Robert L. Katz, an American writer, in his well-known article "Skills of an Effective Administrator," published in the Harvard Business Review in 1955, suggested that the success of a manager depends mainly on three types of skills—technical, human and conceptual. These three skills are required by managers at all levels of the organisation, but their relative importance varies from level to level.

3.3.1 Technical Skills

Technical skill is the knowledge of and proficiency in a specific kind of work or activity. It involves the use of specialised methods, processes, procedures and techniques. A doctor uses his technical skill in diagnosing a patient, an engineer in designing a bridge, a chartered accountant in auditing the books, and a computer programmer in writing a software code. Technical skills are most important at the lower levels of management, where the supervisors and foremen are in direct contact with the operative work.

3.3.2 Human Skills

Human skill is the ability to work effectively with other people, both as an individual and as a member of a group. It includes the capacity to understand others, to communicate with them, to motivate them and to build a sense of team spirit. Human skill is needed in dealing with superiors, subordinates and colleagues alike. Since management is essentially the art of getting things done through others, human skills are important at all levels of management.

3.3.3 Conceptual Skills

Conceptual skill is the mental ability to see the organisation as a whole and to understand how its various parts depend upon and influence one another. It includes the ability to think in terms of abstract ideas, to grasp complex relationships, to analyse problems and to plan for the future. A manager with conceptual skill is able to see the wood for the trees. Conceptual skills are most important at the top levels of management, where major policy decisions are taken.

The relative importance of these three skills at different levels of management may be shown in the form of the following table:

Level of Management	Technical Skills	Human Skills	Conceptual Skills
Top Management	Less Important	Important	Most Important
Middle Management	Important	Most Important	Important
Lower (Supervisory) Management	Most Important	Important	Less Important

Some writers have added two more skills to Katz's list, namely the diagnostic skill (the ability to identify the real cause of a problem) and the design skill (the ability to work out a practical solution to the problem). These are particularly required at the higher levels of management.

3.4 Qualities of an Effective Manager

The success of an organisation depends, to a great extent, on the qualities of its managers. A manager who possesses the right combination of personal qualities can inspire his team to achieve extraordinary results. The qualities that go into the making of an effective manager may be discussed under the following heads:

1. Vision and Foresight. An effective manager has the ability to see ahead of his time. He can anticipate future developments and prepare his organisation to meet them. The vision of Dhirubhai Ambani in setting up Reliance and that of N.R. Narayana Murthy in building Infosys are striking examples of managerial foresight.

2. Sound Knowledge and Education. A manager must have a good knowledge of his field of work and a general understanding of business, economics and the social environment. Formal education in management adds to his knowledge and gives him a systematic way of looking at problems.

3. Intelligence and Sound Judgement. He must be intelligent enough to understand complex problems, and must have the maturity of judgement to take wise decisions on the basis of the facts before him.

4. Integrity and Strong Character. Honesty, truthfulness and a strong sense of ethics are essential for any manager who wishes to win the respect of his subordinates and of the society. As J.R.D. Tata used to say, no success that is achieved by unfair means is worth having.

5. Decisiveness. A good manager has the courage to take decisions, even in the face of uncertainty, and the willingness to accept responsibility for the consequences. Indecision can paralyse an organisation.

6. Communication Skills. He must be able to express his ideas clearly, listen patiently to others, write effectively and conduct meetings with skill. Communication is the lifeblood of management.

7. Leadership Qualities. A manager must have the ability to inspire and guide others. He should be able to win the willing cooperation of his subordinates rather than rely only on the formal authority of his position.

8. Self-Confidence. Confidence in one's own abilities is essential for taking bold decisions and for handling difficult situations. At the same time, the manager must not be overconfident or arrogant.

9. Sense of Responsibility. A good manager owns up the results of his actions. He does not blame others for his failures and is willing to share the credit for his successes with his team.

10. Initiative and Drive. He has the energy and the eagerness to take up new tasks and to work hard for their accomplishment. He does not wait for things to happen; he makes them happen.

11. Emotional Stability. A manager works under heavy pressure and faces criticism, opposition and failure from time to time. He must be able to keep his cool and not lose his temper or his patience.

12. Adaptability and Flexibility. The business environment keeps changing. A good manager is willing to change his methods, his style and even his ideas when the situation so demands.

13. Empathy and Human Understanding. He understands the feelings, problems and aspirations of his subordinates and treats them with sympathy and respect. As Mahatma Gandhi taught, a leader must put himself in the shoes of the people he leads.

14. A Habit of Continuous Learning. Knowledge becomes outdated very quickly in the modern world. An effective manager makes it a habit to read, to attend training programmes and to keep himself up-to-date with the latest developments in his field.

3.5 Challenges Faced by Modern Managers

The world in which the manager works today is very different from the world of even thirty or forty years ago. New developments in technology, in the economy and in society have created a host of new challenges. Some of the major challenges faced by modern managers are discussed below:

1. Globalisation. Since the economic reforms of 1991, the Indian economy has become a part of the global economy. Indian companies now compete with multinational giants both in the home market and abroad. Managers have to deal with international customers, suppliers and competitors, and must understand different cultures and legal systems.

2. Rapid Technological Change. Artificial intelligence, robotics, the Internet of Things, big data analytics, cloud computing and blockchain are bringing about sweeping changes in every industry. Managers must be willing to learn new technologies and to apply them in their own work.

3. Workforce Diversity. The workforce of today is far more diverse than ever before. It includes men and women of different ages, regions, religions, languages and educational backgrounds. The manager must be able to bring together this diverse workforce and create a sense of unity among them.

4. Ethical Challenges. The pressure of competition sometimes tempts managers to compromise on ethics. Cases of corporate fraud, such as the Satyam scandal of 2009, have shaken public confidence in business. Maintaining high standards of ethics and corporate governance is, therefore, a major challenge before the modern manager.

5. Sustainability and the Environment. Concerns about climate change, pollution and the depletion of natural resources have forced businesses to think beyond mere profits. Managers must now find ways of producing goods and services without harming the environment. "Green management" is no longer a fashionable phrase but a real necessity.

6. Remote Working and Virtual Teams. The COVID-19 pandemic showed that a great deal of office work can be done from home. Many companies have adopted a hybrid model of working. Managing teams whose members rarely meet in person, and keeping them motivated and well-coordinated, is a new challenge for managers.

7. Work-Life Balance. Long working hours, constant connectivity through mobile phones and e-mails, and tight deadlines have led to high levels of stress among employees. Managers must help their teams strike a proper balance between work and personal life.

8. Knowledge Management. In a knowledge-based economy, the most important asset of an organisation is the knowledge possessed by its employees. The manager must find ways of capturing this knowledge, sharing it across the organisation and using it to gain a competitive advantage.

9. Cyber Security. With the growing use of the internet and digital technologies, the risk of cyber attacks has increased manifold. Protecting the data and information systems of the organisation has become an important responsibility of management.

10. Changing Customer Expectations. Customers today are far more aware, far more demanding and far less loyal than they used to be. They want quality, variety, fair price and quick service all at the same time. Meeting these expectations consistently is a great challenge for the managers of modern business.

In dealing with these challenges, the manager of today has to be more skilled, more learned, more flexible and more value-oriented than ever before. The role of the manager is becoming more complex with each passing year, but at the same time it is also becoming more interesting and more rewarding.

Summary

Management is performed through a set of functions which include planning, organising, staffing, directing and controlling. Luther Gulick described these functions through the acronym POSDCORB. Each function is closely linked with the others, and coordination runs through all of them as the essence of management.

Henry Mintzberg, on the basis of his study of chief executives at work, identified ten managerial roles grouped under three heads—interpersonal, informational and decisional. Robert L. Katz suggested that managers require three types of skills, namely technical, human and conceptual, and that the relative importance of these skills varies with the level of management.

An effective manager is one who possesses a combination of personal qualities such as vision, knowledge, integrity, decisiveness, communication skills, leadership, self-confidence and the habit of continuous learning. The manager of today, however, has to operate in a fast-changing world and is faced with new challenges such as globalisation, technological change, workforce diversity, ethical issues, sustainability, remote working and cyber security. Meeting these challenges requires a new breed of managers who are both knowledgeable and value-driven.

Key Terms

Functions of Management, POSDCORB, Planning, Organising, Staffing, Directing, Controlling, Coordination, Mintzberg, Interpersonal Roles, Informational Roles, Decisional Roles, Figurehead, Liaison, Monitor, Disseminator, Spokesperson, Entrepreneur, Disturbance Handler, Resource Allocator, Negotiator, Katz, Technical Skills, Human Skills, Conceptual Skills, Globalisation, Workforce Diversity, Knowledge Management.

Review Questions

A. Short Answer Questions (2 marks each)

1. What does the acronym POSDCORB stand for?
2. Why is coordination called the essence of management?
3. Name the three groups of managerial roles given by Henry Mintzberg.
4. What is meant by the figurehead role of a manager?
5. State the three types of skills suggested by Robert L. Katz.
6. Give any four qualities of an effective manager.

B. Long Answer Questions (10 marks each)

7. Explain the various functions of management with suitable examples.
8. Discuss the ten managerial roles given by Henry Mintzberg.
9. Describe the three managerial skills suggested by Robert L. Katz. Which skill is most important at each level of management and why?
10. "An effective manager is born, not made." Discuss this statement in the light of the qualities of an effective manager.
11. What are the major challenges faced by managers in the modern business environment? How can these challenges be met?

CHAPTER 4
PLANNING

Learning Objectives

After studying this chapter, the reader should be able to:

- understand the concept, nature and importance of planning;
- describe the various types of plans used in business;
- explain the different steps involved in the planning process;
- state the principles of sound planning and its limitations; and
- appreciate the concept and process of Management by Objectives (MBO).

Introduction

Planning is the first and the most basic function of management. Whether it is a housewife preparing the weekly grocery list, a farmer deciding which crop to sow, a student preparing the timetable for examinations, or the Government of India framing its five-year plans, the act of planning is found everywhere. In the field of business, planning has assumed even greater importance because of the heavy investment involved, the long gestation periods and the uncertain nature of the future.

Planning is the activity by which the manager decides today what is to be done tomorrow. It is the bridge between where the organisation is at present and where it wishes to be in the future. Without planning, the activities of the organisation would proceed in a haphazard manner, and the achievement of goals would be left to chance. As Henri Fayol observed, the lack of planning is the worst form of mismanagement. The famous saying that "a person who fails to plan, plans to fail" sums up the importance of this function in just a few words.

This chapter examines the concept, nature and importance of planning, describes the different types of plans, explains the steps of the planning process, discusses the principles of sound planning and its limitations, and finally throws light on the well-known technique of

Management by Objectives, popularly known as MBO.

4.1 Concept, Nature and Importance of Planning

4.1.1 Meaning and Definition

Planning may be defined as the process of deciding, in advance, what is to be done, how it is to be done, when it is to be done, where it is to be done, and by whom it is to be done. It is essentially a process of thinking before doing. It involves the setting of objectives, the gathering of information about the future, the working out of alternative courses of action, and the selection of the best course among them.

Different writers have defined planning in slightly different ways. A few of the well-known definitions are given below:

1. Henri Fayol— "Planning is deciding the best alternatives among others to perform different managerial functions in order to achieve the predetermined goals."

2. Koontz and O'Donnell— "Planning is deciding in advance what to do, how to do it, when to do it and who is to do it. Planning bridges the gap from where we are to where we want to go."

3. George R. Terry— "Planning is the selecting and relating of facts and the making and using of assumptions regarding the future in the visualisation and formulation of the proposed activities believed necessary to achieve the desired results."

4. Theo Haimann— "Planning is the function that determines in advance what should be done. It consists of selecting the enterprise objectives, policies, programmes, procedures and other means of achieving these objectives."

5. Louis A. Allen— "Management planning involves the development of forecasts, objectives, policies, programmes, procedures, schedules and budgets."

From these definitions, it is clear that planning is a purposeful, intellectual and forward-looking activity which seeks to achieve specific objectives through the careful selection of suitable courses of action.

4.1.2 Nature and Characteristics of Planning

The nature of planning is brought out by the following characteristics:

1. Planning is the Primary Function. Planning is the first function of management. All other functions—organising, staffing, directing and controlling—follow planning. The plans must be ready before the structure can be built, the people can be appointed, the work can be directed or the results can be controlled.

2. Planning is a Pervasive Activity. Planning is required at all levels of management and in all departments of the enterprise. The Board of Directors plans the long-term policy; the middle managers plan the activities of their departments; and the supervisors plan the day-to-day work of their teams.

3. Planning is Goal-Oriented. Every plan is prepared with some objective in mind. Without a clear goal, planning becomes meaningless. The very purpose of planning is to provide a roadmap for the achievement of goals.

4. Planning is a Continuous Process. Planning is not a one-time activity. As old plans are completed, new plans must be prepared. Even during the implementation of a plan, changes in the situation may require revision of the plan. Planning, therefore, goes on continuously.

5. Planning is an Intellectual Activity. Planning involves thinking, analysing, forecasting and decision-making. It is, therefore, an intellectual or mental activity. A good planner is one who has a clear and far-sighted mind.

6. Planning is Forward-Looking. Planning is concerned with the future. It involves looking ahead and preparing for what is to come. A planner must, therefore, have the ability to forecast and to think in terms of the long run.

7. Planning Involves Choice. Whenever there is more than one way of doing a thing, planning becomes necessary. The planner has to choose, from among many alternatives, the course of action which is most likely to achieve the objective. Where there is no alternative, there is no planning.

8. Planning is Flexible. The plans must be flexible enough to be modified in the light of changing circumstances. A rigid plan that cannot be adjusted may do more harm than good. At the same time, flexibility should not be confused with looseness.

9. Planning Aims at Efficiency. A good plan is one which achieves its objective with the minimum use of resources. The principle of efficiency demands that the benefits of the plan should outweigh its costs.

10. Planning is an Integrated Process. The various plans of an organisation—long-term and short-term, departmental and divisional—must all fit together as parts of an integrated whole. The plans of one department must not run counter to those of another.

4.1.3 Importance of Planning

The importance of planning in the modern business enterprise can scarcely be overstated. Its main advantages are as follows:

1. Provides Direction. Planning gives a clear sense of direction to the activities of the organisation. The employees know what is expected of them and how their efforts will contribute to the common goal.

2. Reduces Uncertainty. Although the future cannot be made fully certain, planning helps in reducing the uncertainty by forecasting the future conditions and by preparing in advance to meet them.

3. Reduces Wastage and Overlapping. When the work is properly planned, there is little wastage of effort, money or material. Duplication of work among different departments is avoided.

4. Promotes Innovation. Planning encourages the manager to think of new ideas, new methods and new products. It is the process of planning that gave us new ventures such as Reliance Jio, which redefined the telecom market in India.

5. Facilitates Decision-Making. Planning lays down the framework within which decisions are to be taken. With a clear plan before him, the manager can take quicker and better decisions.

6. Provides the Basis for Control. The standards against which actual performance is to be measured are laid down at the planning stage. Without planning, control becomes impossible.

7. Improves Coordination. When the goals and the plans of the various departments are clearly stated and well-integrated, coordination among them becomes easy.

8. Boosts Morale. When the workers see that the management has carefully planned the work and that their efforts are properly directed towards a worthwhile goal, their morale and motivation receive a boost.

9. Helps in Anticipating Opportunities and Threats. Planning enables the organisation to look ahead and to take timely advantage of the opportunities that arise in the environment, while preparing for the threats that may come its way.

4.2 Types of Plans

Plans can be classified in various ways. The most common classifications are based on time, use, and the level at which they are prepared.

4.2.1 Classification on the Basis of Time

- Long-term plans, which cover a period of five years or more. They lay down the broad direction of the enterprise.
- Medium-term plans, which cover a period of one to five years.
- Short-term plans, which cover a period of one year or less. They deal with the day-to-day operations of the enterprise.

4.2.2 Classification on the Basis of Use

On the basis of frequency of use, plans may be divided into two broad categories:

(a) Single-Use Plans, which are prepared for one particular occasion or project and are not used again. Examples are a budget, a programme or a project.

(b) Standing Plans, which are used again and again over a long period. Examples are objectives, policies, procedures, rules and strategies.

4.2.3 Classification on the Basis of Hierarchy or Level

On the basis of the level at which they are prepared, plans are of three types—strategic, tactical and operational.

(a) Strategic Plans. These are prepared by the top management. They lay down the long-term direction of the enterprise and cover the entire organisation. The vision and mission of the company, its policies regarding new markets, new products and major investments are all part of strategic planning. The decision of the Tata Group to enter the passenger car business with the Indica, or that of Reliance to enter telecommunications with Jio, are examples of strategic decisions.

(b) Tactical Plans. These are prepared by the middle-level managers. They translate the broad strategy of the top management into specific plans for the various departments. Tactical plans usually cover a period of one to three years and deal with matters such as production targets, sales quotas and personnel requirements.

(c) Operational Plans. These are prepared at the lower levels of management. They cover the day-to-day operations of the enterprise and deal with the specific activities of individual workers and small groups. The daily production schedule of a workshop and the weekly duty roster of a hospital are examples of operational plans.

4.2.4 Major Components of Planning

Within these broad categories, the actual plans take many specific forms. The most important among these are the following:

1. Objectives or Goals. These are the desired results which the organisation seeks to achieve. They give a sense of direction and serve as the starting point of all planning. Good objectives should be specific, measurable, attainable, realistic and time-bound (often remembered by the acronym SMART).

2. Strategy. A strategy is a comprehensive plan for the achievement of the long-term objectives of the enterprise in the face of competition and other environmental factors. The aggressive pricing strategy of Reliance Jio and the rural marketing strategy of Hindustan Unilever are examples of corporate strategies.

3. Policy. A policy is a general statement which guides the decision-making of managers. It marks out the boundaries within which decisions are to be taken. For example, the policy of a company to recruit only graduates is a guide to the personnel manager.

4. Procedure. A procedure is a series of steps to be followed in a definite order to perform a particular activity. The procedure for granting leave to an employee or for placing an order for raw materials is an example.

5. Rule. A rule is a definite statement of what is to be done or not to be done in a given situation. "No smoking in the factory" and "Office hours from 10 a.m. to 5 p.m." are examples of rules. Rules do not leave any scope for discretion.

6. Programme. A programme is a comprehensive plan that combines goals, policies, procedures, rules and resources to carry out a course of action. The literacy programme of the government and the training programme of a company are examples.

7. Project. A project is a single, definite piece of work, usually with a specific time-frame and a separate budget. The construction of a new factory or the launching of a new product is an example of a project.

8. Budget. A budget is a plan expressed in numerical or financial terms. It states the expected results in terms of rupees, units of production or hours of work. The sales budget, the production budget and the cash budget are common examples.

9. Method. A method is the prescribed manner of performing a single step of a procedure. For example, the method of mixing concrete in a construction project is different from the method of welding two steel pieces.

10. Schedule. A schedule is a plan which fixes the time at which each part of an activity is to be performed. A railway timetable and a class timetable are simple examples of schedules.

4.3 Steps in the Planning Process

Planning is not a single act but a series of related steps. The number of steps may vary from one writer to another, but the following are generally accepted:

1. Analysis of the Environment. The first step in planning is the study of the external and internal environment of the enterprise. The external environment consists of factors such as the economy, the government, competition, technology and society. The internal environment consists of the resources and weaknesses of the enterprise itself. The well-known SWOT analysis (Strengths, Weaknesses, Opportunities and Threats) is a popular tool used at this stage.

2. Setting of Objectives. Once the environment has been studied, the next step is to set the objectives. The objectives must be clearly stated, properly communicated and accepted by the people who have to achieve them. Both the overall objectives of the enterprise and the specific objectives of each department are determined.

3. Developing Planning Premises. Premises are the assumptions about the future on which planning is based. They include forecasts about market conditions, prices, costs, government policies, the actions of competitors and so on. Without proper premises, planning is no better than guesswork. All those concerned with planning must work on the basis of the same premises.

4. Identifying the Alternative Courses of Action. Usually there is more than one way of achieving a goal. The planner must list out all the possible alternatives before him. The greater the number of alternatives considered, the better the chance of finding the best one.

5. Evaluating the Alternatives. Each alternative is examined in the light of the objectives and the premises. The expected costs and benefits, the risks involved, the resources required and the suitability to the situation are all weighed carefully.

6. Selecting the Best Alternative. On the basis of this evaluation, the manager selects the alternative which is best suited to the achievement of the objectives. The selected alternative becomes the master plan.

7. Formulating Derivative or Subsidiary Plans. The master plan is then broken down into smaller, departmental and functional plans. The production plan, the sales plan, the financial plan, the manpower plan and the materials plan are all derivative plans which support the main plan.

8. Securing Cooperation and Implementation. Plans are of no value unless they are put into action. The plan must be communicated to all the concerned employees, their cooperation must be secured, and the necessary resources must be made available.

9. Follow-up and Review. After the plan has been put into action, its working is constantly watched. The actual results are compared with the planned results, and any necessary changes in the plan are made. This step links planning with the function of control and provides the input for the next cycle of planning.

4.4 Principles of Sound Planning

Koontz and O'Donnell and other writers have laid down a number of principles for sound planning. The more important among them are the following:

1. Principle of Contribution to Objectives. The primary purpose of every plan is to help in the achievement of the objectives of the enterprise. Any plan which does not contribute to the objectives is a wasteful plan.

2. Principle of Primacy of Planning. Planning is the first function of management and is the basis of all other functions. The other functions cannot be performed properly unless planning is done first.

3. Principle of Pervasiveness. Planning is required at all levels of management. It is the responsibility of every manager, from the Chief Executive down to the supervisor.

4. Principle of Efficiency. A plan is efficient when it achieves its objective with the least cost in terms of money, time and effort. The benefits of the plan must always exceed its costs.

5. Principle of Flexibility. Plans must be flexible enough to be modified in the light of changes in the environment. A rigid plan may quickly become out of date.

6. Principle of Navigational Change. Just as the captain of a ship keeps a constant watch on the course and makes corrections from time to time, the manager too must review his plan periodically and make whatever changes the situation may require.

7. Principle of Commitment. A plan must cover a period of time long enough to fulfil the commitments involved in the decision. For example, if a factory is being set up with a life of twenty years, the planning horizon must extend over twenty years and not merely over one or two years.

8. Principle of the Limiting Factor. In the choice among alternatives, the manager must focus on the factor which is most critical to the achievement of the goal—for example, the availability of finance, the supply of raw material, or the skill of the workforce. This factor is called the limiting factor or the strategic factor.

9. Principle of Timing. Plans must be properly timed. The various plans of the enterprise must be coordinated in such a way that they reinforce one another. Plans introduced at the wrong time may do more harm than good.

10. Principle of Simplicity. A plan must be simple, clear and easy to understand. Complicated plans confuse the employees and are difficult to implement.

4.5 Limitations of Planning

In spite of its many advantages, planning is not free from limitations. The major limitations of planning are the following:

1. Costly and Time-Consuming. Good planning requires the collection of a great deal of information, the holding of many meetings and the services of experts. All this is costly. For small businesses, the cost of elaborate planning may even exceed the benefits.

2. Uncertainty of the Future. Planning is based on forecasts of the future, but the future cannot be predicted with full accuracy. A sudden change in government policy, a war, a pandemic such as COVID-19, or a financial crisis can render the best of plans useless overnight.

3. Rigidity. Once a plan has been put into action, it tends to develop a life of its own. Managers and workers become committed to it and may find it difficult to make changes even when the situation demands them.

4. Resistance to Change. Planning often involves changes in the existing methods of working. Employees and managers, who are comfortable with the old ways, may resist these changes.

5. False Sense of Security. A well-prepared plan sometimes creates the feeling that the future has been taken care of. This false sense of security may make the managers complacent and may prevent them from being alert to new developments.

6. Limited Scope in a Dynamic Environment. In industries where conditions change very rapidly—such as fashion, software and consumer electronics—the scope of long-term planning is limited.

7. Lack of Reliable Information. The quality of a plan depends on the quality of the information on which it is based. In many cases, reliable and up-to-date information is not easily available, and the planner has to work with incomplete data.

8. Internal Inflexibilities. Long-term contracts with suppliers, large investments in fixed assets, capital structure and existing manpower are some of the internal factors that may restrict the freedom of the planner.

9. External Inflexibilities. Government policies, labour laws, trade union pressure, social attitudes and the actions of competitors are some of the external factors that may set limits on what the planner can do.

4.6 Management by Objectives (MBO)

4.6.1 Concept of MBO

Management by Objectives, or MBO, is a well-known technique of planning and performance appraisal which gained great popularity during the 1960s and 1970s. The concept was first put forward by Peter F. Drucker in his book The Practice of Management, published in 1954. It was later developed by writers such as George S. Odiorne, Douglas McGregor and John W. Humble.

MBO is sometimes called Management by Results, because it focuses on the results to be achieved rather than on the activities to be performed. Under MBO, the superior and the subordinate together set the goals which the subordinate is to achieve during a given period, the subordinate is then given the freedom to work towards these goals in his own way, and at the end of the period his performance is reviewed jointly by both. The emphasis is on what is to be achieved, not on how it is to be achieved.

Peter Drucker defined MBO as "a process whereby the superior and the subordinate managers of an organisation jointly identify its common goals, define each individual's major areas of responsibility in terms of results expected of him, and use these measures as guides for operating the unit and assessing the contribution of each of its members."

4.6.2 Features of MBO

- It is a goal-setting and goal-getting technique.
- Goals are set jointly by the superior and the subordinate.
- The goals are specific, measurable and time-bound.
- The subordinate is given freedom to choose the means of achieving the goals.
- Performance is judged on the basis of the results achieved, not on

the personality of the employee.

- Periodic review of progress is built into the system.
- The whole approach emphasises participation, communication and self-control.

4.6.3 Process of MBO

The MBO process generally consists of the following steps:

1. Setting the overall objectives of the organisation by the top management.
2. Breaking down these overall objectives into specific objectives for each department, division and individual manager.
3. Joint setting of objectives between the superior and the subordinate.
4. Matching the available resources with the agreed objectives.
5. Implementation of the agreed action plan, with freedom of action to the subordinate.
6. Periodic review of progress at fixed intervals.
7. Performance appraisal at the end of the period, on the basis of the results achieved.
8. Use of the appraisal in decisions regarding rewards, promotions, training and the setting of the next round of objectives.

4.6.4 Benefits of MBO

The main benefits of MBO are as follows:

- It compels the manager to think clearly about what he wants to achieve.
- It improves the planning process of the enterprise.
- It develops a sense of involvement and commitment among the subordinates.
- It provides a fair basis for performance appraisal.
- It helps in the identification of training needs.
- It improves communication between the superior and the subordinate.
- It encourages self-control and self-development.

4.6.5 Limitations of MBO

MBO is not free from limitations. The chief limitations are:

- Setting clear and measurable objectives for every job is not always easy, especially for jobs of a creative or research nature.
- MBO involves a lot of paperwork, meetings and reviews, all of which are time-consuming.
- Both the superior and the subordinate must be properly trained in the technique. If they are not, MBO becomes merely a form-filling exercise.
- There is a tendency to set only those goals which can be easily measured, while ignoring the qualitative aspects of the job.
- If the top management is not committed to MBO, the system soon collapses.

In spite of these limitations, MBO continues to be a valuable management tool. When implemented with sincerity and with the right kind of training, it can lead to better planning, better appraisal and better results.

Summary

Planning is the function of deciding in advance what is to be done, how it is to be done, when it is to be done and by whom it is to be done. It is a goal-oriented, pervasive, continuous, intellectual and forward-looking activity which provides the basis for all the other functions of management. Planning provides direction, reduces uncertainty, encourages innovation, facilitates decision-making, provides the basis for control and improves coordination.

Plans may be classified on the basis of time, use or level. They include such specific forms as objectives, strategies, policies, procedures, rules, programmes, projects, budgets, methods and schedules. The process of planning consists of a series of steps starting from the analysis of the environment, through the setting of objectives, the development of premises, the identification and evaluation of alternatives, the selection of the best one, the formulation of derivative plans, and ending with implementation and review.

Sound planning is guided by certain well-recognised principles such as contribution to objectives, primacy, pervasiveness, efficiency, flexibility, the limiting factor and simplicity. Planning has its own limitations—it is costly, it is based on uncertain premises, it may give rise to rigidity, and it may meet with resistance to change. The technique of Management by Objectives, given by Peter Drucker, is a participative method of planning and performance appraisal under which the superior and the subordinate jointly set goals and review the results. When properly applied, MBO leads to clearer thinking, greater commitment and better performance.

Key Terms

Planning, Premises, SWOT Analysis, Strategic Plans, Tactical Plans, Operational Plans, Single-Use Plans, Standing Plans, Objectives, Strategy, Policy, Procedure, Rule, Programme, Project, Budget, Method, Schedule, Principle of Limiting Factor, Principle of Navigational Change, Management by Objectives (MBO), Management by Results, Peter Drucker, SMART Goals.

Review Questions

A. Short Answer Questions (2 marks each)

9. Define planning.
10. Mention any four characteristics of planning.
11. What is meant by planning premises?
12. Distinguish between a policy and a rule.
13. What is the difference between a strategic plan and an operational plan?
14. Who is the originator of the concept of Management by Objectives?
15. Expand the acronym SMART in the context of objectives.

B. Long Answer Questions (10 marks each)

16. Explain the meaning, nature and importance of planning in modern business.
17. Describe the various types of plans with suitable examples.
18. Discuss the steps involved in the planning process.
19. State and explain the principles of sound planning.
20. "Planning is not free from limitations." In the light of this

statement, discuss the limitations of planning.

21. Explain the concept of Management by Objectives. Describe its process, benefits and limitations.

C. Practical / Case-Based Questions

22. Take the case of any well-known Indian company (such as Reliance Industries, Tata Motors or Infosys) and discuss how planning has contributed to its success.

23. Prepare a simple plan for organising a one-day cultural programme in your college. Show the various steps you would follow and the specific plans (objectives, procedures, budget, schedule) that would be required.

CHAPTER 5

DECISION MAKING

Learning Objectives

After studying this chapter, the reader should be able to:

- understand the meaning, nature and importance of decision making;
- classify managerial decisions into various types;
- describe the steps in the decision-making process;
- explain the traditional and modern techniques used in decision making;
- compare individual decision making with group decision making; and
- distinguish between the rational and the bounded-rational models of decision making.

Introduction

Every working day, a manager is required to take decisions, big and small. Whether to launch a new product or not, whether to expand the factory or to lease additional capacity, whether to grant leave to an employee, what price to charge for a product, which supplier to choose for raw materials—all these are decisions that managers have to take. It is no exaggeration to say that the entire work of management is, in one way or another, a process of decision making. Herbert A. Simon, the Nobel laureate, went so far as to say that decision making is the essence of management.

A decision is a conscious choice between two or more alternative courses of action with the aim of achieving a desired result. Where there is only one course of action, there is no decision to be made. Where there are several courses of action, the manager must use his judgement, his experience and his analytical ability to pick the one that is most likely to lead to the desired result.

The quality of the decisions taken by managers determines, to a great extent, the success or failure of the enterprise. A few good decisions can transform an ordinary company into a market leader, while a few bad decisions can ruin a once-flourishing business. The decision of Henry Ford to produce a low-priced car for the masses, the decision of J.R.D. Tata to start an airline in India, the decision of Dhirubhai Ambani to enter petrochemicals, and the decision of Sunil Bharti Mittal to provide mobile telephony at low prices are some of the well-known decisions that have shaped the course of business history.

This chapter discusses the meaning and importance of decision making, the different types of managerial decisions, the steps of the decision-making process, the various techniques and tools used in decision making, the relative merits of individual and group decision making, and the rational and bounded-rational models of decision making.

5.1 Meaning and Importance of Decision Making

5.1.1 Meaning and Definition

Decision making is the process of selecting the best course of action from among several alternatives in order to achieve a definite objective. It is the act of making up one's mind. The word "decision" comes from the Latin word "decidere" which means "to cut off." To take a decision is, in fact, to cut off other possibilities and to commit oneself to a particular course of action.

Some of the well-known definitions of decision making are as follows:

1. Peter F. Drucker— "Whatever a manager does, he does through making decisions."

2. George R. Terry— "Decision making is the selection based on some criteria from two or more possible alternatives."

3. Trewatha and Newport— "Decision making involves the selection of a course of action from among two or more possible alternatives in order to arrive at a solution for a given problem."

4. Dalton E. McFarland— "A decision is an act of choice wherein an executive forms a conclusion about what must be done in a given situation."

5. Henry Sigmund— "Decision making is a moment, in an ongoing process of evaluating alternatives related to a goal, at which the decision-maker's expectations about a particular course of action impel him to make a selection."

From these definitions, it is evident that decision making is a goal-directed, conscious and rational choice from among alternatives. It is not a sudden act but a thoughtful process.

5.1.2 Characteristics of Decision Making

The nature of decision making is reflected in the following characteristics:

1. Goal-Oriented. Every decision is taken with some objective in view. The decision is judged by how well it helps in achieving that objective.

2. Choice among Alternatives. Decision making implies that there is more than one course of action open to the manager. Where no alternatives exist, no decision is required.

3. Continuous Process. Decision making is not a one-time activity. From the moment a manager enters his office in the morning till he leaves in the evening, he keeps taking one decision after another.

4. Intellectual or Mental Activity. Decision making involves thinking, analysing, comparing and judging. It is, therefore, primarily a mental activity. The body acts only after the mind decides.

5. Pervasive Function. Decisions are taken at all levels of management and in all functional areas. The peon decides which file to deliver first, and the Managing Director decides on the future course of the company. Both are decisions, though of different importance.

6. Involves Commitment. Once a decision has been taken, the manager and the organisation become committed to it. The resources of the enterprise begin to be spent in the direction chosen. A wrong decision can, therefore, prove costly.

7. Positive or Negative. A decision may take the form of doing something (a positive decision) or of not doing something (a negative decision). The decision "not to enter a particular market" is also a decision.

8. Future-Oriented. Decisions are taken today, but their effects are felt in the future. The manager must, therefore, possess the ability to look ahead and to anticipate future developments.

5.1.3 Importance of Decision Making

The importance of decision making in business may be appreciated from the following points:

- It helps in the achievement of the objectives of the enterprise.
- It ensures the best use of the limited resources of the enterprise.
- It improves the overall efficiency of management.
- It promotes innovation and creativity, since the manager has to look for new and better courses of action.
- It increases the confidence and morale of the employees, who are guided by clear decisions of the management.
- It is the basis for all other functions of management—planning involves choice, organising involves choice, staffing involves choice, and so on.
- It paves the way for growth and expansion of the enterprise through wise strategic decisions.

5.2 Types of Managerial Decisions

Managerial decisions may be classified in a number of ways. The more important classifications are described below.

5.2.1 Programmed and Non-Programmed Decisions

This classification, given by Herbert A. Simon, is one of the most useful. Programmed decisions are routine, repetitive decisions which arise out of day-to-day operations. They can be handled by following an established procedure. Examples include the granting of casual leave to an employee, the placing of routine orders for stationery, or the payment of regular bills. Once a procedure has been laid down, such decisions almost take themselves.

Non-programmed decisions, on the other hand, are unique, complex and unstructured. They arise out of situations which are new or out of the ordinary. There is no ready-made procedure for handling them. The decision of a company to enter a new line of business, or to merge with another company, is a non-programmed decision. Such decisions call for judgement, intuition and creative thinking on the part of the manager.

5.2.2 Strategic and Operational Decisions

Strategic decisions are those which deal with the long-term direction of the enterprise. They are taken at the top level and have a wide impact. The decision to set up a new factory, to enter the export market or to acquire a competitor is a strategic decision. Operational decisions, in contrast, deal with the day-to-day functioning of the enterprise. They are taken at the lower levels of management and have a limited impact. The decision of the foreman to assign a particular worker to a particular machine is an operational decision.

5.2.3 Policy and Operating Decisions

Policy decisions lay down the broad rules within which the work of the enterprise is to be carried out. They are taken at the top level. Operating decisions are taken within the framework of these policies, by the lower levels of management. For example, the decision of a bank that all employees will be transferred every three years is a policy decision; the decision of the General Manager to transfer a particular employee from Indore to Bhopal is an operating decision.

5.2.4 Organisational and Personal Decisions

A manager takes some decisions in his capacity as an officer of the enterprise; these are organisational decisions. He also takes some decisions in his personal capacity; these are personal decisions. The decision of a manager to grant promotion to a subordinate is an organisational decision. The decision of the same manager to invest his own savings in shares is a personal decision.

5.2.5 Individual and Group Decisions

When a decision is taken by a single person, it is an individual decision. When it is taken by a group of persons working together, it is a group decision. The decision of the Board of Directors, or of a committee, or of a panel of experts is a group decision. Group decisions are usually taken on important matters where the views of more than one person are valuable.

5.2.6 Routine and Basic Decisions

Routine decisions are taken frequently and deal with day-to-day matters. They require little time or thought. Basic decisions, on the other hand, are taken occasionally and deal with important matters. They call for careful study and analysis. The decision to give an annual bonus is a routine decision; the decision to introduce a new pension scheme is a basic decision.

5.2.7 Decisions under Certainty, Risk and Uncertainty

This classification is based on the amount of information available to the decision-maker.

(a) Decisions under Certainty—The manager has full information about the alternatives and their outcomes. The choice is, therefore, easy. For example, the decision to deposit money in a fixed deposit at a known rate of interest is taken under conditions of certainty.

(b) Decisions under Risk—The outcomes of the alternatives are not certain, but the manager knows the probability of each outcome. For example, the manager may know that there is a 70 per cent chance of a new product succeeding and a 30 per cent chance of its failing.

(c) Decisions under Uncertainty—Neither the outcomes nor their probabilities are known. The manager has to rely heavily on judgement and intuition. Most strategic decisions in a fast-changing environment, such as the launch of a completely new technology, are taken under conditions of uncertainty.

5.3 Decision-Making Process

Decision making is not a sudden act. It is a systematic process consisting of several steps. The following steps are generally followed in arriving at a sound decision:

1. Identifying the Problem. The first and the most important step is to recognise that a problem exists and to define it clearly. A problem well defined is a problem half solved. Many decisions go wrong because the real problem is not properly understood. The manager must distinguish between the symptoms of the problem and the problem itself. For example, falling sales may be the symptom; the real problem may lie in the quality of the product, the pricing policy, or the conduct of the salesmen.

2. Analysing the Problem. Once the problem has been identified, it must be analysed in depth. The manager must gather all the relevant facts and figures, examine the various factors that have a bearing on the problem, and study the constraints under which the decision is to be taken.

3. Developing Alternative Solutions. Few problems have only one solution. The manager must, therefore, list out all the possible alternative courses of action open to him. The greater the number of alternatives considered, the better the chance of selecting a good one. Brainstorming sessions, group discussions and consultation with experts may help in generating new alternatives.

4. Evaluating the Alternatives. Each alternative is then weighed in the light of the objectives, the available resources, the constraints and the likely consequences. The advantages, disadvantages, costs and risks of each alternative are assessed carefully. Various quantitative techniques such as cost-benefit analysis and decision-tree analysis may be used at this stage.

5. Selecting the Best Alternative. On the basis of the evaluation, the manager selects the alternative which appears to be the best in the given situation. The choice may be based on experience, research, experimentation or simply on judgement. The selected alternative becomes the decision.

6. Implementing the Decision. A decision, however good, is of no value unless it is properly put into action. The manager must communicate the decision to all concerned, secure their cooperation, arrange the necessary resources and supervise the execution of the decision.

7. Follow-up and Review. After the decision has been implemented, its results must be watched carefully. The actual results are compared with the expected results. If there are any deviations, suitable corrective action is taken. The experience gained from one decision becomes a useful input for future decisions.

5.4 Techniques and Tools of Decision Making

Over the years, managers have developed a wide variety of techniques to help them in taking sound decisions. These techniques may be divided into two broad categories—traditional or qualitative techniques and modern or quantitative techniques.

5.4.1 Traditional Techniques

1. Experience. Experience is the best teacher. Managers often draw upon their past experience in similar situations. However, blind reliance on experience can be dangerous, since the situation today may be quite different from that of the past.

2. Intuition. Intuition is the ability to know something without conscious reasoning. Many successful managers and entrepreneurs are said to have a strong sense of intuition. Intuitive decisions may be quick, but they may also be wrong.

3. Facts. Sound decisions are based on facts. Facts are gathered through observation, records, surveys and reports. The greater the volume and accuracy of the facts available, the better the decision is likely to be.

4. Considered Opinion. The opinion of experienced and knowledgeable persons, given after careful thought, is a valuable input in decision making.

5. Brainstorming. This is a group technique developed by Alex F. Osborn. A small group of people is invited to come up with as many ideas as possible on a particular problem. No criticism is allowed during the session. Free flow of ideas, however wild, is encouraged. The ideas are evaluated later.

6. Nominal Group Technique. In this technique, the members of a group first write down their ideas independently. The ideas are then shared, discussed and ranked. This avoids the danger of one or two dominant members influencing the others.

7. Delphi Technique. This technique, developed by the Rand Corporation, makes use of a panel of experts who do not meet face to face. They are asked to give their opinions in writing through a series of questionnaires. Thc summarised replies are circulated among them, and a consensus is gradually arrived at. The Delphi technique is particularly useful in long-range forecasting.

8. Devil's Advocacy. Under this technique, one member of the group is given the role of opposing the proposal under consideration. His objections force the group to think more carefully about the weaknesses of the proposal before taking a final decision.

5.4.2 Modern or Quantitative Techniques

These techniques use mathematics, statistics and computer technology to aid decision making. The leading techniques are:

1. Operations Research. A general term covering the use of scientific methods to solve managerial problems. It includes a variety of techniques such as those listed below.

2. Linear Programming. A mathematical technique used to find the best allocation of limited resources among competing demands. It is widely used in product mix, transportation and assignment problems.

3. Decision-Tree Analysis. A pictorial method of showing the various alternatives and their possible outcomes in the form of a tree. It is particularly useful for decisions taken under conditions of risk.

4. Game Theory. A mathematical study of situations in which two or more competitors interact, each trying to outwit the other. It is useful in dealing with competitive situations in business.

5. Queuing Theory. Used to study problems of waiting lines, such as those that arise at bank counters, petrol pumps, hospitals and railway booking offices.

6. Simulation. A computer-based technique in which a real-life situation is imitated by means of a mathematical model. The manager can try out different decisions on the model before applying them in real life.

7. Cost-Benefit Analysis. A technique under which the total expected costs of a proposal are compared with its total expected benefits. The proposal is accepted if the benefits exceed the costs.

8. Break-Even Analysis. A technique used to determine the level of output at which total revenue equals total cost. It is widely used in pricing and production decisions.

9. PERT and CPM. Programme Evaluation and Review Technique (PERT) and Critical Path Method (CPM) are network techniques used for planning and controlling large projects.

10. Marginal Analysis. A technique borrowed from economics. The manager compares the additional cost of producing one more unit with the additional revenue from selling it, and goes on producing as long as the marginal revenue exceeds the marginal cost.

5.5 Individual versus Group Decision Making

Decisions in an organisation are taken sometimes by individuals and sometimes by groups. Each approach has its own advantages and limitations.

5.5.1 Advantages of Group Decision Making

- A group brings together a greater amount of knowledge, experience and information than a single individual can possess.
- A larger number of alternatives can be generated by a group.
- The members of the group, having participated in the decision, are more likely to accept it and to work for its success.
- A group decision is generally seen as more democratic and is, therefore, better received by the employees.
- The discussion among group members helps in improving their understanding of the problem and in building team spirit.

5.5.2 Disadvantages of Group Decision Making

- Group decision making takes more time, as members must be brought together and discussions must be held.
- The cost of group decision making is high.
- The decisions are often a compromise and may not be the best possible decisions.
- A few dominant members may sway the entire group, and the views of quieter members may not be heard.
- Groups may suffer from "groupthink," a phenomenon in which the desire for harmony within the group leads members to suppress dissenting views and to arrive at hasty decisions.
- Responsibility for the decision becomes diffused, since no single person can be held accountable.

5.5.3 When to Use Group Decision Making

Group decision making is suitable when the problem is complex, when the acceptance of the decision is more important than its speed, when the situation involves a great deal of uncertainty, and when the views of different specialists are required. Individual decision making, on the other hand, is preferable when speed is essential, when the problem is simple, when the manager has the necessary expertise, and when secrecy is required.

5.6 Rational and Bounded-Rational Models of Decision Making

5.6.1 The Rational Model

The classical or rational model of decision making is based on the assumption that the manager is a perfectly rational being, with complete information about all the alternatives and their consequences. According to this model, the manager:

- has clear and unambiguous goals;
- has full information about all the available alternatives;
- knows the consequences of each alternative with certainty;
- can rank the alternatives in order of preference; and
- always selects the alternative that maximises his goal.

This model treats the manager as an "economic man" whose only concern is to maximise the benefit. The model is appealing because of its simplicity and logical consistency. However, it is unrealistic, because in real life no manager can ever have full information, ample time and unlimited mental capacity to consider all the alternatives.

5.6.2 The Bounded-Rationality Model

Herbert A. Simon, who was awarded the Nobel Prize in Economics in 1978, proposed the model of bounded rationality to overcome the unrealistic assumptions of the rational model. According to Simon, the manager is not an "economic man" but an "administrative man" whose rationality is limited or "bounded" by several factors:

- Incomplete information about the alternatives;
- Limited time available for taking the decision;
- Limited cognitive ability of the human mind;
- The complexity of the situation; and
- The personal values, beliefs and biases of the decision-maker.

Because of these limitations, the manager does not search for the best possible alternative. Instead, he searches for an alternative that is "good enough"—one that satisfies the minimum requirements of the situation. Simon coined the term "satisficing" (a combination of satisfy and suffice) to describe this behaviour. The manager, in other words, does not optimise; he satisfices.

5.6.3 Other Models of Decision Making

Two other models deserve a brief mention here:

(a) The Incremental Model, given by Charles E. Lindblom, suggests that managers do not make big, sweeping decisions but proceed by making small, incremental changes to existing policies. Lindblom called this the "science of muddling through."

(b) The Garbage-Can Model, developed by Cohen, March and Olsen, holds that decision making in organisations is often a chaotic and unpredictable process in which problems, solutions, participants and opportunities mix together in a "garbage can" and decisions emerge in a more or less random fashion. This model is particularly useful in describing decision making in highly uncertain and turbulent environments.

5.6.4 Rational versus Bounded-Rational—A Comparison

Basis	Rational Model	Bounded-Rational Model
Assumption about Manager	Manager is fully rational (economic man).	Manager has limited rationality (administrative man).
Information	Complete information available.	Information is incomplete and imperfect.
Alternatives Considered	All possible alternatives are considered.	Only a limited number of alternatives are considered.
Goal	Maximising the benefit.	Satisficing, that is, finding an alternative

Basis	Rational Model	Bounded-Rational Model
		that is good enough.
Realism	Theoretical and ideal.	More realistic and closer to actual practice.
Proposed By	Classical economists and writers.	Herbert A. Simon.

In actual practice, most managers follow neither the pure rational model nor the pure bounded-rational model. They use a combination of analysis and judgement, of fact and intuition, of careful calculation and quick reaction, depending on the situation before them.

Summary

Decision making is the process of choosing the best course of action from among several alternatives in order to achieve a particular objective. It is goal-oriented, continuous, intellectual and pervasive in nature, and is the very essence of management. Decisions may be classified as programmed and non-programmed, strategic and operational, policy and operating, organisational and personal, individual and group, and as decisions taken under conditions of certainty, risk or uncertainty.

The decision-making process generally consists of seven steps—identifying the problem, analysing it, developing alternatives, evaluating them, selecting the best alternative, implementing the decision, and following up on the results. Managers use a variety of techniques to aid decision making, ranging from traditional techniques such as experience, intuition and brainstorming to modern techniques such as linear programming, decision-tree analysis, simulation and break-even analysis.

Decisions may be taken by individuals or by groups. Group decision making brings more knowledge and greater acceptance but is also more time-consuming and may suffer from groupthink. The rational model of decision making assumes a fully informed and fully rational manager seeking to maximise the benefit. The bounded-rationality model of Herbert A. Simon, which is more realistic, recognises the limitations of the human mind and suggests that managers, in practice, look for a satisfactory rather than the best alternative—a behaviour Simon called "satisficing."

Key Terms

Decision Making, Programmed and Non-Programmed Decisions, Strategic Decisions, Operational Decisions, Policy Decisions, Decisions under Certainty, Decisions under Risk, Decisions under Uncertainty, Brainstorming, Nominal Group Technique, Delphi Technique, Devil's Advocacy, Linear Programming, Decision Tree, Game Theory, Queuing Theory, Simulation, Cost-Benefit Analysis, Break-Even Analysis, PERT and CPM, Rational Model, Bounded Rationality, Satisficing, Herbert A. Simon, Economic Man, Administrative Man, Incremental Model, Garbage-Can Model.

Review Questions

A. Short Answer Questions (2 marks each)

1. Define decision making in your own words.
2. Distinguish between programmed and non-programmed decisions.
3. What is meant by decision making under risk?
4. Briefly describe the technique of brainstorming.
5. What is the Delphi technique?
6. Explain the term "satisficing."
7. Who is regarded as the propounder of the bounded-rationality model?

B. Long Answer Questions (10 marks each)

8. "Decision making is the essence of management." Discuss.
9. Explain the various types of managerial decisions with suitable examples.

10. Describe the steps involved in the decision-making process.

11. Discuss the traditional and modern techniques of decision making.

12. Compare individual decision making with group decision making. Under what circumstances is each more suitable?

13. Distinguish between the rational and the bounded-rational models of decision making.

C. Practical / Case-Based Questions

14. You are the marketing manager of a small company manufacturing readymade garments. The sales of your product have been falling for the last three quarters. Identify the steps you would follow to arrive at a decision regarding the future course of action.

CHAPTER 6

FORECASTING AND STRATEGIC PLANNING

Learning Objectives

After studying this chapter, the reader should be able to:

- understand the meaning, importance and techniques of forecasting;
- distinguish between the vision, mission and objectives of an enterprise;
- conduct a SWOT analysis and a PESTLE analysis of an organisation;
- describe the process of strategy formulation and implementation; and
- explain the three levels of strategy—corporate, business and functional.

Introduction

In the last two chapters, we discussed planning as a function of management and the process by which decisions are taken. Both planning and decision making, however, are not made in a vacuum. They are based on certain assumptions about the future and on a clear understanding of the broad direction in which the organisation wishes to move. Forecasting is the activity by which the manager looks ahead and tries to estimate what the future is likely to bring. Strategic planning is the activity by which the top management lays down the long-term course of the enterprise and the broad means of achieving it.

Forecasting and strategic planning have become extremely important in the modern business world. The environment in which business operates is changing rapidly. New technologies are emerging, customer preferences are shifting, competitors are entering the market from every corner of the globe, and government policies are being revised from time to time. In such a fluid environment, no enterprise can afford to drift along without a clear strategy. The companies that have grown and prospered in India over the last three decades—such as Reliance Industries, Infosys, HDFC Bank and Asian Paints—are all known for their careful forecasting and their clear strategic direction.

This chapter discusses the concept and techniques of forecasting, the meaning and significance of vision, mission and objectives, the well-known tools of SWOT and PESTLE analysis, the process of strategy formulation and implementation, and the three levels at which strategies are developed within an organisation.

6.1 Concept and Techniques of Forecasting

6.1.1 Meaning and Definition

Forecasting is the activity of estimating, in advance, the events that are likely to take place in the future. It is the careful study of the past and the present in order to throw light on the future. Forecasting does not aim at predicting the future with absolute certainty; it aims only at reducing the uncertainty by giving the manager a reasonably good picture of what the future is likely to be.

Some of the well-known definitions of forecasting are:

1. **Henri Fayol**— "Forecasting is the examination of the future and drawing up of the plan of action."

2. **George R. Terry**— "Forecasting is the systematic attempt to probe the future by inference from known facts. The purpose is to provide management with information on which it can base planning decisions."

3. **Allen**— "Forecasting is a systematic attempt to probe the future by inference from known facts."

4. **Henry Sisk**— "Forecasting is the process of estimating the future by causal, conjectural and extrapolative methods."

6.1.2 Features of Forecasting

- Forecasting deals with future events that are expected to influence the business.
- It is based on past data, present trends and certain assumptions.
- It involves an element of probability; absolute certainty is never possible.

• It is a pre-requisite of planning. Without forecasts, plans cannot be made.

• It is a continuous activity. Forecasts have to be revised from time to time as new information becomes available.

• It makes use of personal judgement as well as scientific techniques.

6.1.3 Importance of Forecasting

The importance of forecasting in modern business may be appreciated from the following points:

• It helps in planning by providing reliable information about future conditions.

• It reduces the uncertainty surrounding business decisions.

• It enables the manager to take timely action in respect of opportunities and threats.

• It facilitates coordination among the various departments of the enterprise, all of which can plan on the basis of common forecasts.

• It provides the basis for setting standards against which actual performance can later be measured.

• It promotes innovation and growth by drawing attention to new markets, new products and new technologies.

• It gives a competitive edge to those enterprises which are able to forecast better than their rivals.

6.1.4 Areas of Forecasting in Business

Forecasting is required in almost every area of business. The chief areas are:

1. Economic Forecasting. The general state of the economy—the rate of growth of GDP, the rate of inflation, the level of interest rates, the foreign exchange rate, government policy and the like—has a direct bearing on every business and must be carefully forecast.

2. Demand or Sales Forecasting. This is the most common type of forecasting. It estimates the future demand for the product or service of the enterprise and provides the basis for production planning, inventory control and marketing strategy.

3. Technological Forecasting. It deals with the likely future developments in technology that may affect the product, the process or the industry of the enterprise. The rise of electric vehicles, for instance, is a development that every automobile company in India is closely watching.

4. Manpower Forecasting. This estimates the future requirements of personnel—both in terms of numbers and of skills—and provides the basis for recruitment, training and career planning.

5. Financial Forecasting. It estimates the future requirement of funds, the expected revenues and the likely costs. It is the basis of capital budgeting and cash management.

6.1.5 Techniques of Forecasting

The techniques of forecasting may be divided into two broad groups—qualitative or judgemental techniques and quantitative or statistical techniques.

(A) Qualitative or Judgemental Techniques

1. Jury of Executive Opinion. Under this technique, the senior executives of the enterprise come together, share their views on the future and arrive at a forecast on the basis of their collective wisdom. It is simple and quick but suffers from the bias of senior officers.

2. Sales Force Composite. Each salesman estimates the likely sales in his territory. These estimates are aggregated, reviewed and adjusted by the sales managers to arrive at the company's total sales forecast. The strength of this method is that the salesmen are in direct touch with the customers.

3. Survey of Buyers' Intentions. A sample of potential customers is asked, through interviews or questionnaires, what they plan to buy and in what quantity. This is widely used for industrial goods and for major consumer durables.

4. Delphi Method. A panel of experts is asked to give their forecasts in writing through a series of rounds. The results of each round are circulated among them, and a consensus is gradually arrived at. The method is particularly useful for long-term and technological forecasting.

5. Historical Analogy. The future of a new product is estimated on the basis of the past history of a similar product. For example, the future of electric two-wheelers in India may be estimated on the basis of the past growth of CNG vehicles.

6. Scenario Planning. Several possible scenarios of the future are imagined—an optimistic, a pessimistic and a most likely scenario—and a plan is prepared for each. The technique is useful when the future is highly uncertain.

(B) Quantitative or Statistical Techniques

1. Time Series Analysis. The past data on a variable is studied over a period of time, and the trend is projected into the future. The method assumes that the past pattern will continue.

2. Trend Projection. A line is fitted through the past data, by the method of least squares or otherwise, and extended into the future. It is suitable when the trend is more or less stable.

3. Regression Analysis. A statistical method that examines the relationship between the variable being forecast (the dependent variable) and one or more other variables (the independent variables). For example, the sales of refrigerators may be related to the average household income and to the price of electricity.

4. Moving Averages and Exponential Smoothing. These are simple techniques that smooth out the random fluctuations in the data and bring out the underlying trend.

5. Econometric Models. These are large mathematical models that capture the relationships among many variables in the economy. They are used by governments and large corporations for forecasting GDP, inflation and other macroeconomic variables.

6. Input-Output Analysis. Developed by Wassily Leontief, this method studies the flow of goods and services among the different sectors of the economy. It is useful for estimating the demand for the output of one industry on the basis of the activity in another.

6.2 Vision, Mission and Objectives

Every well-managed enterprise has a clear idea of what it stands for and what it wishes to achieve. This idea is generally expressed at three levels of generality—the vision, the mission and the objectives. These three concepts are closely related but should not be confused with one another.

6.2.1 Vision

The vision of an organisation is a mental picture of the desired future state of the enterprise. It describes, in broad and inspiring terms, what the organisation wishes to become over the long run. A good vision statement is short, clear and motivating. It does not merely describe what the company does; it describes what the company aspires to be.

The vision of the Tata Group, for example, is "to be the most respected and valuable Indian multinational by the year 2025." The vision of Infosys is "to be a globally respected corporation that provides best-of-breed business solutions, leveraging technology, delivered by best-in-class people." The vision of the Indian Space Research Organisation is "to harness space technology for national development."

6.2.2 Mission

The mission of an organisation defines its basic purpose or reason for existence. While the vision tells us where the company is going, the mission tells us what business the company is in and whom it serves. A good mission statement answers four basic questions—who we are, what we do, for whom we do it, and how we do it.

The mission of the Tata Group, for instance, is "to improve the quality of life of the communities we serve globally, through long-term stakeholder value creation based on Leadership with Trust." The mission of Amul is "to provide quality products of dairy and food to consumers at reasonable prices, ensuring fair returns to producers."

6.2.3 Objectives and Goals

Objectives are the specific results that the organisation seeks to achieve in the pursuit of its mission. They are more concrete and more measurable than the mission. Goals are sometimes treated as equivalent to objectives, and sometimes as the short-term breakdown of objectives. Whatever the terminology, all good objectives and goals should be SMART, that is, Specific, Measurable, Attainable, Realistic and Time-bound.

An example may help. The mission of a private hospital may be "to provide affordable and quality healthcare to the people of central India." Its objectives may include increasing the number of beds from 100 to 250 within three years, opening two new specialty departments within two years, and reducing the average length of patient stay from seven days to five days within one year.

6.2.4 Vision versus Mission—A Comparison

Basis	**Vision**	**Mission**
Meaning	Picture of the future the organisation aspires to.	Statement of the basic purpose of the organisation.
Question Answered	What do we want to become?	What business are we in, and whom do we serve?
Time Horizon	Long-term and futuristic.	Present and continuing.
Nature	Inspirational and idealistic.	Specific and operational.
Audience	Mainly internal—meant to motivate employees.	Both internal and external—communicates with all stakeholders.

6.3 SWOT and PESTLE Analysis

Before formulating its strategy, an organisation must have a clear understanding of itself and of its environment. Two well-known tools used for this purpose are SWOT analysis and PESTLE analysis.

6.3.1 SWOT Analysis

SWOT analysis is a tool for systematically studying the strengths, weaknesses, opportunities and threats that face an organisation. The technique was developed at the Stanford Research Institute in the 1960s by Albert S. Humphrey and his colleagues. The first two factors—strengths and weaknesses—relate to the internal environment of the organisation, while the last two—opportunities and threats—relate to the external environment.

1. Strengths. These are the internal positive features of the organisation which give it an advantage over its competitors. Examples include a strong brand image, a wide distribution network, sound financial position, skilled workforce and patented technology. The brand image of Tata, the dealer network of Maruti Suzuki and the IT manpower of Infosys are well-known strengths.

2. Weaknesses. These are the internal negative features which place the organisation at a disadvantage. Examples include outdated technology, poor cash flow, high employee turnover, weak management and a narrow product range.

3. Opportunities. These are the favourable factors in the external environment which the organisation can exploit. Examples include a growing market, favourable government policy, declining competition, technological change and changing consumer preferences. The Government of India's "Make in India" initiative, for instance, has opened up new opportunities for domestic manufacturers.

4. Threats. These are the unfavourable factors in the external environment which may harm the organisation. Examples include new competitors, adverse government regulation, economic recession, rising input costs and changing consumer tastes.

Once the SWOT analysis has been carried out, the strategist tries to match strengths with opportunities (the so-called SO strategies), to use strengths to counter threats (ST strategies), to overcome weaknesses by taking advantage of opportunities (WO strategies), and to minimise weaknesses while protecting against threats (WT strategies).

6.3.2 PESTLE Analysis

PESTLE analysis is a tool for the systematic study of the macro-environment of business. The six letters of the word PESTLE stand for Political, Economic, Social, Technological, Legal and Environmental factors. (Some writers prefer to use PEST, while others use STEEPLE or PESTLED to include further factors such as Ethical and Demographic.)

1. Political Factors. These include the stability of the government, the political ideology of the ruling party, the relations of the country with other countries, and the policies of the government towards business. Major policy initiatives in India in recent years, such as the Goods and Services Tax (GST) and the Production-Linked Incentive (PLI) Scheme, are examples of political factors with deep impact on business.

2. Economic Factors. These include the rate of growth of GDP, inflation, interest rates, exchange rates, the level of employment and the distribution of income. The economic reforms of 1991 transformed the Indian economy and gave a fresh direction to Indian business.

3. Social Factors. These include population growth, age distribution, education levels, family structure, lifestyle and cultural values. The rapid urbanisation of India, the rise of the nuclear family, the growth of the middle class and the increasing role of women in the workforce are all social changes with major implications for business.

4. Technological Factors. These include the rate of technological change, the development of new products and processes, the use of information technology, automation and research and development activities. The arrival of 4G and 5G mobile networks and the rise of artificial intelligence are examples.

5. Legal Factors. These include the laws and regulations under which business operates—the Companies Act, the Income-tax Act, the Consumer Protection Act, labour laws, intellectual property laws and so on. Changes in these laws, such as the introduction of the new labour codes, directly affect business operations.

6. Environmental Factors. These include the concern for the natural environment, climate change, pollution control, the conservation of resources and the demand for sustainable products. The pressure to reduce carbon emissions and the growing acceptance of electric vehicles are illustrations.

A careful PESTLE analysis helps the strategist to identify the major opportunities and threats in the external environment, which then feed into the SWOT analysis described above.

6.4 Strategy Formulation and Implementation

6.4.1 Meaning of Strategy

The word "strategy" has its origin in the Greek word "strategos," which means the art of the general. It was originally used in the context of war, but in the modern business world, it refers to the long-term plan of action by which an enterprise seeks to achieve its objectives in the face of competition and other environmental factors.

Some of the well-known definitions of strategy are:

1. **Alfred Chandler**— "Strategy is the determination of the basic long-term goals and objectives of an enterprise, and the adoption of the courses of action and the allocation of resources necessary for carrying out these goals."

2. **William F. Glueck**— "Strategy is a unified, comprehensive and integrated plan designed to assure that the basic objectives of the enterprise are achieved."

3. **Igor Ansoff**— "Strategy is the common thread among the firm's activities and product-markets."

6.4.2 Process of Strategy Formulation

Strategy formulation is a systematic process which generally consists of the following steps:

1. Defining the vision, mission and broad objectives of the enterprise.
2. Scanning the external environment through PESTLE analysis to identify opportunities and threats.
3. Conducting an internal appraisal of the enterprise through SWOT analysis to identify strengths and weaknesses.
4. Setting specific long-term and short-term objectives in the light of the analysis.
5. Identifying alternative strategies that may help in achieving these objectives.
6. Evaluating each alternative in terms of its suitability, feasibility and acceptability.
7. Selecting the strategy or the combination of strategies that is most suitable.
8. Communicating the chosen strategy to all concerned and preparing the necessary action plans.

6.4.3 Strategy Implementation

A strategy, however brilliant, is of no value if it is not properly implemented. Strategy implementation involves translating the chosen strategy into action and ensuring that it produces the desired results. The following aspects of implementation deserve special attention:

1. Organisational Structure. The structure of the organisation must be aligned with the strategy. A growth strategy may require a divisional structure, while a cost-leadership strategy may call for a functional structure.

2. Allocation of Resources. Money, manpower, materials and other resources must be allocated to the various activities in accordance with the requirements of the strategy. Capital budgeting, manpower planning and the preparation of operating budgets are part of this step.

3. Leadership and Culture. Strategy implementation calls for a strong commitment from the top management and for a supportive organisational culture. The leadership must communicate the strategy clearly, motivate the employees and overcome resistance to change.

4. Systems and Procedures. The information systems, control systems, reward systems and operating procedures must all be adjusted to support the strategy.

5. Strategic Control. Once the strategy has been put into action, its progress must be monitored closely. The actual results are compared with the targets, and any deviations are corrected in time. If necessary, the strategy itself is reviewed and revised.

6.5 Corporate, Business and Functional Strategies

In a large organisation, strategies are formulated at three different levels—the corporate level, the business level and the functional level. These three levels of strategy are interrelated and must work together for the success of the enterprise.

6.5.1 Corporate-Level Strategy

Corporate-level strategy is formulated by the top management and deals with the overall direction of the enterprise. It answers the basic question, "What business should we be in?" In a diversified company such as the Tata Group, the corporate-level strategy decides whether the group should be in steel, automobiles, hotels, software, retail or all of these. The chief types of corporate strategy are:

(a) Stability Strategy. The enterprise continues to do what it is already doing, without any major change. This is suitable in an environment where the company is doing well and where major changes appear risky.

(b) Growth or Expansion Strategy. The enterprise seeks to grow in size, sales, market share or geographical reach. Growth may be achieved internally—by launching new products, by entering new markets, or by vertical integration—or externally, through mergers, acquisitions and joint ventures. The growth of Reliance Industries from a small textile mill into a giant in petrochemicals, telecommunications and retail is a classic example of an aggressive growth strategy.

(c) Retrenchment Strategy. When an enterprise is in difficulty, it may have to reduce its scale of operations. Retrenchment may take the form of a turnaround (improving efficiency and cutting costs), divestment (selling off a part of the business) or, in the extreme case, liquidation.

(d) Combination Strategy. A large, diversified enterprise may pursue different strategies in different units. It may follow a growth strategy in one business, a stability strategy in another and a retrenchment strategy in a third, all at the same time.

6.5.2 Business-Level Strategy

Business-level strategy is formulated at the level of a Strategic Business Unit (SBU) or a single business of the enterprise. It answers the question, "How shall we compete in this particular business?" Michael E. Porter, the well-known Harvard professor, has identified three generic business-level strategies:

(a) Cost-Leadership Strategy. The enterprise seeks to become the lowest-cost producer in its industry, so that it can either offer the lowest prices or earn the highest margins. The success of Reliance Jio in capturing the Indian telecom market through aggressively low prices is an example of cost leadership.

(b) Differentiation Strategy. The enterprise offers a product or service that is perceived by the customers as being unique or superior in some way—quality, design, brand image, after-sales service. Apple and Mercedes-Benz are well-known practitioners of differentiation. In India, Asian Paints differentiates itself through superior service and a wide range of colours and finishes.

(c) Focus Strategy. The enterprise concentrates on a particular segment of the market—a particular customer group, a particular product line or a particular geographical area—and serves it better than its broader-based rivals. Examples are companies that focus on rural customers, on luxury consumers or on a single regional market.

6.5.3 Functional-Level Strategy

Functional-level strategies are formulated by the heads of various departments to support the business-level strategy. They are more specific in nature and cover a shorter period of time. The main functional strategies are:

- Marketing strategy, dealing with the product, price, place and promotion (the well-known four P's of marketing).
- Production strategy, dealing with the location of the factory, the choice of technology, the level of capacity and the management of quality.
- Financial strategy, dealing with the sources of funds, the capital structure, the dividend policy and the working-capital management.
- Human resource strategy, dealing with manpower planning, recruitment, training, compensation and industrial relations.
- Research and development strategy, dealing with new products, process improvements and patents.

The three levels of strategy must be carefully aligned with one another. The functional strategies must support the business-level strategy, and the business-level strategies must support the corporate-level strategy. Only then can the enterprise move forward as a unified whole.

Summary

Forecasting is the activity of estimating future events on the basis of past and present information. It is the foundation on which all planning is built. Forecasts are required in such areas as the economy, demand, technology, manpower and finance. The techniques of forecasting are of two main types—qualitative, such as the jury of executive opinion and the Delphi method, and quantitative, such as time series analysis, regression and econometric models.

Every well-managed enterprise has a clear vision (what it aspires to become), a clear mission (its basic purpose) and clear objectives (specific results to be achieved). SWOT analysis is a tool for studying the strengths, weaknesses, opportunities and threats of the enterprise, while PESTLE analysis examines the political, economic, social, technological, legal and environmental factors in the external environment. Together, these tools provide the input for strategy formulation.

Strategy is the long-term plan of action by which the enterprise seeks to achieve its objectives in a competitive environment. The process of strategy formulation includes the setting of the mission and objectives, environmental scanning, the identification and evaluation of alternatives, and the selection of the best strategy. Strategy implementation requires careful attention to organisational structure, resource allocation, leadership, culture, systems and strategic control. Strategies are formulated at three levels—corporate (what business to be in), business (how to compete) and functional (how to support the business strategy)—and all three must work together for the success of the enterprise.

Key Terms

Forecasting, Demand Forecasting, Technological Forecasting, Jury of Executive Opinion, Sales Force Composite, Delphi Method, Time Series Analysis, Regression Analysis, Vision, Mission, Objectives, SMART Goals, SWOT Analysis, PESTLE Analysis, Strategy, Strategy Formulation, Strategy Implementation, Strategic Control, Stability Strategy, Growth Strategy, Retrenchment Strategy, Combination Strategy, Porter's Generic Strategies, Cost Leadership, Differentiation, Focus, Corporate Strategy, Business Strategy, Functional Strategy, Strategic Business Unit (SBU).

Review Questions

A. Short Answer Questions (2 marks each)

9. Define forecasting.
10. State any four features of forecasting.
11. What is the difference between vision and mission?
12. What does the acronym SWOT stand for?
13. Explain any two factors covered under PESTLE analysis.
14. Name the three generic strategies given by Michael Porter.
15. What is meant by a Strategic Business Unit?

B. Long Answer Questions (10 marks each)

16. Discuss the importance of forecasting in modern business. Explain the various techniques of forecasting.

17. Explain the concepts of vision, mission and objectives with suitable examples.

18. What is SWOT analysis? Conduct a SWOT analysis of any Indian company of your choice.

19. Explain PESTLE analysis as a tool for studying the external environment of business.

20. Describe the process of strategy formulation and implementation in an enterprise.

21. Discuss the three levels of strategy with suitable examples from Indian business.

C. Practical / Case-Based Questions

22. Pick up the annual report of any listed Indian company and identify its vision statement, mission statement and major strategic objectives. Comment on their clarity and quality.

23. Imagine you are the strategic planner of a new herbal cosmetics company starting operations in Madhya Pradesh. Prepare a brief SWOT and PESTLE analysis to guide the launch.

CHAPTER 7

ORGANIZING

Learning Objectives

After studying this chapter, the reader should be able to:

- understand the meaning and nature of organising as a function of management;
- state and explain the principles of organising;
- describe the various steps in the process of organising;
- distinguish between the formal and the informal organisation;
- appreciate the importance and the limitations of organising; and
- understand the use of organisation charts and organisation manuals.

Introduction

Once the plans have been prepared, the next step is to put them into action. This requires the creation of a structure within which the work of the enterprise can be carried out in a smooth and orderly manner. The activities of the enterprise have to be identified, grouped together, assigned to suitable persons, and linked with one another through proper relationships of authority and responsibility. The function of management which accomplishes all this is known as organising.

Organising is sometimes compared to the building of a house. After the architect has prepared the plan, the builder must lay the foundation, erect the walls, fit the doors and windows, and link the various rooms through corridors and staircases. In the same way, after the plans have been drawn up, the manager must build the structure of the enterprise, link its various parts and prepare it for the work that is to come.

A well-organised enterprise is one in which every employee knows what he is expected to do, to whom he is to report, who is to report to him, and how his work is connected with that of others. In such an enterprise, the resources are used efficiently, the work moves forward smoothly and the goals are achieved without unnecessary friction. A poorly organised enterprise, on the other hand, is marked by confusion, duplication, conflict and waste. The success of every business, therefore, depends in no small measure on the quality of its organisation.

This chapter discusses the meaning and the nature of organising, lays down the principles on which a sound organisation is built, describes the process by which an organisation is created, distinguishes between the formal and the informal organisation, examines the importance and the limitations of the function, and finally explains the use of organisation charts and organisation manuals.

7.1 Meaning, Nature and Principles of Organising

7.1.1 Meaning and Definition

The word "organisation" is used in two distinct senses. In the first sense, it refers to the process or the function by which the structure of an enterprise is built. In the second sense, it refers to the structure itself, that is, the network of positions and relationships that has been brought into being. In this chapter, we are mainly concerned with the first sense, that is, organising as a process.

Organising may be defined as the process of identifying and grouping the work to be performed, defining and delegating the responsibility and authority, and establishing the relationships among the various positions for the purpose of enabling people to work together effectively in the accomplishment of the objectives of the enterprise.

Some of the well-known definitions of organising are:

1. Louis A. Allen— "Organising is the process of identifying and grouping the work to be performed, defining and delegating responsibility and authority, and establishing relationships for the purpose of enabling people to work together most effectively in accomplishing objectives."

2. Henri Fayol— "To organise a business is to provide it with everything useful to its functioning—raw material, tools, capital and personnel."

3. Koontz and O'Donnell— "Organising involves the grouping of activities necessary to accomplish the goals and plans, the assignment of these activities to appropriate departments, and the provision of authority, delegation and coordination."

4. Mooney and Reiley— "Organisation is the form of every human association for the attainment of a common purpose."

5. Theo Haimann— "Organising is the process of defining and grouping the activities of the enterprise and establishing the authority relationships among them."

7.1.2 Nature and Characteristics of Organising

The nature of organising is brought out by the following characteristics:

1. A Process or Function. Organising is a continuous process. It is not a one-time activity. As the size, the products and the environment of the enterprise change, the organisation must be modified accordingly.

2. Goal-Oriented. Organising is undertaken for the achievement of the objectives of the enterprise. Without clear goals, the act of organising loses its meaning.

3. Group Activity. Organising deals with the activities of two or more people working together. A single individual working alone has no need for an organisation.

4. Identification and Grouping of Activities. The total work of the enterprise is broken down into smaller jobs and activities, which are then grouped together on the basis of similarity into departments, sections and units.

5. Division of Labour. Different persons are entrusted with different jobs according to their qualifications, skills and experience. This brings about specialisation and increases efficiency.

6. Authority and Responsibility. Each position in the organisation is given a definite amount of authority and is held responsible for the performance of certain duties.

7. Hierarchy of Positions. An organisation has a clear hierarchy, from the top management to the operative staff, with each level having its own role to play.

8. Coordination. Since the work has been divided among many persons and departments, their efforts must be carefully coordinated so that they work together as a unified whole.

9. Common Objective. All the activities and all the positions in the organisation are directed towards the achievement of a common objective.

10. Communication. An organisation cannot function without a proper system of communication, both upward and downward, and also horizontally among departments.

7.1.3 Principles of Organising

Over the years, writers such as Henri Fayol, Lyndall Urwick, James Mooney and Koontz and O'Donnell have laid down certain guiding principles for sound organising. The more important among them are the following:

1. Principle of Objective. Every organisation, and every part of it, must contribute to the attainment of the objectives of the enterprise. Activities that do not contribute should be eliminated.

2. Principle of Division of Work. The total work of the enterprise should be divided among individuals and departments on the basis of specialisation. Specialisation increases efficiency and skill.

3. Principle of Authority and Responsibility. Authority and responsibility must always go together. A person who is given the responsibility for a job must also be given the authority to carry it out.

4. Principle of Unity of Command. Each subordinate should receive orders from one superior only. Receiving orders from two or more superiors leads to confusion, conflict and inefficiency.

5. Principle of Unity of Direction. All activities having the same objective should be placed under the direction of one manager. This ensures unity of action.

6. Principle of Scalar Chain. There should be a clear line of authority from the top to the bottom. All communications should ordinarily flow through this chain.

7. Principle of Span of Control. The number of subordinates that a manager can effectively supervise is limited. This number, known as the span of control or span of management, varies according to the nature of the work and the abilities of the manager.

8. Principle of Delegation. Authority should be delegated to the lowest level at which a competent decision can be taken. Excessive centralisation of authority should be avoided.

9. Principle of Exception. Routine matters should be handled at the lower levels, and only the exceptional cases should be brought to the attention of the higher management. This saves the time of the top managers for more important work.

10. Principle of Coordination. The activities of various individuals and departments must be coordinated so that they work together for the common goal. Coordination, as we have already seen, is the very essence of management.

11. Principle of Balance. There should be a proper balance between the various parts of the organisation—between centralisation and decentralisation, between line and staff, between the various departments and so on.

12. Principle of Flexibility. The structure of the organisation should be flexible enough to be adjusted in the light of changing circumstances. A rigid organisation soon becomes unsuitable to the times.

13. Principle of Continuity. The organisation must be designed in such a way that it can continue its operations smoothly even when there are changes of personnel at the top.

14. Principle of Simplicity. The organisation structure should be as simple as possible. Unnecessary complexity creates confusion and increases cost.

15. Principle of Efficiency. The structure should enable the organisation to achieve its objectives at the minimum possible cost.

7.2 Process of Organising

Organising is not a single act but a series of well-defined steps. The number of steps may vary slightly from one writer to another, but the following are generally accepted:

1. Determination of Objectives. The first step in organising is to identify the objectives that the enterprise wishes to achieve. The objectives must be clearly defined, since they determine the nature and the volume of work that has to be done.

2. Identification of Activities. On the basis of the objectives, the various activities required to achieve them are identified and listed. For example, in a manufacturing company, the activities may include purchasing of raw material, production, marketing, finance, accounting, personnel and so on.

3. Grouping of Activities. Similar activities are grouped together so that they may be handled by a single person or department. This step is known as departmentation. The grouping may be done on the basis of function, product, territory, customer or process.

4. Assignment of Duties. After the activities have been grouped, the next step is to assign them to suitable persons. The right job is given to the right person, having regard to his qualifications, experience and aptitude. The duties of each person are clearly defined and reduced to writing in the form of a job description.

5. Delegation of Authority. Along with the duties, the necessary authority is also delegated to each person so that he may carry out his duties effectively. The authority of each position is also reduced to writing wherever possible.

6. Establishing Relationships. The relationships among the various positions are clearly defined. Each person knows who his immediate superior is, who his subordinates are, and which other persons or departments he must consult or coordinate with. The result is a clear chain of command from the top to the bottom of the organisation.

7. Providing Physical Facilities and a Proper Environment. An organisation cannot function without suitable office space, equipment, machinery, technology and a healthy working environment. The provision of these facilities is also a part of the organising function.

8. Coordinating the Activities. Finally, all the activities, departments and persons must be linked together so that they work in harmony towards the common goal. Coordination runs through the entire process of organising.

7.3 Formal and Informal Organisation

Within every enterprise, two types of organisation exist side by side—the formal organisation, which is deliberately created by the management, and the informal organisation, which grows spontaneously out of the personal relationships among the employees.

7.3.1 Formal Organisation

The formal organisation is the official structure that the management of the enterprise consciously brings into being for the purpose of achieving its objectives. It is reflected in the organisation chart, the job descriptions, the manuals and the rule books. The formal organisation has the following features:

- It is deliberately created by the management.
- It has a clearly defined structure with positions, departments, levels and lines of authority.
- The duties and the authority of each position are clearly laid down.
- Rules, procedures and policies govern the conduct of the work.
- It is goal-oriented and impersonal.
- Communication generally flows along the established channels.

Examples of formal organisations include all companies, government departments, banks, hospitals, universities and the armed forces.

7.3.2 Informal Organisation

The informal organisation is the network of personal relationships that develops naturally among the members of the formal organisation. It is not planned by the management, nor is it shown on any chart. It arises out of the human need for friendship, recognition and a sense of belonging. Its existence was first brought to light by the Hawthorne experiments, which we have already discussed in Chapter 2.

The features of the informal organisation are:

- It comes into being spontaneously, without any official sanction.
- It is based on personal friendships, common interests, common backgrounds and informal interactions.
- It has no defined structure or hierarchy, though informal leaders do emerge.
- Communication in the informal organisation, often called the "grapevine," travels through word of mouth and spreads very rapidly.
- It satisfies the social and the psychological needs of the employees.

The lunch-hour groups in an office, the cricket team of a company, the WhatsApp group of fellow employees and the union of office workers are all examples of the informal organisation.

7.3.3 Formal versus Informal Organisation

Basis	**Formal Organisation**	**Informal Organisation**
Origin	Deliberately created by the management.	Arises spontaneously out of personal relationships.
Purpose	To achieve the goals of the enterprise.	To meet the social and psychological needs of the employees.
Structure	Clearly defined and shown in the organisation chart.	No defined structure; informal leaders emerge.
Rules	Governed by formal rules, policies and procedures.	Governed by group norms and customs.
Communication	Through official channels.	Through the grapevine.
Authority	Flows from the top downwards.	Emerges from the group itself.
Permanence	Stable and continuing.	Changes frequently as members come and go.

7.3.4 Benefits and Drawbacks of Informal Organisation

The informal organisation, though not officially created, has both benefits and drawbacks.

Benefits: The informal organisation fulfils the social needs of the employees. It provides a fast channel of communication. It supplies useful feedback to the management about the feelings and the problems of the workers. It often supports the formal authority by encouraging cooperation among employees. It also helps in the emergence of natural leaders, who may later be useful to the management.

Drawbacks: The grapevine can also spread rumours and misinformation. Strong informal groups may resist legitimate changes proposed by the management. Group pressures may force individual members to conform, leading to a loss of personal initiative. In extreme cases, the goals of the informal group may run counter to those of the formal organisation.

A wise manager does not try to suppress the informal organisation. He recognises its existence, understands its working and tries to make use of its strengths in the interest of the enterprise.

7.4 Importance and Limitations of Organising

7.4.1 Importance of Organising

Good organising offers a number of benefits to the enterprise, of which the following are the most important:

1. Facilitates Administration. A clear organisation structure makes the work of administration easy. Every person knows what he has to do and to whom he has to report.

2. Specialisation. By dividing the work and grouping similar activities together, organising brings about specialisation. A specialist worker is more efficient than a jack-of-all-trades.

3. Optimum Use of Resources. Good organising ensures that men, money, materials and machines are used in the most efficient manner, with little wastage.

4. Coordination. Organising provides the means by which the various activities are coordinated and the efforts of different individuals and departments are directed towards the common goal.

5. Avoidance of Duplication. When work is properly organised, the duplication of effort and overlapping of responsibility are avoided.

6. Facilitates Growth and Expansion. A sound organisation provides the framework within which the enterprise can grow. New activities can be added, new departments can be created and new markets can be entered without disrupting the existing structure.

7. Channel for Communication. The organisation provides clear channels through which information can flow from the top to the bottom and from the bottom to the top.

8. Encourages Initiative and Creativity. By delegating authority and by encouraging employees to participate in decisions, a good organisation brings out the best in them.

9. Scope for Training and Development. A well-organised enterprise provides ample opportunities for the training and development of its employees, who can be moved from one job to another and from one department to another as part of their growth.

10. Adaptation to Change. A flexible organisation can adapt itself quickly to changes in the environment, in technology and in customer preferences.

7.4.2 Limitations of Organising

Like every other function of management, organising too has its limitations:

1. Cost. The creation and maintenance of a sound organisation involves cost—in terms of money, time and effort. For very small enterprises, this cost may not be justified by the benefits.

2. Rigidity. Once an organisation has been created, it tends to develop a momentum of its own. Established positions, departments and procedures resist change, even when change is necessary.

3. Bureaucratic Tendencies. Large organisations may develop excessive rules, red tape and a slow style of decision-making. This is the well-known problem of bureaucracy.

4. Inter-Departmental Conflict. Departments may begin to compete with one another for resources, status and recognition. This may harm the overall interest of the enterprise.

5. Problems of the Informal Organisation. The informal organisation, if not properly handled, may create problems for the formal organisation.

6. Excessive Specialisation. Too much specialisation may make the work monotonous, reduce the worker's sense of involvement and narrow his outlook.

7. Difficulty in Adapting to a Dynamic Environment. An

organisation that has been carefully built for one set of conditions may find it difficult to adapt when those conditions change rapidly.

7.5 Organisation Charts and Manuals

7.5.1 Organisation Chart—Meaning

An organisation chart is a diagrammatic representation of the structure of the organisation. It shows the various positions, the departments, the levels of management and the lines of authority and communication. In a single picture, the chart gives a clear view of the formal organisation.

Some definitions of an organisation chart are given below:

1. George R. Terry— "An organisation chart is a diagrammatic form which shows the important aspects of an organisation, including the major functions and their respective relationships, the channels of supervision, and the relative authority of each employee who is in charge of his respective function."

2. Henry G. Hodges— "The organisation chart is a picture of arrangements and inter-arrangements of positions within an organisation."

7.5.2 Types of Organisation Charts

Organisation charts may be of three types:

1. Vertical Chart. This is the most common type of chart. The highest position is shown at the top, with the lower positions placed below it in descending order. The lines of authority run from the top downwards.

2. Horizontal Chart. Here, the highest position is shown on the left, with the lower positions arranged to the right in order of decreasing authority. The lines of authority run from left to right.

3. Circular Chart. In a circular chart, the highest position is shown at the centre, with the lower positions arranged in concentric circles around it. The lines of authority run from the centre outwards. This type of chart is less common but is sometimes used to suggest that all positions in the organisation are equally important.

7.5.3 Uses of the Organisation Chart

- It gives a clear picture of the structure of the enterprise at a glance.

- It helps the employees in understanding their own position and that of others.
- It is a useful aid in the training of new employees.
- It helps the management in spotting overlaps, gaps and weaknesses in the structure.
- It serves as a useful tool for planning future changes in the organisation.

7.5.4 Limitations of the Organisation Chart

- It shows only the formal relationships and not the informal ones.
- It does not indicate the degree of authority enjoyed by each position.
- It quickly becomes out of date if not regularly revised.
- It may create rigidity in the minds of the employees, who may refuse to do anything not specifically shown in the chart.
- It may also lead to a feeling of inferiority among those at the lower levels and of superiority among those at the higher levels.

7.5.5 Organisation Manual

An organisation manual is a booklet which contains, in a single document, all the important information about the organisation—its history, its objectives, its structure, its policies, its procedures, the duties and authority of each position, and the relationships among the various positions. The organisation chart is generally included in the manual.

Different writers have identified several types of manuals, of which the more common are:

- the policy manual, which sets out the policies of the company;
- the operating manual, which describes the procedures for various operations;
- the organisation manual, which describes the structure of the organisation;
- the departmental manual, which deals with the working of a particular department; and
- the employee handbook, which is meant for the use of the employees and contains information about their rights, duties and benefits.

7.5.6 Advantages and Limitations of Manuals

The organisation manual offers a number of advantages. It is a ready source of information about the organisation. It reduces confusion and disputes about responsibilities. It standardises practices across the various units of the enterprise. It is a useful aid in the training and induction of new employees. It serves as a reference document for decisions and is particularly useful when there are frequent changes in personnel.

At the same time, manuals have certain limitations. They are costly to prepare and to keep up to date. They may create rigidity, since employees may stick to the letter of the manual even when the situation calls for flexibility. No manual can cover every possible situation, and excessive reliance on it may stifle the use of judgement and initiative.

Summary

Organising is the process by which the activities required for the achievement of the objectives of the enterprise are identified, grouped together, assigned to suitable persons, and linked through proper relationships of authority and responsibility. It is a goal-oriented, group-based, continuous process which involves division of labour, delegation of authority, hierarchy, coordination and communication.

Sound organising is guided by a number of principles, including the principles of objective, division of work, authority and responsibility, unity of command, scalar chain, span of control, delegation, exception, coordination, balance, flexibility and simplicity. The process of organising consists of eight steps, beginning with the determination of objectives and ending with the coordination of activities.

Within every enterprise, both formal and informal organisations exist side by side. The formal organisation is deliberately created by the management, while the informal organisation grows out of the personal relationships among the employees. A wise manager recognises both and tries to harmonise them. Organising offers many benefits—administration, specialisation, coordination, growth and adaptation—but it also has its limitations such as cost, rigidity, bureaucracy and inter-departmental conflict. The organisation chart and the organisation manual are two useful tools that, between them, document the entire structure and working of the formal organisation.

Key Terms

Organising, Formal Organisation, Informal Organisation, Grapevine, Division of Labour, Authority, Responsibility, Hierarchy, Span of Control, Departmentation, Principles of Organising, Principle of Exception, Coordination, Organisation Chart, Vertical Chart, Horizontal Chart, Circular Chart, Organisation Manual, Policy Manual, Operating Manual, Employee Handbook.

Review Questions

A. Short Answer Questions (2 marks each)

1. Define organising in your own words.
2. State any four characteristics of organising.
3. What is meant by unity of command?
4. Distinguish between formal and informal organisation.
5. What is the grapevine?
6. Explain the principle of exception.
7. Name any three types of organisation charts.

B. Long Answer Questions (10 marks each)

8. Explain the meaning, nature and characteristics of organising.
9. Discuss the major principles of organising.
10. Describe the steps involved in the process of organising.
11. Distinguish between formal and informal organisation. What are the benefits and drawbacks of the informal organisation?
12. Discuss the importance and the limitations of organising.
13. Explain the meaning, types, uses and limitations of an organisation chart.
14. What is an organisation manual? Discuss its contents, advantages and limitations.

C. Practical / Case-Based Questions

15. Visit any college, bank or hospital in your locality, study its

working and prepare an organisation chart showing its various positions, departments and levels of authority.

CHAPTER 8

ORGANISATIONAL STRUCTURE AND DESIGN

Learning Objectives

After studying this chapter, the reader should be able to:

- describe the traditional structures of organisation—line, functional, and line and staff;
- explain the more recent structures such as matrix, project and network;
- understand the working of virtual and boundaryless organisations;
- identify the factors that influence the design of an organisation; and
- distinguish between mechanistic and organic forms of organisation.

Introduction

In the previous chapter, we have discussed organising as a function of management. Once the manager has decided that he must organise, the next question that arises is—what kind of structure should the organisation have? Should it follow the simple chain of command of a traditional army, or should it be built around specialist departments, or should it bring together a team of specialists from different fields for a particular project? Different structures suit different situations, and the choice of the right structure is a matter of careful judgement.

The structure of an organisation is the formal pattern of positions and relationships through which its work is carried out. It tells us who is responsible for what, who reports to whom, and how the various activities are linked together. The structure provides the skeleton on which the flesh and blood of the enterprise rest. A well-designed structure makes the work easy and smooth; a poorly designed structure becomes a source of constant friction and inefficiency.

Over the years, several types of organisational structures have been developed. The older types, such as the line, the functional and the line and staff, were suited to the relatively simple businesses of the past. The newer types, such as the matrix, the project, the network, the virtual and the boundaryless organisations, have come into being to meet the needs of the modern, fast-changing and technology-driven world. This chapter discusses each of these structures in turn and concludes with a discussion of the factors that influence the choice of the right structure for a particular enterprise.

8.1 Line, Functional, and Line and Staff Structures

8.1.1 Line Organisation

The line organisation, also known as the scalar, vertical or military organisation, is the oldest and the simplest form of organisation. The lines of authority run in a straight line from the top to the bottom of the enterprise. Each subordinate has one and only one superior, and each superior has direct authority over his subordinates. The army, the navy, the police and most small businesses follow this type of structure.

The line organisation may be of two types. In the pure line type, all the persons at a given level perform similar work. In the departmental line type, the activities are divided into departments, but within each department the line structure is followed.

Features. Authority flows from the top downwards in a clear chain. Each manager is responsible for all the activities of his unit. The unity of command is fully maintained. Communication takes place through the line, and the final authority for all decisions rests at the top.

Advantages. The line organisation is simple and easy to understand. Decisions can be taken quickly. Discipline is easy to maintain. Authority and responsibility are clearly fixed. The cost of running such an organisation is low. It is most suitable for small enterprises and for activities requiring strict discipline.

Disadvantages. The line manager is overloaded with work, since he has to look after every aspect of his unit. There is no scope for specialisation, and the manager may have to take decisions in areas where he has little expertise. There is a tendency for the manager to become autocratic. The structure does not suit large and complex enterprises.

8.1.2 Functional Organisation

The functional organisation owes its origin to F.W. Taylor. He felt that the line manager could not be an expert in every function, and that the worker should, therefore, receive orders from different specialist managers, each of whom would be responsible for one particular function. Taylor called this arrangement "functional foremanship." Although the original eight-foreman system of Taylor is not followed in its pure form anywhere today, the basic idea—that activities should be grouped on the basis of function and that each function should be headed by a specialist—has found wide acceptance.

Features. The activities of the enterprise are grouped on the basis of function, such as production, marketing, finance and personnel. Each function is headed by an expert. The same worker may receive orders from several specialist managers in respect of different aspects of his work. Authority is based on functional knowledge rather than on hierarchical position alone.

Advantages. Specialisation is the chief advantage. Each function is handled by an expert, leading to higher quality of work and better decisions. Standardisation of methods becomes possible. The burden on the top management is reduced, since the specialists take care of their own areas. Innovation and creative thinking are encouraged.

Disadvantages. The principle of unity of command is violated, since the same worker receives orders from several superiors. This may lead to confusion and conflict. Accountability for results is difficult to fix. Coordination among the various functional heads may be hard to achieve. The structure is costly to operate.

8.1.3 Line and Staff Organisation

The line and staff organisation is a combination of the line and the functional types. It seeks to combine the strengths of both while avoiding their weaknesses. Under this structure, the line officers retain the responsibility for taking decisions and for getting the work done, while specialist officers, known as staff officers, advise and assist them in their respective fields. Most large enterprises today follow some form of the line and staff organisation.

Features. There are two types of authority—line authority and staff authority. Line authority is the direct authority to take decisions and to issue orders. Staff authority is the authority to advise, to recommend and to provide expert assistance. The line is concerned with execution, while the staff is concerned with advice. Specialisation is achieved through the staff without violating the unity of command in the line.

The staff itself may be of different kinds:

- Personal staff, such as a personal secretary or an executive assistant to the chief executive;
- Specialist staff, such as the legal, financial, human resource, public relations and information technology departments; and
- General staff, who assist the manager in a wide variety of matters.

Advantages. The line and staff organisation brings together the simplicity of the line and the specialisation of the functional structure. The line officer has the benefit of expert advice from the staff. Decisions are better-informed. The unity of command is preserved. The structure is suitable for large and complex enterprises.

Disadvantages. Conflict often arises between line and staff officers. The line officers may regard the advice of the staff as interference, while the staff may complain that the line does not pay heed to its suggestions. The structure is also expensive to operate, since it involves a large number of staff officers in addition to the line.

8.2 Matrix, Project and Network Structures

8.2.1 Matrix Organisation

The matrix organisation came into being during the 1960s in the American aerospace industry, where the National Aeronautics and Space Administration (NASA) had to coordinate large and complex projects involving a number of specialists from different functions. The structure has since spread to many industries and is widely used in consulting firms, automobile companies and information technology companies.

The matrix structure combines the functional and the project structures. Each employee has two reporting relationships—one to the head of his functional department (such as engineering, marketing or finance) and the other to the head of the project on which he is working. Authority is, therefore, shared between the functional manager and the project manager. The result, when drawn on paper, looks like a matrix or a grid, with functions running across one direction and projects running across the other.

Advantages. The matrix structure makes for better use of resources, since the same specialists can be deployed on different projects at different times. It brings flexibility, since project teams can be assembled and disbanded as needed. It improves coordination among functions and gives sharper focus to each project. It is particularly suitable for complex projects involving many disciplines.

Disadvantages. The structure violates the principle of unity of command. The employee, with two bosses, may face conflicting demands. Power struggles between functional and project managers are common. Decision-making may slow down because of the need for joint approval. The structure is costly to operate.

8.2.2 Project Organisation

The project organisation is a temporary structure created for the execution of a specific project. Once the project is completed, the structure is dissolved and the employees return to their original departments or are reassigned to other projects. The project organisation is common in industries such as construction, defence, research and development, and large information technology assignments.

Familiar examples in India include the building of the Delhi Metro and other metro rail projects, the construction of major dams and expressways, and the planning and execution of space missions by the Indian Space Research Organisation (ISRO) such as Chandrayaan and Mangalyaan. Each of these projects is set up as a separate entity with its own project director, its own team of specialists drawn from various functions, its own budget and its own time schedule.

Features. The project organisation is goal-specific and time-bound. The project manager has full authority and responsibility for the project. The team is drawn from different functions and works exclusively on the project till its completion.

Advantages. Focused attention on the project, quick decision-making, better coordination among team members and clear accountability for results are the chief advantages. The structure is particularly well suited to unique, one-time tasks.

Disadvantages. Resources may be duplicated across projects. Specialists may face career uncertainty when their project ends. Good project managers, who combine technical knowledge with administrative ability, are not easy to find.

8.2.3 Network Organisation

The network organisation is a relatively recent development, born of the information technology revolution. Under this structure, a small core company carries out only the activities at which it is most skilled, while a wide network of independent companies, linked by information technology, performs the rest of the work. The core company acts as the hub, with the various outside partners forming the spokes of the wheel.

The classic example is Nike, the American sports goods company. Nike designs and markets its products but does not manufacture them itself. The manufacturing is carried out by hundreds of independent factories in various countries. Apple too designs its products in California but has them manufactured in China and elsewhere by partner companies. Many Indian companies have adopted similar arrangements, contracting out manufacturing, logistics, information technology and customer service to specialised firms.

Advantages. The network structure offers great flexibility, since partners can be added or replaced as needed. Costs are kept low, as the company does not have to invest in every activity. It can focus on its core competence—design, marketing, branding—while leaving the rest to specialists. It also enables rapid global expansion.

Disadvantages. The core company loses direct control over the activities outsourced to others. Quality and timely delivery depend on the reliability of the partners. There are risks to confidentiality, particularly when the partner is in another country. The structure may also weaken the long-term competitive position of the company, since key skills are no longer developed in-house.

8.3 Virtual and Boundaryless Organisations

8.3.1 Virtual Organisation

The virtual organisation is a temporary network of independent companies—suppliers, customers, even competitors—linked by information technology to share skills, costs and access to one another's markets. It has no permanent physical office in the traditional sense. Its employees may work from home, from co-working spaces or from various locations across the globe, connected by the internet.

The COVID-19 pandemic of 2020 gave a great push to virtual ways of working in India and across the world. Companies that had earlier been hesitant to allow employees to work from home discovered that much of the office work could indeed be done virtually. Many information technology firms in India now follow a hybrid model in which employees come to the office only for a few days a week and work virtually for the rest. Online education platforms such as BYJU'S, Unacademy and Vedantu, online consulting firms, freelancer-based companies and many start-ups operate largely as virtual organisations.

Advantages. The overhead costs of office space and other facilities are sharply reduced. Talent can be hired from anywhere in the world. The organisation can respond very quickly to new opportunities. Employees enjoy flexibility in their work arrangements.

Disadvantages. Communication can be difficult, particularly across different time zones and cultures. The lack of face-to-face contact may weaken team spirit and reduce informal exchange of ideas. Security and confidentiality of data become major concerns. Supervising the work and maintaining discipline are harder than in a physical office.

8.3.2 Boundaryless Organisation

The term "boundaryless organisation" was coined by Jack Welch, the legendary Chief Executive of General Electric (GE), during the 1990s. Welch wanted to break down the traditional walls that separate the various parts of a large company and to bring about free flow of ideas and information. The boundaryless organisation seeks to eliminate four kinds of boundaries:

1. Vertical Boundaries—those between the various levels of the hierarchy. The aim is to bring the top management close to the operating staff.

2. Horizontal Boundaries—those between the various departments. The aim is to promote cross-functional teamwork.

3. External Boundaries—those between the company and its customers, suppliers and other outside parties. The aim is to build strong partnerships.

4. Geographical Boundaries—those between the various countries in which the company operates. The aim is to function as a single, global enterprise.

Features. The boundaryless organisation typically has a flat structure with few levels of management. It makes wide use of cross-functional teams. The employees are empowered to take decisions on their own. Communication is open in all directions. Strategic alliances with other companies are used freely.

Advantages. Decisions are taken faster. Innovation is encouraged through the free flow of ideas across boundaries. Coordination among departments improves. The organisation becomes more flexible and responsive to change.

Disadvantages. When boundaries are removed, accountability may become unclear. Employees may feel confused about their roles. The structure requires highly skilled, self-motivated employees, who may not always be available. Managers who have grown up in traditional structures often find it difficult to adjust to the boundaryless way of working.

8.4 Factors Affecting Organisational Design

Organisational design refers to the choice of the structure most suited to the situation in which the enterprise operates. The contingency approach to management, discussed in Chapter 2, tells us that there is no one best design that fits every situation. The right design depends on a number of factors, the more important of which are described below.

1. Strategy. The structure of an organisation must support its strategy. Alfred Chandler, after his famous study of large American corporations, concluded that "structure follows strategy." A company pursuing a growth strategy needs a flexible structure that can easily accommodate new units. A company following a cost-leadership strategy may prefer a functional structure that allows tight control over costs. A company pursuing differentiation may need a structure that encourages creativity and innovation.

2. Size of the Organisation. Small organisations can operate with a simple line structure, with the owner-manager taking most of the decisions. As the organisation grows in size, the structure must become more elaborate, with more departments, more levels and more specialists.

3. Technology. Joan Woodward, a British researcher, studied a hundred manufacturing firms in southern England and found that the structure that suited them depended on the technology they used. Firms using unit or small-batch production (such as custom-built machinery) had simple, flat structures. Firms using mass-production technology (such as automobile assembly) had functional, more rigid structures with many levels. Firms using continuous process technology (such as petroleum refining) had complex structures with a higher proportion of managers.

4. Environment. Tom Burns and G.M. Stalker, two British scholars, classified organisations into two types on the basis of their environment—mechanistic and organic. Mechanistic organisations, with their rigid hierarchies, clear rules and specialised jobs, are suited to stable and predictable environments. Organic organisations, with their flexible structures, broad jobs and free flow of information, are suited to dynamic and uncertain environments. The Indian information technology industry, with its fast-changing technology, has by and large adopted organic structures.

5. People and Culture. The skills, education, experience and cultural values of the workforce influence the choice of structure. An educated and highly motivated workforce can handle the freedom of an organic structure, while a less skilled workforce may need the discipline of a mechanistic structure.

6. Nature of Activity. Manufacturing companies often use functional structures, service organisations often use matrix or team-based structures, and construction or consulting firms often use project structures. The type of activity, in other words, has a major bearing on the choice of structure.

7. Geographic Spread. A company operating from a single location can manage with a simple structure. A company spread across regions or countries will need a divisional or regional structure, with each region enjoying considerable autonomy.

8. Life-Cycle Stage. The structure of an organisation often changes with its stage of development. A start-up usually has a simple, informal structure. As it grows, it adopts a functional structure. On reaching maturity, it may move to a divisional or matrix structure. In times of decline, restructuring becomes necessary.

9. Government Regulations. Some industries, such as banking and insurance, operate under detailed regulations laid down by the government and the regulator (the Reserve Bank of India, the Insurance Regulatory and Development Authority and others). These regulations may dictate certain features of the structure.

10. Philosophy of Top Management. The personal beliefs of the top management about centralisation and decentralisation, about delegation, about employee participation and about risk-taking, all influence the choice of structure. The same business activity can be organised quite differently by two leaders with different management philosophies.

8.4.1 Mechanistic and Organic Structures

As we have seen, Burns and Stalker drew a useful distinction between mechanistic and organic structures. The chief differences between the two are summarised in the table below:

Basis	Mechanistic Structure	Organic Structure
Hierarchy	Tall, with many levels.	Flat, with few levels.

Basis	Mechanistic Structure	Organic Structure
Specialisation	High; jobs are narrow and clearly defined.	Low; jobs are broad and flexible.
Authority	Centralised at the top.	Decentralised; widely shared.
Rules and Procedures	Numerous and strictly enforced.	Few; flexibility is encouraged.
Communication	Vertical, along formal channels.	Free flow in all directions.
Suitable Environment	Stable and predictable.	Dynamic and uncertain.
Typical Example	Government departments, banks, manufacturing units.	Information technology firms, start-ups, research laboratories.

In actual practice, very few organisations are purely mechanistic or purely organic. Most are a blend of the two, with different parts of the same organisation leaning more towards one type or the other. The challenge before the modern manager is to find the right blend for his particular situation.

Summary

The structure of an organisation is the formal pattern of positions and relationships through which its work is carried out. The traditional structures include the line, the functional and the line and staff. The line organisation is simple, with a clear chain of command, but offers no scope for specialisation. The functional organisation, given by F.W. Taylor, provides specialisation but violates the unity of command. The line and staff organisation, used by most large enterprises, combines line authority for decisions with staff advice for specialisation.

The newer structures include the matrix, the project and the network. The matrix organisation, which originated in the American aerospace industry, has employees reporting both to a functional head and to a project head. The project organisation is a temporary arrangement built around a specific assignment, as seen in the Delhi Metro and ISRO missions. The network organisation, of which Nike and Apple are well-known examples, is built around a small core company that outsources most of its activities to a network of partners.

The virtual organisation, made possible by information technology, has no permanent office and links its employees through the internet. The boundaryless organisation, a concept developed by Jack Welch at GE, seeks to remove the boundaries between levels, between departments, between the company and the outside world, and between countries.

The choice of the right structure depends on a number of factors—strategy, size, technology, environment, people, nature of activity, geographic spread, life-cycle stage, government regulation and the philosophy of top management. Burns and Stalker drew a useful distinction between mechanistic structures, suitable for stable environments, and organic structures, suitable for dynamic environments. Most modern organisations are a blend of the two, designed to suit the particular needs of the situation.

Key Terms

Organisational Structure, Organisational Design, Line Organisation, Functional Organisation, Line and Staff Organisation, Personal Staff, Specialist Staff, Matrix Organisation, Project Organisation, Network Organisation, Virtual Organisation, Boundaryless Organisation, Jack Welch, Mechanistic Structure, Organic Structure, Burns and Stalker, Joan Woodward, Alfred Chandler, Structure Follows Strategy.

Review Questions

A. Short Answer Questions (2 marks each)

1. What is meant by line organisation?
2. Who is the originator of the functional organisation?
3. Distinguish between line and staff authority.

4. Give two examples of project organisations in India.
5. What is a network organisation? Give one example.
6. Who coined the term "boundaryless organisation"?
7. Distinguish between mechanistic and organic structures.

B. Long Answer Questions (10 marks each)

8. Explain the features, advantages and disadvantages of the line organisation.

9. Discuss the functional organisation as given by F.W. Taylor. State its merits and demerits.

10. Describe the line and staff organisation. Why is it the most widely used structure today?

11. Explain the matrix structure of organisation. Under what circumstances is it most suitable?

12. Write a detailed note on the virtual and boundaryless organisations.

13. Discuss the various factors that affect the design of an organisation.

CHAPTER 9

AUTHORITY, RESPONSIBILITY AND DELEGATION

Learning Objectives

After studying this chapter, the reader should be able to:

- understand the concept and the various sources of authority;
- distinguish between responsibility and accountability;
- describe the process and the principles of delegation;
- identify the major barriers to effective delegation and the ways of overcoming them; and
- distinguish between centralisation and decentralisation of authority.

Introduction

An organisation, as we have seen in the previous two chapters, is built up of various positions, each with its own set of duties. These positions, however, do not operate in isolation. They are linked together through relationships of authority and responsibility. Authority is what gives a manager the right to command his subordinates and to expect compliance with his orders. Responsibility is the obligation of the subordinate to perform the duties assigned to him. Without authority, no manager can function; without responsibility, no work would be done.

As an organisation grows in size, no single person—not even the Managing Director—can perform all the duties himself. He must delegate, that is, hand over some of his work and the authority needed for its performance to others. Delegation is the means by which the work of an organisation gets divided among many shoulders. Without delegation, the manager would soon collapse under the burden of work, and the organisation itself would cease to grow.

Closely related to delegation are the concepts of centralisation and decentralisation. When most of the authority is concentrated at the top, the organisation is said to be centralised. When the authority is spread widely across the various levels, it is said to be decentralised. Modern industries such as the Tata Group, ITC and the Mahindra Group have moved towards a high degree of decentralisation, while many family-run businesses and public-sector enterprises continue to be centralised.

This chapter examines the concept and the sources of authority, the closely related ideas of responsibility and accountability, the process and the principles of delegation, the barriers that come in the way of effective delegation, and the relative merits of centralisation and decentralisation.

9.1 Concept and Sources of Authority

9.1.1 Meaning and Definition of Authority

Authority may be defined as the right of a manager to take decisions, to issue orders to his subordinates and to expect them to be carried out. It is the cement that holds an organisation together. Every position in an organisation, from the office boy to the chairman, carries with it a certain amount of authority—the office boy has the authority to deliver files, and the chairman has the authority to approve a multi-crore investment.

Some well-known definitions of authority are given below:

1. Henri Fayol— "Authority is the right to give orders and the power to exact obedience."

2. Koontz and O'Donnell— "Authority is the power to command others to act or not to act in a manner deemed by the possessor of the authority to further enterprise objectives."

3. Louis A. Allen— "Authority is the sum of the powers and the rights entrusted to make possible the performance of the work delegated."

4. Mooney and Reiley— "Authority is the power and the right to lead, to command and to require action from others."

9.1.2 Characteristics of Authority

- Authority is the right to take decisions and to give orders.
- It is attached to the position, not to the person holding it. When a person leaves the position, the authority remains with the position and passes on to his successor.
- Authority flows from the top downwards along the scalar chain.

- Authority is always limited. No manager has unlimited authority; he must operate within the limits laid down by law, by company policy and by the customs of the organisation.
- Authority must be balanced by an equal amount of responsibility.
- Authority is essentially a relationship between a superior and a subordinate.

9.1.3 Sources of Authority

Different writers have given different explanations of the source from which the authority of a manager flows. The chief theories on this subject are the following:

1. Formal or Traditional Authority Theory. According to this theory, authority flows from the top of the organisation downwards. In a joint stock company, for example, the source of all authority is the law and the Memorandum of Association. The shareholders, who are the owners, elect the Board of Directors, who in turn appoint the Managing Director, who then delegates authority to the General Manager, and so on down the line. This is the most widely accepted view.

2. Acceptance Theory. This theory was propounded by Chester I. Barnard. According to him, the authority of a manager has reality only when his orders are accepted by his subordinates. If the order is not accepted, there is, in effect, no authority. Barnard pointed out that most orders fall within what he called the "zone of indifference" of the subordinate—the zone within which he is willing to comply without questioning. Orders that fall outside this zone may be resisted, and in such cases the authority of the manager is in fact challenged.

3. Competence Theory. According to this theory, authority arises out of the personal knowledge, skill and competence of an individual. A doctor, a chartered accountant, a software architect or any other specialist has authority over those who consult him because of his expertise. This kind of authority is also known as the authority of knowledge.

4. Charismatic Theory. Some persons command authority because of their personal magnetism and their inspiring qualities of character. Such leaders are followed willingly by others, even in the absence of any formal position. Mahatma Gandhi, who held no government office, exercised tremendous moral authority over the entire nation. In modern business, the personal charisma of leaders such as Dhirubhai Ambani and Steve Jobs gave them an authority that went far beyond what their positions alone could have provided.

9.1.4 Types of Authority

Authority in an organisation may be of three main types:

(a) Line Authority—the direct authority of a superior over his subordinates in the chain of command. The Production Manager has line authority over the assistant production managers and the foremen working under him.

(b) Staff Authority—the authority to advise, to recommend and to assist, but not to command. The legal adviser of a company has staff authority over the General Manager in legal matters.

(c) Functional Authority—the limited line authority given to a staff specialist in his own area of expertise. The personnel manager, for instance, may be given functional authority to issue uniform rules regarding leave to be followed by all departments.

9.2 Responsibility and Accountability

9.2.1 Responsibility

Responsibility is the obligation of a subordinate to perform the duties assigned to him by his superior to the best of his ability. It is the other side of the coin of authority. While authority gives a person the right to command, responsibility imposes on him the duty to perform.

Some well-known definitions of responsibility are:

1. Koontz and O'Donnell— "Responsibility may be defined as the obligation of a subordinate to whom a duty has been assigned to perform the duty."

2. Dalton E. McFarland— "Responsibility is the obligation of an individual to perform assigned duties to the best of his ability under the direction of his executive leader."

3. Davis— "Responsibility is an obligation of an individual to perform assigned duties."

The chief features of responsibility are as follows:

- It arises out of the superior-subordinate relationship.
- It flows upwards—the subordinate is responsible to his superior.
- It cannot be delegated. A superior may delegate the duty to his subordinate, but he himself remains finally responsible to his own superior.
- It is a continuing obligation; it does not end with one act.

9.2.2 Accountability

Accountability is the state of being answerable for the discharge of one's duties. The subordinate, having accepted the duty and the authority, is now accountable to his superior for the results. He must report back on what he has done and explain any failures.

Accountability differs from responsibility in the following ways. Responsibility is the obligation to perform; accountability is the obligation to report on performance. Responsibility starts the moment a duty is accepted; accountability comes into play after the duty has been performed. A subordinate cannot escape his accountability by passing on the duty to someone else.

9.2.3 Relationship between Authority, Responsibility and Accountability

Authority, responsibility and accountability are three closely related concepts. A sound organisation requires that the three should always remain in balance. This is known as the principle of parity of authority and responsibility. If authority is greater than responsibility, the manager may become arbitrary and even tyrannical, since there are no duties to balance his powers. If responsibility is greater than authority, the manager becomes frustrated, since he is held answerable for results which he does not have the powers to achieve.

The principle, therefore, is that the amount of authority granted to a person and the amount of responsibility imposed on him must be equal. Both, in turn, give rise to accountability, by which the person becomes answerable for the use he makes of his authority and for the discharge of his responsibility.

9.3 Delegation—Process and Principles

9.3.1 Meaning and Concept of Delegation

Delegation is the process by which a manager assigns a portion of his work to his subordinate, gives him the necessary authority to perform that work and holds him accountable for the results. In other words, delegation is the downward sharing of authority between a superior and a subordinate.

Some well-known definitions of delegation are:

1. Louis A. Allen— "Delegation is the entrustment of responsibility and authority to another and the creation of accountability for performance."

2. Theo Haimann— "Delegation of authority means the granting of authority to subordinates to operate within prescribed limits."

3. F.G. Moore— "Delegation means assigning work to others and giving them authority to do it."

9.3.2 Process or Elements of Delegation

Louis A. Allen identified three essential elements of delegation, which together form the process:

1. Assignment of Duties. The first step is to entrust the subordinate with the duties or tasks to be performed. The superior decides what is to be done, breaks it down into smaller jobs and assigns them to his subordinates according to their capacity.

2. Grant of Authority. Along with the duties, the necessary authority is granted to the subordinate so that he is able to perform them. The authority granted should be sufficient to enable the subordinate to discharge his duty, but it should not exceed the requirements of the duty.

3. Creation of Accountability. Having accepted the duty and the authority, the subordinate becomes accountable to his superior for the discharge of his duty and for the use he makes of his authority. The superior, in turn, remains accountable to his own superior for the work of his subordinate.

Some writers add a fourth step—the determination of the results expected from the subordinate. The expected results are clearly stated at the time of delegation so that the subordinate knows exactly what he is to achieve.

9.3.3 Importance of Delegation

Delegation is of vital importance to every manager and to every organisation. Its benefits include the following:

- It relieves the manager of routine and detailed work, and gives him time to attend to important matters of policy and planning.
- It enables the work of the enterprise to be divided among many persons, so that no one is over-burdened.
- It develops the subordinates, by giving them the experience of taking decisions and of bearing responsibility.
- It identifies future leaders for higher positions in the organisation.
- It speeds up decision-making, since the decisions are taken at the point closest to the action.
- It improves the morale and the motivation of the employees, who feel trusted and valued.
- It makes possible the growth and the expansion of the enterprise, since no single person can manage a large organisation single-handedly.

9.3.4 Principles of Delegation

Effective delegation is governed by the following well-established principles:

1. Principle of Functional Definition. The duties, authority and expected results of each position should be clearly defined in writing. The subordinate must know exactly what is expected of him.

2. Principle of Delegation by Results Expected. The amount of authority delegated should be sufficient to achieve the results expected from the subordinate. Too little authority makes the duty impossible to perform; too much creates problems of its own.

3. Principle of Parity of Authority and Responsibility. The authority granted and the responsibility imposed must be equal. Neither should exceed the other.

4. Principle of Absolute Responsibility. While authority can be delegated, responsibility cannot. The superior remains finally responsible for the acts of his subordinate to his own superior. As Louis Allen has put it, "responsibility cannot be delegated, only the work can be."

5. Principle of Unity of Command. A subordinate should receive orders from, and should be accountable to, one superior only. Delegation should not violate this principle.

6. Principle of Scalar Chain. Delegation should follow the established chain of command, from the top downwards.

7. Principle of Authority Level. Decisions within the authority of a particular position should be taken at that position and should not be sent up to the higher levels.

8. Principle of Exception. Only those matters which are beyond the authority of the subordinate, or which are out of the ordinary, should be referred to the superior. Routine matters should be decided at the level of the subordinate.

9.4 Barriers to Effective Delegation

Although delegation is a great help to the manager, many managers find it hard to delegate effectively. The barriers to delegation may arise from three sources—the superior, the subordinate and the organisation.

9.4.1 Barriers on the Part of the Superior

- The feeling that "I can do it better myself." Some managers are convinced that no subordinate can match the quality of their own work and, therefore, refuse to delegate.
- Lack of confidence in the ability or the integrity of the subordinates.
- Fear of being overshadowed by a competent subordinate.
- Reluctance to take the risk of mistakes by the subordinate, for which the superior would still be answerable.
- Inability to plan, organise and direct the work of others.
- Personal insecurity and a feeling that delegation will reduce one's own importance.
- A conservative attitude that does not welcome new ways of working.

9.4.2 Barriers on the Part of the Subordinate

- Fear of criticism in case of failure.
- Lack of self-confidence and of the necessary experience.
- Preference for being told what to do rather than having to decide for oneself.

• Already heavy workload, which makes the subordinate unwilling to take on more.

• Lack of adequate information, training or resources to handle the delegated task.

• Absence of any incentive or reward for accepting additional responsibility.

9.4.3 Barriers on the Part of the Organisation

• A highly centralised culture in which all decisions are taken at the top.

• Absence of clear job descriptions and authority limits.

• Inadequate planning, which leaves the superior himself unclear about what to delegate.

• Lack of a proper control system, which makes the superior fearful of losing track of the work.

• Splintered authority, in which the same matter has to be approved by several officers.

• Poor systems of communication and information sharing.

9.4.4 Overcoming the Barriers

Effective delegation can be brought about by the following measures:

• careful selection of the right person for the right job;

• adequate training and orientation of the subordinates;

• clear definition of the duties, authority and results expected;

• free and effective communication between the superior and the subordinate;

• creating an atmosphere of trust, in which honest mistakes are tolerated and learning is encouraged;

• establishing a sound control system that does not interfere with the day-to-day work; and

• suitably rewarding good performance and counselling poor performance.

9.5 Centralisation versus Decentralisation

9.5.1 Concept of Centralisation

Centralisation refers to the concentration of decision-making authority at the top levels of management. In a highly centralised organisation, the lower levels have very little freedom; they merely carry out the orders received from above.

In the words of Henri Fayol, "Everything that goes to increase the importance of the subordinate's role is decentralisation; everything that goes to reduce it is centralisation." According to Allen, "Centralisation is the systematic and consistent reservation of authority at the central points within the organisation."

9.5.2 Concept of Decentralisation

Decentralisation is the opposite of centralisation. It refers to the systematic dispersal of decision-making authority to the lower levels of the organisation. In a decentralised set-up, the lower-level managers enjoy considerable freedom in taking decisions within their own areas of work.

Allen defined decentralisation as "the systematic effort to delegate to the lowest levels all authority except that which can be exercised at central points." Henri Fayol described it in terms of the relative importance of the role of the subordinate.

9.5.3 Delegation and Decentralisation—A Comparison

Delegation and decentralisation are closely related concepts but are not the same thing. The chief differences between them are as follows:

Basis	Delegation	Decentralisation
Nature	A process; takes place between a superior and a subordinate.	A philosophy; spreads throughout the organisation.
Necessity	Compulsory in every organisation, however small.	Optional; depends on the choice of top management.
Scope	Narrow; covers a particular task or duty.	Wide; covers all or most of the work of the enterprise.
Reversibility	Authority cannot be	Top management may

Basis	Delegation	Decentralisation
	withdrawn easily once delegated.	withdraw decentralised authority at any time.
Responsibility	The superior remains responsible for the delegated work.	The unit head becomes responsible for his unit's performance.

9.5.4 Factors Favouring Centralisation and Decentralisation

Factors favouring centralisation: (i) small size of the enterprise; (ii) few products and limited geographical spread; (iii) need for uniformity of policy and action; (iv) lack of competent and trained subordinates; (v) tight regulatory environment; and (vi) a top management that prefers tight personal control.

Factors favouring decentralisation: (i) large size of the enterprise; (ii) diversified product range; (iii) wide geographical spread, both within India and abroad; (iv) availability of competent and trained subordinates; (v) need for quick decision-making in a competitive environment; (vi) need for innovation and adaptation to local conditions; and (vii) a top management that believes in employee participation.

9.5.5 Advantages of Decentralisation

- It reduces the burden on the top management.
- It enables quicker decisions, since the decisions are taken closer to the point of action.
- It develops the abilities of the lower-level managers and prepares them for higher responsibilities.
- It improves the morale and the motivation of the employees.
- It helps the organisation to adapt itself to local conditions and to customer needs.
- It encourages a spirit of healthy competition among the various units.
- It makes possible the growth of large and diversified enterprises.

9.5.6 Disadvantages of Decentralisation

- It may lead to a lack of uniformity in policies and practices across the various units.
- It increases the cost of operation, since each decentralised unit requires its own set of managers and supporting staff.
- Coordination among the various units may become difficult.
- Healthy competition may sometimes turn into harmful rivalry among units.
- Quick action during an emergency or a crisis may be difficult under a fully decentralised system.
- It requires competent managers at all levels, who may not always be easily available.

Most large Indian business houses today follow a fair degree of decentralisation. The Tata Group, with its many independent operating companies; ITC, with its various business divisions; and the Aditya Birla Group, with its widely spread global operations, are good examples. Smaller family-run businesses and many public-sector enterprises, on the other hand, continue to be highly centralised, with most major decisions being taken at the top.

Summary

Authority is the right of a manager to take decisions, to issue orders to his subordinates and to expect compliance. It is attached to the position, flows from the top downwards and is always limited. The various theories of authority—the formal, the acceptance, the competence and the charismatic—explain its source from different points of view. Authority in an organisation is of three main types—line, staff and functional.

Responsibility is the obligation of a subordinate to perform the duties assigned to him. It flows upwards and cannot be delegated. Accountability is the state of being answerable for one's performance. The three concepts of authority, responsibility and accountability must always be kept in balance. This is known as the principle of parity of authority and responsibility.

Delegation is the process by which a superior assigns a part of his work to his subordinate, grants him the necessary authority and creates accountability for the performance of the work. Louis Allen identified three essential elements of delegation. The major principles of delegation include the principles of functional definition, delegation by results expected, parity of authority and responsibility, absoluteness of responsibility, unity of command, scalar chain, authority level and exception.

Effective delegation is often hindered by barriers arising from the superior, the subordinate and the organisation. These barriers can be overcome by careful selection and training, clear definition of duties and authority, free communication, an atmosphere of trust, sound control systems and suitable rewards.

Centralisation refers to the concentration of authority at the top, while decentralisation refers to the systematic dispersal of authority to the lower levels. The two are different from delegation, which is a process between a particular superior and a particular subordinate. Modern Indian business houses such as the Tata Group, ITC and the Aditya Birla Group are good examples of decentralised organisations.

Key Terms

Authority, Formal Authority Theory, Acceptance Theory of Authority, Zone of Indifference, Chester I. Barnard, Competence Theory, Charismatic Authority, Line Authority, Staff Authority, Functional Authority, Responsibility, Accountability, Parity of Authority and Responsibility, Delegation, Assignment of Duties, Grant of Authority, Creation of Accountability, Absolute Responsibility, Principle of Exception, Centralisation, Decentralisation, Splintered Authority.

Review Questions

A. Short Answer Questions (2 marks each)

1. Define authority.
2. Name the four theories of the source of authority.
3. What is meant by the "zone of indifference"?
4. Distinguish between responsibility and accountability.

5. State any three principles of delegation.
6. Why is it said that "responsibility cannot be delegated"?
7. Distinguish between delegation and decentralisation.

B. Long Answer Questions (10 marks each)

8. Discuss the concept and the various sources of authority.

9. Explain the relationship between authority, responsibility and accountability.

10. Describe the process and the principles of delegation of authority.

11. What are the major barriers to effective delegation? How can they be overcome?

12. Distinguish between centralisation and decentralisation. Discuss the advantages and the disadvantages of decentralisation.

C. Practical / Case-Based Questions

13. Choose any well-known Indian business house (such as the Tata Group, ITC or the Mahindra Group) and discuss the extent to which it is decentralised. What are the benefits that it has gained from decentralisation?

14. You are the owner of a small chain of three coaching institutes in Indore, Bhopal and Ujjain. Until now, you have been taking every important decision yourself. Discuss the steps you would take to decentralise the authority and the benefits you would expect to gain.

CHAPTER 10

DEPARTMENTATION, SPAN OF MANAGEMENT AND COORDINATION

Learning Objectives

After studying this chapter, the reader should be able to:

- understand the concept of departmentation and its various bases;
- explain the meaning of the span of management and the factors that determine it;
- distinguish between tall and flat structures of organisation;
- appreciate the need, the principles and the techniques of coordination; and
- understand why coordination is called the essence of management.

Introduction

Once the basic structure of the organisation has been chosen, the manager faces three further questions of great practical importance. First, on what basis should the activities of the enterprise be grouped together into departments? Should the grouping be by function, by product, by territory, by customer, or by some other basis? Secondly, how many subordinates should report to a single manager? Is there a magic number that produces the best results? And thirdly, how should the various departments and the various subordinates be made to work together as a single team, in spite of their different specialisations and their different points of view?

The first question is answered through the process of departmentation, by which the activities of the enterprise are grouped into smaller, manageable units. The second question is answered by the concept of the span of management, which deals with the number of subordinates that a manager can effectively supervise. The third question is answered by the concept of coordination, by which the efforts of the various departments and individuals are blended into a single, harmonious whole.

This chapter discusses these three closely related topics. The bases of departmentation, the concept and determinants of the span of management, the need and principles of coordination, the techniques of effective coordination, and finally the reasons why coordination is described as the very essence of management—all these are taken up in turn.

10.1 Bases of Departmentation

10.1.1 Meaning and Importance of Departmentation

Departmentation is the process of dividing the activities of an enterprise into smaller and more manageable units called departments, sections or divisions. It is the second step in the process of organising, coming immediately after the identification of activities. According to Koontz and O'Donnell, "Departmentation refers to a distinct area, division or branch of an enterprise over which a manager has authority for the performance of specified activities."

The need for departmentation arises out of the simple fact that a single manager cannot directly supervise all the activities of a large enterprise. Departmentation makes possible the application of the principle of specialisation, fixes the responsibility for each group of activities on a particular manager, brings about better coordination within each group, and provides a clear basis for control and growth.

10.1.2 Bases of Departmentation

The activities of an enterprise can be grouped on the basis of several criteria. The chief bases of departmentation are described below.

1. Departmentation by Function. This is the most common basis of departmentation. The activities of the enterprise are grouped according to the major functions to be performed, such as production, marketing, finance, personnel, and research and development. Each function is placed under the charge of a specialist manager who has expertise in that area. Most small and medium-sized manufacturing companies in India use this basis.

The advantages of functional departmentation are specialisation, economy of operation, easy control by the top management and clear career paths for specialists. The disadvantages include a tendency to develop narrow departmental loyalties, slow decision-making and difficulty in fixing responsibility for the success or failure of any one product.

2. Departmentation by Product or Service. Large multi-product companies often group their activities on the basis of products or product lines. Each product becomes a separate department, with its own production, marketing and finance functions. Hindustan Unilever, for example, has separate divisions for home care, personal care, foods and refreshments. ITC has divisions for cigarettes, hotels, foods, paperboards, agribusiness and information technology. The Tata Group is organised as a federation of independent product companies.

Product-wise departmentation brings sharper focus on each product, fixes accountability clearly and enables faster decision-making. Its drawbacks are the duplication of resources across products and the higher cost of operation.

3. Departmentation by Territory or Geography. Enterprises that operate over wide geographical areas often group their activities by region. The State Bank of India, for instance, is organised into circles such as North, South, East, West and Central. Most insurance companies, fast-moving consumer goods companies and pharmaceutical companies follow a regional structure. Within the state of Madhya Pradesh too, large business houses often have separate offices for the Indore region, the Bhopal region, the Gwalior region and the Jabalpur region.

Territorial departmentation enables the company to remain close to its customers, to take advantage of local knowledge and to respond quickly to local conditions. Its drawbacks include the high cost of running many offices and the difficulty of coordinating the various regions.

4. Departmentation by Customer. Some enterprises group their activities on the basis of the customers they serve. A commercial bank, for example, may have separate divisions for retail banking, corporate banking, agricultural banking and international banking. A textile mill may have one section for the export market and another for the domestic market. A university may have separate units for undergraduate, postgraduate, research and distance-learning programmes.

Customer-wise departmentation enables the company to develop specialised expertise in serving each customer group and to provide better service. Its drawbacks include the under-utilisation of facilities and the temptation to grant special favours to particular customer groups.

5. Departmentation by Process or Equipment. Manufacturing concerns often group their activities on the basis of the production process or the equipment used. A cotton textile mill is generally organised into departments for spinning, weaving, dyeing, finishing and packing. A steel plant is organised into departments for smelting, casting, rolling and finishing. A sugar mill has separate departments for cane crushing, juice extraction, boiling, crystallisation and packing.

Process-wise departmentation makes the best use of specialised machinery and skilled manpower. Its drawbacks include the difficulty of coordinating the various stages of the process and the high cost of moving materials from one department to another.

6. Departmentation by Time. In organisations that work round the clock—such as hospitals, hotels, transport services, telephone exchanges, police stations and certain factories—activities are organised by shifts: the morning shift, the afternoon shift and the night shift. This basis is generally used in combination with one of the others.

The advantage is full utilisation of plant and equipment. The drawbacks include problems of supervision during the night shift, the inconvenience caused to the workers and the higher cost of operation.

7. Departmentation by Number. Under this basis, persons performing similar duties are grouped together on the basis of their number. This is the oldest basis of departmentation and was widely used in the army (a platoon, a company, a battalion) and in primitive labour gangs. In modern industry, it is rarely used in its pure form.

8. Composite or Combined Basis. In actual practice, very few large enterprises use only one basis of departmentation. They use a combination of bases at different levels. At the top, the structure may be functional or product-based; at the middle, it may be territorial or customer-based; and at the lower levels, it may be by process or by shift. This is known as composite departmentation.

10.2 Span of Management

10.2.1 Concept of Span of Management

The span of management, also known as the span of control or the span of supervision, refers to the number of subordinates that a manager can effectively supervise. The capacity of any one person to attend to the work of others is limited by his time, his energy and his mental capacity. There is, therefore, a limit beyond which a manager cannot effectively supervise his subordinates.

The concept is closely linked with the levels in an organisation. If the span is narrow, that is, if each manager supervises only a few subordinates, the organisation will have many levels of management and will look tall like a pyramid. If the span is wide, with each manager supervising a large number of subordinates, the organisation will have few levels and will look flat. Both types have their own advantages and limitations.

10.2.2 Tall and Flat Structures—A Comparison

Basis	Tall Structure	Flat Structure
Span of Management	Narrow; few subordinates per manager.	Wide; many subordinates per manager.
Number of Levels	Many.	Few.
Supervision	Close, detailed supervision.	Loose supervision; greater delegation.
Communication	Slow; many levels to pass through.	Fast and direct.
Cost	Higher, because of	Lower.

Basis	**Tall Structure**	**Flat Structure**
	more managerial positions.	
Suitability	Complex work, less skilled workforce.	Routine work, well-trained workforce.

10.2.3 Graicunas' Theory of Span of Management

V.A. Graicunas, a French management consultant, was among the first to study the span of management on a mathematical basis. Writing in 1933, he pointed out that a superior has not just one but three kinds of relationships with each of his subordinates—direct single relationships, direct group relationships and cross relationships. He developed a formula to calculate the total number of relationships that arise out of a given number of subordinates:

$$\mathbf{N = n\,[\,(2^n / 2) + (n - 1)\,]}$$

where N is the total number of relationships and n is the number of subordinates. Using this formula, the number of relationships grows extremely rapidly. With only four subordinates, the manager has to handle 44 relationships; with six, the number jumps to 222; with twelve, it goes beyond 24,000.

Graicunas' theory brought out the fact that the addition of even one more subordinate increases the workload of the manager much more than is apparent at first sight. The theory has been criticised on the ground that not all the relationships listed by Graicunas actually arise in practice, and that the theory ignores the difference between important and routine relationships. Even so, it serves as a useful warning against the casual addition of subordinates.

10.2.4 The Lockheed Study

During the 1960s, the Lockheed Missiles and Space Company in the United States carried out a practical study of the span of management. The study identified seven factors that influence the appropriate span—the similarity of functions performed by the subordinates, their geographic contiguity, the complexity of the functions, the amount of direction and control required, the extent of coordination needed, the requirement of planning, and the availability of organisational assistance to the manager. Each factor was given a weight, and the total score was used to determine the proper span for a particular position. The Lockheed approach was a more practical and flexible alternative to the rigid formula of Graicunas.

10.2.5 Factors Determining the Span of Management

There is no single correct span of management that suits every situation. The appropriate span depends on a number of factors:

1. Nature of the Work. If the work is simple, routine and repetitive, a wide span is possible. If the work is complex, varied and demanding, a narrow span becomes necessary.

2. Ability of the Manager. A capable, experienced and well-organised manager can handle a wider span than a less capable one.

3. Ability of the Subordinates. Well-trained, motivated and self-disciplined subordinates require less supervision, making a wider span possible.

4. System of Communication. An efficient system of communication—including the use of information technology, mobile phones and electronic mail—enables a manager to deal with a larger number of subordinates.

5. Geographic Location. If the subordinates are located close to one another and to the manager, supervision is easy. If they are spread over distant places, the span has to be narrower.

6. Use of Standard Plans and Procedures. When detailed plans, standard procedures and clear policies are in place, the subordinates can guide themselves to a large extent, and a wider span becomes possible.

7. Extent of Delegation. If the manager is willing to delegate authority freely, he can handle more subordinates. If he insists on taking every decision himself, his span must be narrow.

8. Level of Management. At the top level, the work is complex and the span tends to be narrow. At the lower levels, the work is more routine and the span can be wider.

10.3 Need and Principles of Coordination

10.3.1 Meaning and Definition of Coordination

Coordination is the process of harmonising the activities of different individuals and departments so that they work together as a single team for the achievement of the common goals of the enterprise. It is the force that binds together all the various activities and gives unity of action to the otherwise scattered efforts of the organisation.

Some well-known definitions of coordination are:

1. Mooney and Reiley— "Coordination is the orderly arrangement of group effort to provide unity of action in the pursuit of a common purpose."

2. Henri Fayol— "To coordinate is to harmonise all the activities of a concern so as to facilitate its working and its success."

3. Dalton E. McFarland— "Coordination is the process whereby an executive develops an orderly pattern of group efforts among his subordinates and secures unity of action in the pursuit of a common purpose."

4. Theo Haimann— "Coordination is the orderly synchronising of efforts of the subordinates to provide the proper amount, timing and quality of execution so that their united efforts lead to the achievement of the stated objective."

10.3.2 Features of Coordination

- Coordination is a conscious and deliberate activity, not an accidental occurrence.
- It is a continuous process that runs through all the phases of management.
- It is a pervasive function, required at every level and in every department.
- It is a group activity; a single individual working alone has no need for coordination.
- It is directed towards the achievement of a common purpose.
- It is the responsibility of every manager, from the chief executive down to the supervisor.
- It works both vertically (between the different levels) and

horizontally (between the different departments).

10.3.3 Need and Importance of Coordination

The need for coordination has increased greatly in modern times because of several factors:

- the growing size of business enterprises;
- the increasing specialisation, which tends to make each department concerned only with its own work;
- the wide variety of products, customers and markets handled by modern enterprises;
- the geographical spread of operations both within India and abroad; and
- the rapid pace of change in technology, in customer preferences and in the competitive environment.

Without proper coordination, the various departments may begin to pull in different directions, the efforts of the employees may be wasted, and the goals of the enterprise may not be achieved. Good coordination, on the other hand, ensures that the entire organisation works as a single, well-tuned machine.

10.3.4 Principles of Coordination

Mary Parker Follett, an early American writer on management, laid down four principles which she described as the foundations of effective coordination. These are sometimes called the four principles of coordination:

1. Principle of Direct Contact. Coordination is best achieved through direct personal contact among the people concerned. Memos, files and circulars are no substitute for a face-to-face exchange of views.

2. Principle of Early Stage. Coordination should begin at the earliest stages of planning and policy-making. If the various departments are consulted while the plan is being prepared, conflicts are far less likely to arise during its execution.

3. Principle of Reciprocal Relations. All factors in a situation are reciprocally related; each influences and is influenced by every other. A decision in one department, therefore, may have unforeseen effects on other departments. The manager must keep this interdependence in mind while taking decisions.

4. Principle of Continuity. Coordination is a continuous process. It does not end with the framing of a single plan or with the holding of one meeting. It has to be maintained throughout the working of the enterprise.

To these four principles of Follett, modern writers have added three more:

5. Principle of Self-Coordination. When one department changes its working in some way, the other departments adjust themselves automatically. This self-coordination is possible only when there is good communication and a strong sense of team spirit.

6. Principle of Effective Communication. Sound and timely communication, in both directions, is the lifeblood of coordination.

7. Principle of Leadership. Strong leadership at every level is essential for securing the willing cooperation of the employees and for guiding their efforts in a coordinated manner.

10.4 Techniques of Effective Coordination

To achieve effective coordination, the manager makes use of a number of techniques. The more important of these are listed below:

1. Sound Planning. Plans which are well prepared, internally consistent and properly communicated lay the foundation of coordination. The objectives, policies and procedures of the various departments must all support the overall plan of the enterprise.

2. Clear Definition of Authority and Responsibility. When every employee knows what his duties are, what authority he enjoys and to whom he is accountable, much of the confusion that hampers coordination is removed at the very source.

3. Effective Communication. A sound communication system, with free flow of information both upwards and downwards as well as horizontally, is essential for coordination. The use of e-mail, intranet, video-conferencing and enterprise resource-planning software in modern organisations has greatly improved communication.

4. Effective Leadership and Supervision. A capable leader inspires his team to work together. He resolves conflicts, sorts out misunderstandings and creates a sense of common purpose.

5. Group Meetings and Conferences. Regular meetings of the senior managers, the departmental heads and the project teams help in exchanging views, in spotting problems early and in agreeing on a common course of action.

6. Standard Policies and Procedures. Standard policies, procedures and rules ensure uniformity of action and, therefore, automatic coordination.

7. Coordinating Committees. Many enterprises set up coordinating committees, with members drawn from various departments, to deal with matters that cut across departmental boundaries.

8. Liaison Officers. Special liaison officers are sometimes appointed to keep two or more departments in close touch. For instance, a liaison officer between the production and marketing departments helps to match production with sales.

9. Voluntary Coordination through Indoctrination. When the employees are properly trained to understand and to accept the goals of the enterprise, they coordinate their efforts voluntarily without the need for constant supervision.

10. Use of Information Technology. Modern enterprises make extensive use of computer-based information systems, which integrate the activities of various departments and provide real-time information to all concerned. The Enterprise Resource Planning (ERP) systems used by companies like Infosys, TCS and Wipro are good examples.

10.5 Coordination—The Essence of Management

In Chapter 3, we noted that some writers treat coordination as a separate function of management, while others regard it as the essence of management. The second view is the more widely accepted one today, and is supported by writers such as Mary Parker Follett, James D. Mooney and Dalton E. McFarland.

According to this view, coordination is not a separate activity but is the very purpose for which all the other functions of management are performed. Each function contributes, in its own way, to the larger task of coordinating the efforts of the organisation:

• Planning coordinates the objectives, the premises, the policies and the various courses of action.

• Organising coordinates the duties, the authority and the relationships among the various positions.

• Staffing coordinates the requirements of the various positions with the abilities of the available personnel.

• Directing coordinates the day-to-day efforts of individuals and groups towards the common goal.

• Controlling coordinates the actual results with the planned results and brings about the necessary corrections.

Coordination thus runs through every function of management like a thread that runs through the beads of a necklace. As Mary Parker Follett herself put it, coordination is "the first test of the validity of management."

10.5.1 Coordination and Cooperation—A Distinction

Coordination is sometimes confused with cooperation, but the two are not the same. Coordination is the orderly arrangement of group effort; it is a deliberate, planned activity by the manager. Cooperation is the willing assistance that the employees give to one another in the performance of their work; it is an attitude of mind. Coordination, in other words, is something that the manager does; cooperation is something that the employees feel.

Coordination cannot be brought about merely by cooperation; the manager must consciously plan and direct the efforts of his team. At the same time, coordination is greatly helped when the employees cooperate willingly. The best results are obtained when both coordination and cooperation work together.

Summary

This chapter has dealt with three closely related topics in the field of organising. Departmentation is the process of dividing the activities of an enterprise into smaller and more manageable units. The chief bases of departmentation are by function, by product, by territory, by customer, by process, by time and by number. Most large enterprises use a combination of these bases at different levels.

The span of management is the number of subordinates that a manager can effectively supervise. A narrow span gives rise to a tall structure with many levels, while a wide span gives rise to a flat structure with few levels. Each has its own advantages and limitations. Graicunas drew attention to the rapid increase in the number of relationships as subordinates are added, while the Lockheed study identified seven practical factors that determine the proper span. The actual span depends on the nature of the work, the ability of the manager and the subordinates, the system of communication, the geographic location, the use of standard plans and procedures, the extent of delegation and the level of management.

Coordination is the process of harmonising the activities of different individuals and departments so that they work together as a single team for the achievement of the common goals of the enterprise. The need for coordination has grown with the size of modern business, with specialisation and with the wide geographic spread of operations. Mary Parker Follett laid down four principles of coordination—direct contact, early stage, reciprocal relations and continuity—to which three more have since been added. Effective coordination is brought about through sound planning, clear definition of authority, effective communication, strong leadership, group meetings, standard procedures, coordinating committees, liaison officers and information technology. Most modern writers regard coordination not as a separate function but as the very essence of management, since it runs through every other function as a unifying thread.

Key Terms

Departmentation, Functional Departmentation, Product Departmentation, Territorial Departmentation, Customer Departmentation, Process Departmentation, Composite Departmentation, Span of Management, Span of Control, Tall Structure, Flat Structure, Graicunas' Theory, Lockheed Study, Coordination, Direct Contact, Reciprocal Relations, Continuity, Self-Coordination, Liaison Officer, Coordinating Committee, Cooperation, Coordination versus Cooperation.

Review Questions

A. Short Answer Questions (2 marks each)

1. Define departmentation.
2. Name any four bases of departmentation.
3. What is meant by span of management?
4. Distinguish between a tall and a flat organisation structure.
5. State the four principles of coordination given by Mary Parker Follett.
6. What is the difference between coordination and cooperation?
7. Why is coordination called the essence of management?

B. Long Answer Questions (10 marks each)

8. Discuss the various bases of departmentation with suitable Indian examples.
9. Explain the concept of the span of management. Discuss the Graicunas' theory in this connection.
10. What are the factors that determine the proper span of management?
11. Define coordination. Discuss its features and the need for coordination in modern business.
12. Explain the principles and techniques of effective coordination.
13. "Coordination is the essence of management." Discuss.

C. Practical / Case-Based Questions

14. Visit any departmental store, hospital or college in your locality. Identify the basis on which its activities are departmentalised and the approximate span of management at each level.
15. You have been appointed as the General Manager of a new mid-sized hotel coming up in Indore. The hotel will have departments for housekeeping, food and beverages, front office, security, accounts and personnel. Discuss the steps you would take to ensure effective coordination among them.

CHAPTER 11

STAFFING

Learning Objectives

After studying this chapter, the reader should be able to:

- understand the concept, nature and importance of staffing;
- explain the process of manpower planning;
- describe the sources and the process of recruitment and selection;
- discuss the methods of training and development of employees;
- understand the various techniques of performance appraisal; and
- explain the concepts of promotion, transfer and separation.

Introduction

In the previous chapters, we have studied how the work of an enterprise is planned and how its structure is organised. The plans and the structure, however, are only on paper. They come to life only when human beings—the managers and the workers—breathe their efforts into them. The function of management by which an organisation finds, develops and keeps the right kind of people for its various positions is known as staffing.

It has rightly been said that an organisation is no better than the people who work in it. Buildings, machines, raw materials and money can all be bought from the market, but they remain lifeless until human beings put them to use. The success of every business depends, in the final analysis, upon the quality of its human resource. As J.R.D. Tata observed, the most important asset of a company is the men and women who work for it.

Staffing has, in recent years, grown into a separate field of study known as Human Resource Management or HRM. Large companies today have full-fledged HR departments headed by senior managers. Even in smaller enterprises, the manager spends a great deal of his time on staffing-related activities such as recruiting new employees, training them, appraising their performance, deciding on their promotions and managing their grievances.

This chapter discusses the concept and the importance of staffing, the process of manpower planning, the methods of recruitment and selection, the techniques of training and development, the modern systems of performance appraisal, and the related questions of promotion, transfer and separation.

11.1 Concept, Nature and Importance of Staffing

11.1.1 Meaning and Definition

Staffing is the function of management by which the various positions in an organisation are filled with suitable persons and kept filled. It is concerned with the entire range of activities relating to people—from estimating the requirement of manpower at one end to managing their retirement at the other.

Some well-known definitions of staffing are:

1. Koontz and O'Donnell— "The managerial function of staffing involves manning the organisation structure through proper and effective selection, appraisal and development of personnel to fill the roles designed into the structure."

2. Dalton E. McFarland— "Staffing is the function by which managers build an organisation through the recruitment, selection and development of individuals as capable employees."

3. Theo Haimann— "Staffing pertains to the recruitment, selection, development, training and compensation of subordinate managers."

11.1.2 Nature and Features of Staffing

- Staffing is a pervasive function. It is required in every type of organisation—business, government, hospital, school—and at every level of management.
- It is a continuous process. As new positions are created, old employees retire or resign, and the work of staffing goes on without a break.
- It is people-centred. While the other functions of management deal with abstract concepts such as plans, structures and rules, staffing deals with living human beings, with their feelings, hopes and aspirations.
- It is the responsibility of every manager. Although the personnel

or human resource department plays a leading role, the actual selection, training and appraisal of subordinates is the duty of every line manager.

- It is concerned with both the present and the future. The needs of today have to be met, but the needs of tomorrow also have to be planned for.

11.1.3 Importance of Staffing

- It ensures that the right person is placed in the right job at the right time.
- It improves the efficiency and productivity of the enterprise by making the best use of human resources.
- It develops the abilities of the employees through training, transfer and promotion.
- It builds employee morale and creates a sense of belonging.
- It ensures continuity of work, as new employees are ready to replace those who leave.
- It helps the enterprise to adapt itself to changes in technology, markets and the work environment.
- It contributes to the long-term growth and survival of the enterprise.

11.1.4 Components of Staffing

The staffing function covers the following activities:

- manpower planning;
- recruitment of candidates;
- selection of the right person;
- placement and induction of new employees;
- training and development;
- performance appraisal;
- compensation and wage administration;
- promotion, transfer and demotion;
- industrial relations and grievance handling; and
- separation through resignation, retirement, retrenchment or termination.

11.2 Manpower Planning

11.2.1 Meaning and Definition

Manpower planning, also known as human resource planning, is the process of estimating the future requirement of personnel of an enterprise and of ensuring that suitable persons are available to fill these positions at the right time. It is the first step in the staffing function and provides the basis for all subsequent staffing activities.

Some well-known definitions of manpower planning are:

1. E.W. Vetter— "Manpower planning is the process by which an organisation should move from its current manpower position to its desired manpower position. Through planning, management strives to have the right number and the right kind of people, at the right places and at the right time, doing things which result in long-term benefit to the individual and the organisation."

2. Coleman— "Manpower planning is the process of determining manpower requirements and the means for meeting those requirements in order to carry out the integrated plan of the organisation."

3. Geisler— "Manpower planning is the process by which a firm ensures that it has the right number of people, and the right kind of people, at the right places, at the right time, doing things for which they are economically most useful."

11.2.2 Process of Manpower Planning

The process of manpower planning generally consists of the following steps:

1. Analysis of Organisational Plans and Objectives. The starting point is the overall plan of the enterprise. The expansion plans, the new projects, the introduction of new technology and the diversification programmes all have a direct bearing on manpower needs.

2. Forecasting Manpower Requirements. On the basis of the organisational plans, the future manpower requirements are forecast, both in terms of numbers and of types of skills.

3. Analysing the Existing Manpower. A careful study is made of the manpower already available in the enterprise—their numbers, qualifications, age, experience and likely retirements during the planning period.

4. Identifying the Manpower Gap. The difference between the manpower required and the manpower available is identified. This is the gap that has to be filled through staffing action.

5. Formulating the Action Plan. An action plan is prepared to fill the gap. It may involve recruitment of new employees, training of the existing ones, transfer between departments, or in some cases, retrenchment of surplus staff.

6. Monitoring and Review. The progress of the manpower plan is monitored at regular intervals, and any changes in the situation are taken into account.

11.3 Recruitment and Selection

11.3.1 Recruitment

Recruitment is the process of searching for prospective candidates and of stimulating them to apply for jobs in the organisation. The objective of recruitment is to make available a sufficient number of suitable applicants from whom the right persons can be selected.

Edwin B. Flippo defined recruitment as "the process of searching for prospective employees and stimulating them to apply for jobs in the organisation." Dale Yoder described it as "a process to discover the sources of manpower to meet the requirements of the staffing schedule and to employ effective measures for attracting that manpower in adequate numbers to facilitate effective selection of an efficient workforce."

11.3.2 Sources of Recruitment

(a) Internal Sources.

Internal sources refer to filling the vacancy from within the organisation. The chief internal sources are:

- Promotion of existing employees to higher positions on the basis of merit or seniority.
- Transfer of employees from one department or location to another.
- Re-employment of former employees who had left the organisation.
- Internal advertisement, by which the existing employees are informed of the vacancy and invited to apply.

Internal recruitment is economical, motivates the existing employees and helps in retaining good talent. Its drawback is that it limits the choice of candidates and may lead to inbreeding of ideas.

(b) External Sources.

External sources refer to attracting candidates from outside the organisation. The chief external sources are:

- Advertisement in newspapers, magazines, the internet and television.
- Online job portals such as Naukri.com, Monster, LinkedIn and Indeed.
- Government employment exchanges, which maintain a register of job-seekers.
- Private employment agencies and head-hunting firms, which specialise in finding candidates for executive positions.
- Campus recruitment from colleges, universities and management institutes such as the IIMs, IITs and other professional schools.
- Walk-in interviews, where candidates can come to the company on a fixed date without any prior appointment.
- Recommendations from existing employees and from outside well-wishers.
- Labour contractors, particularly for unskilled and semi-skilled workers in industries such as construction.
- Job fairs and recruitment exhibitions.

External sources provide a wider choice of candidates and bring fresh blood into the organisation. They are, however, more expensive and time-consuming than internal sources.

11.3.3 Selection

Selection is the process of choosing, from among the candidates attracted by recruitment, the persons most suited to the requirements of the job and of the organisation. As Dale Yoder has put it, "Selection is the process by which candidates for employment are divided into two classes—those who will be offered employment and those who will not."

Recruitment is a positive process aimed at attracting as many candidates as possible, while selection is a negative process aimed at rejecting the unsuitable candidates and choosing only the best. The difference between the two is summarised in the table below:

Basis	Recruitment	Selection
Nature	Positive process; aims at attracting candidates.	Negative process; aims at rejecting unsuitable candidates.
Objective	To make available a sufficient pool of candidates.	To choose the most suitable persons from the pool.
Sequence	Comes first.	Follows recruitment.
Method	Through advertisement, campus visits, agencies, etc.	Through tests, interviews and reference checks.
Cost	Comparatively lower.	Comparatively higher.

11.3.4 Process of Selection

The selection process generally consists of the following steps:

1. Screening of the applications received in response to the advertisement.
2. Preliminary interview to eliminate clearly unsuitable candidates.
3. Employment tests, which may include intelligence tests, aptitude tests, personality tests, trade tests and proficiency tests.
4. Main interview by a selection committee or by the concerned department head.
5. Checking of references furnished by the candidate.
6. Medical examination to ensure that the candidate is physically fit for the job.
7. Final selection and issue of the appointment letter.
8. Placement on the job and induction into the organisation.

11.4 Training and Development

11.4.1 Meaning and Concept

Training is the process of imparting specific skills to an employee for the better performance of his present job. Development, on the other hand, is the broader process of improving the overall knowledge, attitudes and abilities of an employee for his future growth in the organisation.

Edwin B. Flippo defined training as "the act of increasing the knowledge and skills of an employee for doing a particular job." Although the two terms are often used together, they differ in their scope. Training is short-term, job-specific and concerned with operative employees, while development is long-term, person-oriented and concerned mainly with managerial employees.

11.4.2 Importance of Training and Development

- It increases the efficiency and productivity of the employees.
- It improves the quality of work and reduces wastage of materials.
- It reduces accidents at the workplace.
- It helps the employees in adapting to new technologies and new methods of working.
- It boosts the morale, the confidence and the job satisfaction of the employees.
- It opens up opportunities for career growth and promotion.
- It prepares the second line of executives for higher responsibilities, ensuring management succession.
- It enables the enterprise to retain its competitive edge in a fast-changing environment.

11.4.3 Methods of Training

(a) On-the-Job Methods.

Under these methods, the employee learns while he works on his regular job. The chief on-the-job methods are:

- Coaching, in which the employee learns under the personal guidance of a senior.
- Apprenticeship, in which a new entrant works under an experienced craftsman for a fixed period.
- Job rotation, in which the employee is moved from one job to another for short periods.

- Internship, in which a student of a professional course is placed in a company for a few months for practical experience.
- Understudy, in which a person is trained to take over the responsibilities of his senior in due course.

(b) Off-the-Job Methods.

Under these methods, the employee is trained away from his actual workplace. The chief off-the-job methods are:

- Classroom lectures, which are useful for explaining concepts and principles.
- Case studies, in which the trainees analyse real-life business situations.
- Role playing, in which the trainees act out the roles of various persons in a business situation.
- Management games, which simulate real-life business decision-making.
- Conferences and seminars, where the trainees interact with experts in their field.
- Programmed instruction and e-learning, which allow the trainee to learn at his own pace through computer-based modules.
- Sensitivity training and behavioural training, which aim at improving inter-personal skills.
- In-basket exercises, in which the trainee is given a set of typical problems faced by a manager and is asked to take decisions on them.

11.5 Performance Appraisal

11.5.1 Meaning and Concept

Performance appraisal is the systematic evaluation of the performance of an employee on the job. It involves the measurement of his output and his behaviour against the standards laid down for his position. The findings of the appraisal are used for taking decisions about promotion, salary, training and the future career of the employee.

Edwin B. Flippo described performance appraisal as "a systematic, periodic and impartial rating of an employee's excellence in matters pertaining to his present job and to his potential for a better job."

11.5.2 Objectives of Performance Appraisal

- To provide feedback to the employees about their performance.
- To identify the strengths and the weaknesses of each employee.
- To assess the training and development needs of the employees.
- To provide a fair basis for decisions about promotion, salary and transfer.
- To identify employees with potential for higher positions.
- To improve the future performance of the employees through counselling.
- To maintain a record of the employees' performance for future reference.

11.5.3 Methods of Performance Appraisal

(a) Traditional Methods.

- Ranking method, in which all employees are arranged in order from best to worst.
- Paired comparison, in which each employee is compared one-on-one with every other employee.
- Grading method, in which the employees are placed in pre-determined grades such as A, B, C and D.
- Forced distribution, in which a fixed percentage of employees is placed in each grade.
- Checklist method, in which the appraiser ticks off statements that apply to the employee.
- Critical-incident method, in which significant good or bad acts of the employee are recorded throughout the year.
- Graphic rating scale, in which the employee is rated on various traits on a numerical scale.
- Essay method, in which the appraiser writes a descriptive note on the employee.
- Confidential reports, traditionally used in government services.

(b) Modern Methods.

- Management by Objectives (MBO), in which the employee is appraised against goals jointly set with his superior.
- Behaviourally Anchored Rating Scale (BARS), in which the employee is rated on specific job behaviours rather than on general traits.

• 360-degree feedback, in which the employee receives feedback from his superiors, his peers, his subordinates and even his customers.

• Assessment centres, in which a group of candidates is observed by trained assessors through a series of exercises.

• Psychological appraisal, which assesses the personality, the intelligence and the potential of the employee.

11.5.4 Common Errors in Performance Appraisal

• Halo effect—allowing one positive trait of the employee to influence the rating of all other traits.

• Horn effect—the opposite of the halo effect, in which one negative trait colours the entire rating.

• Central tendency—the tendency to rate everyone as average.

• Leniency or strictness error—being either too generous or too harsh in rating.

• Recency effect—over-weighing the most recent events while ignoring the rest of the year.

• Personal prejudice and bias on grounds of caste, religion, region or gender.

11.6 Promotion, Transfer and Separation

11.6.1 Promotion

Promotion is the upward movement of an employee from a lower position to a higher position in the organisation, with greater responsibility, status and pay. According to Scott, promotion is "a change in the status of an employee within the same organisation, generally involving an increase in pay and status as well as in the responsibilities of the new job."

Promotion may be of various types. A vertical promotion takes the employee to the next higher position within the same department. A horizontal promotion involves a sideways movement across departments. An upgradation involves an increase in pay and status without a change in the basic job. A dry promotion is one which gives the employee a higher position and greater responsibility but no immediate increase in pay.

Bases of Promotion. Promotion may be based on seniority, on merit, or on a combination of both. Seniority gives weight to the length of service, while merit gives weight to ability and performance. Each has its supporters and critics. Seniority promotes a feeling of security and avoids favouritism, but does not necessarily reward the most able. Merit rewards the able, but is difficult to measure objectively and may give rise to charges of favouritism. The seniority-cum-merit basis seeks to combine the strengths of both, by giving weight first to seniority and then to merit, or vice versa.

11.6.2 Transfer

Transfer is the lateral movement of an employee from one job, department or location to another, of comparable status and pay. Unlike promotion, transfer does not involve a change in the level of the employee in the organisation.

Transfers may take place for various reasons:

- Production transfer, to meet changes in production requirements between departments.
- Replacement transfer, to fill a vacancy caused by the absence of another employee.
- Versatility transfer, to give the employee experience in different kinds of work.
- Remedial transfer, to correct a mistake made in the original placement.
- Shift transfer, from one shift to another.
- Mutual transfer, where two employees exchange their positions.
- Personal transfer, to accommodate the personal or family needs of the employee.
- Punitive transfer, used as a form of mild punishment for misconduct.

11.6.3 Separation

Separation is the end of the employment relationship between the employee and the organisation. It may take various forms:

1. Resignation. The employee voluntarily leaves the organisation, generally to take up another job or for personal reasons.

2. Retirement. The employee leaves the organisation on reaching the age of superannuation, generally sixty years in most Indian companies. The Voluntary Retirement Scheme (VRS), popular in many public-sector enterprises during the 1990s and the 2000s, allowed employees to retire early in exchange for an attractive financial package.

3. Termination or Dismissal. The employer puts an end to the employment for misconduct, inefficiency or other reasons. Termination is governed by labour laws and by the company's standing orders, and requires that the principles of natural justice be followed.

4. Retrenchment. The employer terminates the service of an employee for reasons such as surplus manpower, closure of a unit or a change in technology. Retrenchment compensation has to be paid as required by the Industrial Disputes Act.

5. Lay-off. A temporary inability of the employer to provide work to the employee, due to reasons such as shortage of raw material, breakdown of machinery or accumulation of stock. The employee remains on the rolls of the company and is entitled to lay-off compensation.

6. Suspension. The employee is temporarily kept away from his duties, pending the outcome of an enquiry into alleged misconduct.

7. Death. The employment ends automatically with the death of the employee, and the family of the deceased is entitled to such benefits as may be due under the rules of the company and under the law.

Summary

Staffing is the function of management by which the various positions in an organisation are filled with suitable persons and kept filled. It is a pervasive, continuous and people-centred function. The components of staffing include manpower planning, recruitment, selection, placement, training, performance appraisal, compensation, promotion, transfer and separation.

Manpower planning is the process of estimating the future requirements of personnel and of ensuring that the right people are available at the right time. It involves an analysis of the organisational plans, a forecast of manpower needs, an analysis of the existing manpower, the identification of the gap, the preparation of an action plan and a regular review.

Recruitment is the process of searching for and attracting candidates, while selection is the process of choosing the most suitable persons from among them. Recruitment may be from internal or external sources. The selection process involves screening, preliminary interview, tests, main interview, reference check, medical examination, final decision and placement.

Training is the imparting of specific skills for the present job, while development is the broader process of growing the overall abilities of the employee for the future. Methods of training may be on the job, such as coaching, apprenticeship, job rotation and understudy, or off the job, such as lectures, case studies, role playing, management games and conferences.

Performance appraisal is the systematic evaluation of an employee's performance on the job. Traditional methods of appraisal include ranking, grading, checklist, critical incident and graphic rating, while modern methods include MBO, BARS, 360-degree feedback and assessment centres. Common errors in appraisal are the halo effect, the horn effect, central tendency, leniency and recency effect.

Promotion, transfer and separation are the three major forms of internal movement of employees. Promotion is the upward movement to a higher position, transfer is the lateral movement of similar status, and separation is the end of the employment relationship through resignation, retirement, termination, retrenchment, lay-off, suspension or death.

Key Terms

Staffing, Manpower Planning, Recruitment, Selection, Internal Sources, External Sources, Campus Recruitment, Naukri.com, Training, Development, On-the-Job Training, Off-the-Job Training, Coaching, Apprenticeship, Job Rotation, Understudy, Role Playing, Management Games, Performance Appraisal, Ranking Method, BARS, 360-Degree Feedback, Assessment Centre, Halo Effect, Horn Effect, Central Tendency, Promotion, Seniority, Merit, Dry Promotion, Transfer, Production Transfer, Versatility Transfer, Separation, Resignation, Retirement, VRS, Termination, Retrenchment, Lay-off, Suspension.

Review Questions

A. Short Answer Questions (2 marks each)

9. Define staffing.
10. State any four components of the staffing function.
11. Distinguish between recruitment and selection.
12. Name any four external sources of recruitment.
13. Distinguish between training and development.
14. What is the halo effect in performance appraisal?
15. Distinguish between promotion and transfer.
16. What is a Voluntary Retirement Scheme (VRS)?

B. Long Answer Questions (10 marks each)

17. Discuss the concept, nature and importance of staffing in the modern enterprise.
18. Explain the process of manpower planning.
19. Distinguish between recruitment and selection. Discuss the sources of recruitment and the steps in the selection process.
20. Discuss the various methods of training and development.
21. What is performance appraisal? Explain the traditional and modern methods of performance appraisal.
22. Explain the concepts of promotion, transfer and separation.

C. Practical / Case-Based Questions

23. You have been appointed as the HR Manager of a newly established hospital in Indore with two hundred employees including doctors, nurses, technicians, administrative staff and support staff. Prepare a brief plan covering recruitment, training and performance appraisal for the hospital.
24. Choose any well-known Indian company and study the recruitment process it follows. Comment on its strengths and weaknesses.

CHAPTER 12

DIRECTING

Learning Objectives

After studying this chapter, the reader should be able to:

- understand the meaning, nature and importance of directing;
- state and explain the principles of directing;
- describe the four elements of directing—supervision, motivation, leadership and communication;
- appreciate the role of directing in linking the plans and the people of the organisation; and
- identify the techniques by which a manager can direct his subordinates effectively.

Introduction

In the chapters so far, we have studied four of the five basic functions of management—planning, organising, staffing and a brief reference to coordination. Plans have been prepared, the structure has been built, and the various positions have been filled with suitable persons. None of this, however, produces a single rupee of revenue, a single unit of output or a single satisfied customer. Plans and organisation charts are no more than pieces of paper, and the persons selected for the various positions are no more than potential workers, until someone tells them what to do, motivates them to do it, leads them in the doing, and communicates with them throughout the doing. The function of management that performs all this is called directing.

Directing is rightly described as the heart of management. Just as the body cannot live without the heart, the organisation cannot work without directing. Planning shows the way; organising builds the structure; staffing puts people into place; but it is directing that brings the entire organisation to life. As Marshall Dimock has remarked, "The heart of administration is the directing function."

Directing is the function by which a manager guides, supervises, motivates and leads his subordinates so that they put in their best efforts in the achievement of the objectives of the enterprise. It is a continuous, pervasive and intensely human activity. It runs through every level of management, from the Chairman down to the foreman, and it concerns itself not with files and machinery but with living men and women, with their hopes, fears, ambitions and sentiments.

This chapter discusses the meaning, the nature and the principles of directing, describes its four elements—supervision, motivation, leadership and communication—examines its importance in the modern organisation, and concludes with the techniques by which a manager can direct his subordinates effectively. The three elements of motivation, leadership and communication are introduced here in brief; each of them will be taken up in detail in the chapters that follow.

12.1 Meaning, Nature and Principles of Directing

12.1.1 Meaning and Definition

Directing may be defined as the function of management which involves guiding, supervising, motivating and leading the employees of the organisation so that they perform their assigned tasks effectively and contribute to the achievement of the objectives of the enterprise. It is the action-oriented function of management. The other functions prepare the ground, but it is directing that actually sets things in motion.

Some well-known definitions of directing are:

1. Koontz and O'Donnell— "Directing is the inter-personal aspect of managing by which subordinates are led to understand and contribute effectively to the attainment of enterprise objectives."

2. Theo Haimann— "Directing consists of the process and techniques utilised in issuing instructions and making certain that operations are carried on as originally planned."

3. E.F.L. Brech— "Direction is the continuous task of taking decisions, embodying them in specific and general orders and instructions, and serving as the leader of the enterprise."

4. Marshall E. Dimock— "Direction is the heart of administration, because it is the action-known function which deals chiefly with human relations."

5. Urwick and Brech— "Directing is the guidance, the inspiration, the leadership of those men and women that constitute the real core of the responsibilities of management."

12.1.2 Nature and Characteristics of Directing

The nature of directing is brought out by the following characteristics:

1. Initiating Function. Directing is the function that puts the entire organisation into action. Until the manager begins to direct, the plans and the structure remain mere ideas on paper.

2. Pervasive Function. Directing is performed at every level of management. The Chief Executive directs his senior managers, the senior managers direct their juniors, and the foreman directs the workers. Wherever there is a superior and a subordinate, there is directing.

3. Continuous Activity. Directing is not a one-time act. It is a continuous process that goes on as long as the organisation exists. The manager keeps directing his subordinates day in and day out.

4. Performance through Human Element. Directing deals with human beings, with their feelings, their attitudes and their sentiments. Of all the functions of management, it is the most human and the most personal.

5. Flows from Top to Bottom. Directing follows the scalar chain of authority. Orders and instructions flow from the higher levels to the lower levels, just as authority does.

6. Linking Function. Directing links the planning, organising and staffing functions to the achievement of results. It is the bridge between intention and action.

7. Creative Function. It is through directing that the lifeless plans and the static structure are turned into a living, breathing, working enterprise. There is, therefore, a great deal of creativity involved in directing.

8. Both an Art and a Science. Directing makes use of well-established principles, which give it the character of a science. But its application to actual situations requires a high degree of personal skill, which makes it an art.

12.1.3 Principles of Directing

Effective directing is guided by the following well-established principles:

1. Principle of Maximum Individual Contribution. Directing should be such that each employee is encouraged to contribute his maximum effort and his best abilities to the achievement of the organisational goals.

2. Principle of Harmony of Objectives. There should be harmony between the personal goals of the employees and the organisational goals. When the employees feel that their personal goals are advanced through the achievement of the organisational goals, they put in their wholehearted effort.

3. Principle of Unity of Command. Each subordinate should receive directions from one superior only. Receiving directions from two or more superiors leads to confusion, conflict and inefficiency.

4. Principle of Appropriate Direction Technique. Different situations and different subordinates call for different techniques of direction. A new and inexperienced subordinate may need detailed instructions; an experienced one may need only broad guidance. The manager should choose the technique suited to the situation.

5. Principle of Managerial Communication. Effective direction is impossible without effective communication. The manager must communicate his instructions clearly and must also be a good listener so as to receive the feedback from his subordinates.

6. Principle of the Use of Informal Organisation. The informal organisation, as we saw in Chapter 7, exists in every enterprise. The manager should make use of it in the interest of effective direction, rather than try to suppress it.

7. Principle of Leadership. The manager must function as a leader. He must inspire his subordinates, win their confidence and lead by personal example.

8. Principle of Follow-Through. Direction is not complete until the manager has followed up on his instructions to ensure that they have been understood, accepted and carried out as expected.

12.2 Elements of Directing

The function of directing has four main elements—supervision, motivation, leadership and communication. These four elements are closely related to one another and together make up the work of direction. The first element, supervision, is discussed in some detail in this chapter, while the other three—motivation, leadership and communication—are introduced here briefly and are taken up at length in Chapters 13, 14 and 15 respectively.

12.2.1 Supervision

Supervision is the act of overseeing the work of the subordinates and of guiding them in its performance. It is the most direct form of directing. The supervisor stands face to face with the workers and makes sure that the work proceeds as planned. The foreman in a factory, the office superintendent in an office, the matron in a hospital and the head clerk in a bank are all examples of supervisors.

In the words of G.R. Terry, "Supervision means overseeing the work of subordinates by their superiors." Theo Haimann defined it as "the direct and immediate guidance and control of the subordinates in the performance of their tasks."

Need for Supervision. Supervision is necessary because plans, however carefully prepared, do not execute themselves. Workers, however well selected, may need guidance from time to time. Materials may have to be issued, machinery may have to be set right, doubts may have to be cleared, and quality may have to be checked. All of this is the work of the supervisor.

Role of the Supervisor. The supervisor occupies a unique position in the organisation. He is the link between the management and the workers. He represents the management to the workers and the workers to the management. He explains the plans and the policies of the management to the workers, and conveys the problems and the grievances of the workers to the management. He has been variously called the man in the middle, the marginal man and the first-line manager.

Qualities of a Good Supervisor. A good supervisor possesses certain qualities. He has a good knowledge of the work under his charge.

He is fair and impartial in dealing with his subordinates. He sets a good example by his own conduct. He is firm where firmness is needed and considerate where consideration is needed. He communicates clearly, listens patiently and decides quickly. He has the ability to plan his own work and to plan the work of his subordinates.

12.2.2 Motivation

Motivation is the process of stimulating the employees of the organisation to act in a desired manner and to put in their best efforts in the achievement of the organisational goals. It is concerned with the inner drives and needs of the employees, with the rewards that are offered to them and with the satisfaction that they derive from their work. As Koontz and O'Donnell have put it, "Motivation refers to the urge which a person feels to satisfy his needs."

Motivation may be financial, such as wages, bonuses, allowances and profit-sharing; or non-financial, such as appreciation, recognition, status, participation, job enrichment and opportunities for growth. The role of the manager is to understand what motivates each of his subordinates and to provide the appropriate motivators. The various theories of motivation given by Abraham Maslow, Frederick Herzberg, Douglas McGregor and others will be discussed in detail in Chapter 13.

12.2.3 Leadership

Leadership is the ability of a manager to influence and inspire his subordinates so that they willingly follow him in the achievement of the organisational goals. A leader is one who is able to win the willing cooperation of his followers, not by the use of authority alone but by his personal qualities, his vision and his example.

In the words of Koontz and O'Donnell, "Leadership is the ability of a manager to induce his subordinates to work with confidence and zeal." Leadership is closely related to direction, for it is through leadership that the manager actually gets his subordinates to follow his directions. The various styles of leadership—autocratic, democratic, free-rein—and the theories of leadership—trait theory, behavioural theory, situational theory—will be discussed in Chapter 14.

12.2.4 Communication

Communication is the process of sharing of information, ideas and feelings between two or more persons, with a view to creating a common understanding. It is the lifeblood of every organisation. Without communication, the manager cannot direct, the subordinates cannot perform, and the various departments cannot coordinate.

Newman and Summer defined communication as "an exchange of facts, ideas, opinions or emotions by two or more persons." Communication may be formal or informal, written or oral, verbal or non-verbal, and may flow downwards, upwards or horizontally. The various types of communication and the barriers to effective communication will be discussed in detail in Chapter 15.

12.3 Importance of Directing in Organisations

Directing plays a vital role in every organisation. Its importance can be appreciated from the following points:

1. Initiates Action. Directing is the function that sets the entire organisation in motion. Until the manager begins to direct, the plans of the enterprise remain on paper and the structure remains dormant. As soon as direction begins, the wheels of action start turning.

2. Integrates Individual Effort. Through direction, the manager integrates the efforts of his various subordinates into a single, coordinated whole. He ensures that everyone works towards the common goal of the enterprise and not in his own separate direction.

3. Means of Motivation. Directing is the chief means by which the manager motivates his subordinates. Through his personal example, his words of encouragement, his rewards and recognition, he creates among the employees the desire to put in their best.

4. Provides Leadership. Effective directing requires effective leadership. A good leader, through his vision and his personal qualities, inspires his subordinates to perform beyond what their formal duties require.

5. Facilitates Change. When the enterprise has to adopt new methods, new technologies or new ways of working, the employees often resist the change. Through skilful directing, the manager helps the employees to understand the need for change, to overcome their resistance and to adopt the new ways willingly.

6. Brings Stability and Balance. By providing clear instructions, fair leadership and open communication, directing brings stability to the organisation. The employees know what is expected of them, and there is little scope for confusion or conflict.

7. Helps in the Achievement of Objectives. All the other functions of management are useful only to the extent that they help in the achievement of the objectives of the enterprise. Directing is the function that actually translates the plans into results.

8. Develops People. Through directing, the manager not only gets the immediate work done but also develops his subordinates for the future. He trains them on the job, exposes them to new responsibilities and prepares them for higher positions.

9. Effective Utilisation of Resources. Money, materials, machines and information are all used through the efforts of human beings. Effective directing ensures that the human beings use these resources in the most efficient manner, with minimum waste.

12.4 Techniques of Effective Direction

Although the actual techniques of direction vary from one situation to another, certain broad approaches have emerged from the experience of managers over the years.

12.4.1 Styles or Techniques of Direction

1. Autocratic Direction. Under this style, the manager takes all the decisions himself and gives detailed orders to his subordinates, who are expected to obey without question. This style is suitable in emergencies, in dealing with new or untrained employees, and in some kinds of work such as military operations.

2. Democratic or Participative Direction. Under this style, the manager consults his subordinates before taking decisions and welcomes their views and suggestions. The final decision rests with the manager, but the subordinates feel that they are a part of the process. This style is suitable when the subordinates are educated, experienced and willing to participate.

3. Free-Rein or Laissez-Faire Direction. Under this style, the manager gives broad guidelines and allows his subordinates considerable freedom to plan and execute their work. This style works well with highly skilled and self-motivated employees, such as research scientists, university professors and creative designers.

4. Consultative Direction. A variation of the democratic style, in which the manager actively consults his subordinates on important matters but reserves the right to take the final decision. The consultation may be informal, as in casual discussions, or formal, as in meetings of departmental heads.

12.4.2 Quality of Good Direction

Whatever the style adopted, the directions issued by the manager must possess certain qualities if they are to be effective. A good direction is:

1. Clear and Complete—the subordinate must know exactly what he is to do, when, where and how.

2. Reasonable—it must be capable of being carried out by the subordinate within the available time and resources.

3. Issued at the Right Time—neither so early as to be forgotten nor so late as to cause panic.

4. In Suitable Language—in a language and a manner that the subordinate can understand.

5. In Writing Wherever Necessary—important and complex directions should be put in writing to avoid misunderstanding and to provide a record.

6. Followed Up—the manager must check that the direction has been received, understood, accepted and carried out.

12.4.3 Practical Techniques

In actual practice, managers use a wide variety of techniques to direct their subordinates effectively. Some of the more important of these are:

- clearly defining the duties, the targets and the standards of performance for each subordinate;
- issuing instructions through both formal channels (such as written orders and meetings) and informal channels (such as personal contact and the grapevine);

- setting a good personal example by one's own conduct;
- providing the necessary training, tools and resources to the subordinates;
- recognising good performance through appreciation, awards and rewards;
- counselling the subordinates whose performance falls below the standard;
- using participative methods such as suggestion schemes, quality circles and team meetings;
- maintaining a sound system of communication, both upwards and downwards;
- creating a healthy work atmosphere through fair dealings, open communication and respect for the dignity of the employee; and
- following up on the directions issued to ensure that the desired results are obtained.

Summary

Directing is the function of management by which a manager guides, supervises, motivates and leads his subordinates so that they put in their best efforts in the achievement of the goals of the enterprise. It is rightly described as the heart of management, for it is through directing that the plans, the structure and the people of the organisation are brought to life. Directing is a continuous, pervasive, initiating, creative and people-centred activity, which flows from the top to the bottom and links the other functions of management to actual results.

Effective directing is guided by the principles of maximum individual contribution, harmony of objectives, unity of command, appropriate technique, managerial communication, use of the informal organisation, leadership and follow-up. Its four main elements are supervision, motivation, leadership and communication. Supervision is the act of overseeing the work of subordinates and is performed by the first-line supervisor, who acts as the link between the management and the workers. Motivation is the process of stimulating the employees to put in their best, leadership is the ability to inspire and influence them, and communication is the sharing of information that makes both motivation and leadership possible. The latter three elements are taken up at length in the next three chapters.

The importance of directing lies in the fact that it initiates action, integrates individual efforts, motivates and leads the employees, facilitates change, brings stability, helps in the achievement of objectives, develops people and ensures the effective utilisation of resources. The chief techniques of direction may be autocratic, democratic, free-rein or consultative, depending on the situation. Whatever the style adopted, good direction must be clear, complete, reasonable, well-timed, issued in suitable language, put in writing wherever necessary and followed up by the manager.

Key Terms

Directing, Heart of Management, Initiating Function, Pervasive Function, Linking Function, Principles of Directing, Harmony of Objectives, Supervision, Supervisor, Man in the Middle, First-Line Manager, Motivation, Leadership, Communication, Autocratic Direction, Democratic Direction, Free-Rein Direction, Consultative Direction, Follow-Up.

Review Questions

A. Short Answer Questions (2 marks each)

1. Define directing.
2. State any four characteristics of directing.
3. Name the four elements of directing.
4. Why is supervision called the "man-in-the-middle" function?
5. State any three principles of effective directing.
6. Distinguish between autocratic and democratic direction.
7. State any four qualities of good direction.

B. Long Answer Questions (10 marks each)

8. Discuss the meaning, nature and importance of directing.
9. Explain the principles of effective directing.
10. Describe the four elements of directing with special reference to supervision.

11. "Directing is the heart of management." Comment.

12. Discuss the various styles or techniques of direction. Under what circumstances is each style most suitable?

C. Practical / Case-Based Questions

13. You have recently been appointed as the supervisor of a small workshop with twenty workers in Indore. Describe the steps you would take to direct your team effectively.

14. Identify any successful Indian business leader and discuss the directing techniques that, in your view, contributed to his or her success.

CHAPTER 13

MOTIVATION

Learning Objectives

After studying this chapter, the reader should be able to:

- understand the concept, the nature and the importance of motivation;
- describe the process or the cycle of motivation;
- explain the well-known theories of motivation given by Maslow, Herzberg, McGregor and Vroom;
- distinguish between content theories and process theories of motivation; and
- identify the various financial and non-financial incentives used by modern organisations.

Introduction

Why do some employees work hard, while others, doing the same kind of work for the same kind of pay, do as little as they can get away with? Why does an employee who is excellent in one organisation become indifferent in another? Why do some workers feel inspired to do their best, while others feel that they are merely putting in time? The answer to all these questions lies in the concept of motivation.

Motivation is the inner force that drives a person to act in a particular way. It is what gets a worker up in the morning, brings him to the workplace, makes him put in his best effort during the day and brings him back the next morning to do it all over again. Without motivation, the most carefully prepared plans, the most thoughtfully designed structure and the most skilfully selected employees can produce nothing of value.

In the long history of management thought, no subject has received greater attention than motivation. Beginning with the Hawthorne experiments and continuing through the work of Abraham Maslow, Frederick Herzberg, Douglas McGregor, Victor Vroom and many others, the question of what motivates an employee at the workplace has been studied from many angles. The Indian context too has thrown up valuable insights, drawing on the Bhagavad Gita's teaching of work as a duty (nishkama karma) and on the trusteeship principle of Mahatma Gandhi.

This chapter discusses the concept and the importance of motivation, the process by which motivation works, the leading theories of motivation—the hierarchy of needs of Maslow, the two-factor theory of Herzberg, the X and Y theories of McGregor and the expectancy theory of Vroom—and the various financial and non-financial incentives used by modern organisations.

13.1 Concept and Importance of Motivation

13.1.1 Meaning and Definition

The word "motivation" comes from the Latin word "movere," which means "to move." In simple terms, motivation refers to that which moves a person to act in a particular way. It is the inner urge that prompts a person to do what he does.

Some well-known definitions of motivation are:

1. Koontz and O'Donnell— "Motivation refers to the urge or the drive within a human being to satisfy his needs."

2. Stanley Vance— "Motivation is the emotion or desire operating on a person's will, causing him to act."

3. E.F.L. Brech— "Motivation is a general inspirational process which gets the members of a team to pull their weight effectively."

4. W.G. Scott— "Motivation means a process of stimulating people to action in order to accomplish desired goals."

5. Dalton E. McFarland— "Motivation refers to the way in which urges, drives, desires, aspirations, strivings or needs direct, control or explain the behaviour of human beings."

13.1.2 The Motivation Process or Cycle

Motivation may be understood as a process that runs in the following cycle. Every human being has certain unsatisfied needs or wants. These unsatisfied needs create within him a feeling of tension or drive. The tension prompts him to take some action that he believes will satisfy the need. If the action does satisfy the need, he experiences a sense of satisfaction, and the tension is reduced. He then proceeds to satisfy his next need. This is the basic cycle of motivation—need leads to tension, tension to action, action to satisfaction, and satisfaction to the emergence of a fresh need.

13.1.3 Features of Motivation

- Motivation is an internal feeling. It arises within the individual; it cannot be forced upon him from outside.
- It is a psychological concept. It deals with the mind and the feelings of the person.
- It is goal-oriented. Motivation is directed towards the satisfaction of a particular need or the achievement of a particular goal.
- It is a continuous process, since as one need is satisfied, another arises in its place.
- It influences the entire behaviour of the person, not just one aspect of it.
- It may be positive or negative. Positive motivation uses rewards; negative motivation uses fear or punishment.
- It is a complex phenomenon influenced by many factors—personal, social, economic and cultural.

13.1.4 Types of Motivation

Motivation may be classified in three different ways:

(a) Positive and Negative Motivation. Positive motivation works through rewards such as bonus, promotion, praise and recognition. Negative motivation works through fear of punishment, demotion, transfer to undesirable jobs or even dismissal.

(b) Intrinsic and Extrinsic Motivation. Intrinsic motivation arises from within the work itself—the joy of doing a creative job, the pride of mastering a skill, the satisfaction of helping a customer. Extrinsic motivation arises from outside—the pay, the bonus, the promotion, the title.

(c) Financial and Non-Financial Motivation. Financial motivation works through money and money-related benefits, while non-financial motivation works through rewards that have no direct monetary value, such as recognition, status and responsibility.

13.1.5 Importance of Motivation

- Motivated employees give higher output and better quality of work.
- They are more loyal to the organisation, reducing absenteeism and labour turnover.
- Motivation helps in building a high level of morale and team spirit.
- It makes possible the achievement of the goals of the enterprise.
- It improves industrial relations and reduces the number of disputes and strikes.
- It overcomes the resistance of the employees to changes in technology, methods or organisation.
- It helps in the development of the employees by encouraging them to learn new skills.
- It improves the public image of the company, since motivated employees serve customers better and speak well of their employer.

13.2 Maslow's Hierarchy of Needs Theory

The Hierarchy of Needs theory of motivation was put forward by Abraham H. Maslow (1908–1970), an American psychologist, in his article "A Theory of Human Motivation," published in 1943, and later developed in his book Motivation and Personality (1954). The theory is one of the most widely known and most widely used theories of motivation in the world.

Maslow's theory rests on two basic propositions. The first is that human needs can be arranged in a definite order, from the most basic to the most advanced. The second is that, in general, the lower needs must be satisfied to a reasonable extent before the higher needs become active. A satisfied need is no longer a source of motivation; only an unsatisfied need motivates.

13.2.1 The Five Levels of Needs

Maslow identified five levels of human needs, arranged in the form of a pyramid:

1. Physiological Needs. These are the most basic needs of human life—the needs for food, water, shelter, clothing, sleep and reproduction.

At the workplace, they are satisfied through wages and basic working conditions such as a clean canteen, drinking water and rest pauses.

2. Safety and Security Needs. Once the physiological needs have been reasonably met, the person becomes concerned with his safety and security. He wants protection from physical danger, loss of job, illness, accident and old age. At the workplace, these needs are satisfied through job security, provident fund, gratuity, medical insurance, group life insurance and safe working conditions.

3. Social or Belongingness Needs. When the physiological and safety needs have been reasonably met, the social needs take over. The person now wants love, friendship, affection and a sense of belonging to a group. At the workplace, these needs are met through a friendly atmosphere, team work, cordial superior-subordinate relations and social activities organised by the company.

4. Esteem or Ego Needs. At the fourth level are the needs for self-esteem (the feeling of competence, confidence and achievement) and for external esteem (the recognition, status and prestige granted by others). At the workplace, these needs are satisfied through titles, promotions, awards, public recognition, a private cabin, a company car and similar marks of distinction.

5. Self-Actualisation Needs. At the top of the pyramid are the needs for self-actualisation—the need to realise one's full potential, to be everything that one is capable of becoming. At the workplace, these needs are satisfied through challenging work, autonomy, creative opportunities and the chance to develop one's abilities to the fullest.

13.2.2 Implications and Limitations

Implications. Maslow's theory has many practical implications for the manager. He must understand at what level of need each of his subordinates is operating and must provide the motivators suited to that level. A worker still struggling for his daily bread will not be motivated by a fancy job title; a senior executive who has already achieved everything else will not be inspired by a small increase in salary.

Limitations. The theory has been criticised on several grounds. The hierarchy is not always as rigid as Maslow suggested—some persons may pursue higher needs even before their lower needs are fully satisfied. The same need may motivate different persons differently. Cultural factors play a role; the priorities in the West may differ from those in India. Empirical evidence supporting the theory is limited. In spite of these criticisms, however, Maslow's theory remains the most widely taught theory of motivation, mainly because of its simplicity and its intuitive appeal.

13.3 Herzberg's Two-Factor Theory

The two-factor theory of motivation was put forward by Frederick Herzberg (1923–2000) in his book The Motivation to Work, published in 1959. Herzberg and his associates studied two hundred engineers and accountants in nine companies in the Pittsburgh area of the United States. They asked each respondent to describe a time when he had felt exceptionally good and a time when he had felt exceptionally bad about his job. The findings led Herzberg to a remarkable conclusion: the factors that caused job satisfaction were quite different from the factors that caused job dissatisfaction. The two were not the opposite ends of a single scale but two separate scales altogether.

13.3.1 The Two Factors

1. Hygiene or Maintenance Factors. These are the factors that, when present, prevent dissatisfaction but do not, by themselves, create satisfaction or motivation. Herzberg called them "hygiene" factors by analogy with public hygiene, which prevents disease without curing it. The chief hygiene factors are: company policy and administration, supervision, working conditions, interpersonal relations with superiors, peers and subordinates, salary, status, job security and personal life. If these factors are absent or inadequate, the employee feels dissatisfied. If they are present and adequate, he simply feels not dissatisfied—he does not feel actively motivated to do better.

2. Motivational Factors or Motivators. These are the factors that, when present, actively motivate the employee to put in his best effort. They are concerned with the content of the work itself. The chief motivational factors are: achievement, recognition, the work itself, responsibility, advancement (promotion) and personal growth. If these factors are present, the employee feels truly motivated. If they are absent, he does not feel actively dissatisfied; he simply does not feel motivated.

13.3.2 Implications

The two-factor theory has important implications for the manager. The manager must, first of all, ensure that the hygiene factors are adequately taken care of, so that dissatisfaction is prevented. But the work of motivation does not end there. To create real motivation, the manager must also provide opportunities for achievement, recognition, responsibility and growth—that is, he must enrich the job itself. The concept of job enrichment, which we shall discuss again in the context of incentives, owes much to the work of Herzberg.

13.3.3 Comparison with Maslow

Herzberg's theory is closely related to that of Maslow. The hygiene factors of Herzberg correspond roughly to the lower needs (physiological, safety and social) of Maslow, while the motivators correspond to the higher needs (esteem and self-actualisation). The two theories complement each other rather than contradict each other.

13.3.4 Limitations

Herzberg's theory has been criticised on several grounds. The original study was confined to professional workers in the United States and may not apply equally to all categories of workers in all parts of the world. The methodology, in which the respondent recalls his own past experiences, may suffer from bias—people tend to attribute good outcomes to their own efforts and bad outcomes to factors beyond their control. The role of salary is doubtful: Herzberg classified it as a hygiene factor, but many studies have shown that salary, too, can be a strong motivator, particularly for low-paid workers. In spite of these criticisms, the theory has had a great impact on management thinking, particularly in the field of job design.

13.4 McGregor's Theory X and Theory Y

Douglas McGregor (1906–1964), an American social psychologist, put forward an entirely different way of looking at motivation in his classic work The Human Side of Enterprise, published in 1960. McGregor argued that the way a manager motivates his subordinates depends on the assumptions he makes about human nature. He identified two sets of contrasting assumptions, which he called Theory X and Theory Y.

13.4.1 Theory X—The Traditional View

Theory X represents the traditional view of human nature held by many managers. Its main assumptions are:

- The average human being has an inherent dislike of work and will avoid it if he can.
- Because of this dislike, most people must be coerced, controlled, directed and threatened with punishment to get them to put forth adequate effort.
- The average human being prefers to be directed, wishes to avoid responsibility and has relatively little ambition.
- He wants security above all else.
- He is by nature self-centred, resistant to change and indifferent to the needs of the organisation.

If the manager holds these assumptions, his style of motivation will be authoritarian. He will rely heavily on close supervision, detailed instructions, tight control, financial incentives for good work and threats of punishment for bad work—the famous "carrot and stick" approach.

13.4.2 Theory Y—The Modern View

Theory Y represents the modern view of human nature, supported by the findings of the behavioural sciences. Its main assumptions are:

- The expenditure of physical and mental effort at work is as natural as play or rest. Work, under suitable conditions, can be a source of satisfaction.
- External control and the threat of punishment are not the only means of getting people to work. Most people exercise self-direction and self-control in the service of objectives to which they are committed.
- Commitment to objectives is a function of the rewards associated with their achievement.
- The average human being learns, under proper conditions, not only to accept but also to seek responsibility.
- The capacity to exercise a high degree of imagination, ingenuity

and creativity in the solution of organisational problems is widely, not narrowly, distributed in the population.

- In modern industrial life, the intellectual potential of the average human being is being only partially utilised.

If the manager holds these assumptions, his style of motivation will be democratic and participative. He will provide his subordinates with challenging work, opportunities for growth, recognition and a share in decision-making. He will create the conditions in which the natural creativity and the natural sense of responsibility of his subordinates can find expression.

13.4.3 Implications and Limitations

Implications. McGregor's theory tells us that the assumptions a manager makes about his subordinates have a profound effect on the style of motivation he adopts. A Theory X manager and a Theory Y manager, dealing with the same group of employees, will produce very different results. McGregor strongly favoured Theory Y as more in keeping with the realities of modern industrial life. People, he said, generally rise to the expectations placed on them; if the manager treats them as responsible adults, they behave responsibly.

Limitations. Critics have pointed out that no person is wholly an X or wholly a Y; most of us are a mixture of the two. The right approach also depends on the situation, the nature of the work and the cultural background. The factory floor of the 1950s, with its largely uneducated workers, may have called for some elements of Theory X; the software development unit of today, with its highly trained engineers, certainly calls for Theory Y. In actual practice, the wise manager varies his style with the situation.

13.5 Vroom's Expectancy Theory

All the theories discussed so far—those of Maslow, Herzberg and McGregor—are known as content theories of motivation, because they try to identify the specific things that motivate people. Victor H. Vroom, a Canadian-American psychologist, took a different approach in his book Work and Motivation, published in 1964. He proposed what is known as a process theory, which tries to explain not what motivates people but how the process of motivation actually works.

13.5.1 The Three Variables

According to Vroom, the strength of a person's motivation to perform an act depends on three variables:

1. Expectancy (E). This is the belief of the person that a particular effort on his part will result in a particular level of performance. Expectancy depends on his confidence in his own ability, on the resources available to him and on the difficulty of the task. Its value ranges from 0 (no chance) to 1 (certainty).

2. Instrumentality (I). This is the belief of the person that a particular level of performance will result in a particular reward. Instrumentality depends on the fairness of the appraisal system and on the credibility of the manager's promises. Its value also ranges from 0 to 1.

3. Valence (V). This is the value or importance that the person attaches to the reward. A reward may be highly valued (positive valence), of no value (zero valence) or even unwelcome (negative valence).

13.5.2 The Vroom Formula

Vroom expressed the relationship among these three variables in the following formula:

Motivation = Expectancy × Instrumentality × Valence

The three variables are multiplied, not added. This means that if any one of them is zero, the level of motivation will also be zero. A worker who is confident of his ability (high expectancy), but who does not believe that good performance will be rewarded (zero instrumentality), will not be motivated. A worker who believes that good performance will be rewarded (high instrumentality), but who does not value the reward offered (zero valence), will also not be motivated.

13.5.3 Implications

Vroom's theory has several practical implications for the manager:

- The manager must ensure that his subordinates have the ability, the training and the resources needed to perform well, so that the expectancy is high.

• He must ensure that good performance is fairly and visibly rewarded, so that the instrumentality is high.

• He must understand what each subordinate values—some may value money, some recognition, some growth opportunities—and must offer rewards that match these values, so that the valence is high.

Only when all three variables are present in good measure will the worker be strongly motivated to perform.

13.5.4 Limitations

Vroom's theory has been criticised as being too complex for everyday use. It assumes that people behave in a strictly rational manner, which is not always the case. Measuring the three variables is also difficult in practice. Nevertheless, the theory has greatly enriched our understanding of motivation by drawing attention to the cognitive processes that lie behind it.

13.5.5 Other Theories—A Brief Mention

Besides the four major theories discussed above, several other theories of motivation deserve a brief mention:

• The Equity Theory of J. Stacy Adams, which holds that an employee is motivated when he feels that he is being treated fairly in comparison with others.

• The Reinforcement Theory of B.F. Skinner, which holds that behaviour that is rewarded tends to be repeated, while behaviour that is punished tends to be avoided.

• The Achievement Motivation Theory of David C. McClelland, which identifies three basic needs that drive human behaviour—the need for achievement (nAch), the need for power (nPow) and the need for affiliation (nAff).

13.6 Financial and Non-Financial Incentives

Incentives are the means by which motivation is put into practice. They are the rewards offered to the employees in return for desired performance. Incentives are broadly of two types—financial and non-financial.

13.6.1 Financial Incentives

Financial incentives are those that have a direct monetary value. The chief financial incentives used by modern enterprises are:

- Wages and salaries, which are the basic financial reward for work.
- Dearness allowance and other allowances such as house rent allowance, medical allowance and travelling allowance.
- Bonus, both statutory (as required under the Payment of Bonus Act) and ex gratia bonus paid voluntarily by the company.
- Profit-sharing, under which a portion of the profits of the company is distributed among the employees.
- Co-partnership, under which the employees are given a share in the ownership of the company. The Employee Stock Option Plan (ESOP), widely used by Indian information technology companies such as Infosys and TCS, is a modern form of co-partnership.
- Commission, generally paid to salesmen as a percentage of the sales made by them.
- Productivity-linked incentives, which reward the worker for output above a standard level.
- Suggestion awards, given to employees whose suggestions are accepted and implemented.
- Retirement benefits such as provident fund, gratuity, pension and group insurance, which provide financial security in later years.
- Perquisites, such as a company car, a company house, club membership, leave travel concession and reimbursement of telephone and internet expenses—generally provided to senior managers.

13.6.2 Non-Financial Incentives

Non-financial incentives are those that do not have a direct monetary value but appeal to the psychological, social and ego needs of the employee. Their importance has been brought home by the work of Maslow, Herzberg and others. The chief non-financial incentives are:

- Job security, which gives the employee the assurance that he will not lose his job arbitrarily.
- Status and recognition, conveyed through titles, a private cabin, a company car and other marks of distinction.
- Praise and appreciation by the superior, especially when given in public.

- Awards such as "Best Employee of the Year", "Employee of the Month", gold medals and certificates of merit.
- Promotion to a higher position with greater responsibility and prestige.
- Job enrichment, which makes the work itself more challenging, meaningful and rewarding.
- Job rotation, which provides variety and broadens the experience of the employee.
- Participation in decision-making through works committees, joint management councils, suggestion schemes and quality circles.
- Empowerment, by which the employee is given the authority to take decisions about his own work.
- Opportunities for career development through training and education.
- Pleasant working conditions, including good lighting, ventilation, cleanliness, safety and rest facilities.
- Healthy interpersonal relations, including fair dealings with superiors, friendly relations with colleagues and a culture of mutual respect.
- Flexible working hours and the option of working from home, which has become a powerful non-financial incentive after the COVID-19 pandemic.
- Sports, cultural and recreational activities organised by the company.

13.6.3 Choice of Incentives

The choice of the right mix of financial and non-financial incentives depends on a number of factors—the nature of the work, the level of the employee, the stage of his career, the financial position of the company and the cultural environment. Lower-paid workers and those in the early stages of their careers are generally more responsive to financial incentives. Senior managers and professionals, whose basic financial needs have been well taken care of, often respond more strongly to non-financial incentives such as status, recognition and challenging work. The wise manager studies his employees, understands what each of them values, and offers a combination of incentives that brings out the best in them.

Summary

Motivation is the inner force that drives a person to act in a particular way. It is a goal-oriented, psychological and continuous process that runs in the cycle of need, tension, action and satisfaction. Motivation may be positive or negative, intrinsic or extrinsic, financial or non-financial. Its importance lies in the higher productivity, better quality, lower absenteeism, greater loyalty, better industrial relations and easier adaptation to change that it brings about.

Of the many theories of motivation, four stand out as the most influential. Maslow's hierarchy of needs places human needs in five levels—physiological, safety, social, esteem and self-actualisation—and holds that the lower needs must be reasonably satisfied before the higher ones become active. Herzberg's two-factor theory distinguishes between hygiene factors, which only prevent dissatisfaction, and motivators, which actually produce motivation. McGregor's Theory X and Theory Y describe two contrasting sets of assumptions about human nature and the styles of motivation that flow from each. Vroom's expectancy theory is a process theory which holds that motivation depends on the product of expectancy, instrumentality and valence; if any one of these is zero, motivation too will be zero.

Incentives put the theories of motivation into practice. Financial incentives include wages, allowances, bonus, profit-sharing, ESOPs, commission, productivity-linked rewards, retirement benefits and perquisites. Non-financial incentives include job security, status, recognition, awards, promotion, job enrichment, participation in decisions, empowerment, career development, pleasant working conditions and flexible work arrangements. The wise manager combines the two in proportions that suit the situation and the individuals involved.

Key Terms

Motivation, Motivation Cycle, Positive and Negative Motivation, Intrinsic and Extrinsic Motivation, Maslow's Hierarchy, Physiological Needs, Safety Needs, Social Needs, Esteem Needs, Self-Actualisation,

Herzberg's Two-Factor Theory, Hygiene Factors, Motivators, Job Enrichment, Theory X, Theory Y, McGregor, Vroom's Expectancy Theory, Expectancy, Instrumentality, Valence, Adams' Equity Theory, Skinner's Reinforcement Theory, McClelland's Need Theory, Financial Incentives, ESOP, Non-Financial Incentives, Job Security, Recognition.

Review Questions

A. Short Answer Questions (2 marks each)

1. Define motivation.
2. Describe the motivation cycle in brief.
3. Name the five levels of needs given by Maslow.
4. Distinguish between hygiene factors and motivators.
5. State any four assumptions of Theory X.
6. Write the Vroom formula and explain its three variables.
7. Give any four examples of non-financial incentives.
8. What is an Employee Stock Option Plan (ESOP)?

B. Long Answer Questions (10 marks each)

9. Discuss the concept, the nature and the importance of motivation.

10. Explain Maslow's hierarchy of needs theory. What are its strengths and limitations?

11. Describe Herzberg's two-factor theory of motivation.

12. Distinguish between Theory X and Theory Y as given by Douglas McGregor.

13. Explain Vroom's expectancy theory of motivation with the help of his formula.

14. Discuss the various financial and non-financial incentives used by modern organisations.

C. Practical / Case-Based Questions

15. You are the manager of a software company in Indore with about fifty engineers. The performance of some of them has been falling in recent months. On the basis of any motivation theory of your choice, suggest steps for motivating them.

16. Take the case of any successful Indian company (such as Infosys, TCS or Tata Steel) and discuss the financial and non-financial incentives that it offers to its employees.

CHAPTER 14

LEADERSHIP

Learning Objectives

After studying this chapter, the reader should be able to:

- understand the concept, the nature and the importance of leadership;
- distinguish between leadership and management;
- describe the various styles of leadership;
- explain the trait, behavioural and situational theories of leadership;
- distinguish between transactional and transformational leadership; and
- identify the emerging concepts of leadership such as servant, ethical and charismatic leadership.

Introduction

Of all the elements of the directing function, none is more important than leadership. Plans, structures and systems do not lead human beings; they merely lay down what is to be done and how. The actual task of getting human beings to put in their best effort, day after day and year after year, rests on the shoulders of leaders. As Peter Drucker observed, management is doing things right, but leadership is doing the right things.

The history of the world is, in many ways, a history of its leaders. Mahatma Gandhi led India to freedom through the power of his moral example. J.R.D. Tata built one of the largest business houses of India on the foundations of trust and quality. Verghese Kurien transformed the dairy industry of India through the cooperative movement at Anand. Sam Manekshaw led the Indian Army to victory in 1971. In every field of human activity—politics, business, the army, religion, science, sport—leadership is what makes the difference between ordinary results and extraordinary results.

This chapter examines the concept, the nature and the importance of leadership, distinguishes it from the more general function of management, describes the well-known styles of leadership, presents the trait, behavioural and situational theories of leadership, discusses the modern ideas of transformational and transactional leadership, and concludes with a brief survey of the emerging concepts such as servant, ethical and charismatic leadership.

14.1 Concept, Nature and Importance of Leadership

14.1.1 Meaning and Definition

Leadership is the ability of a person to influence and guide the activities of others, with their willing cooperation, towards the achievement of a common goal. A leader is one who is followed not because of his formal position or authority alone, but because of his personal qualities, his vision and his ability to inspire confidence in those around him.

Some well-known definitions of leadership are:

1. Koontz and O'Donnell— "Leadership is the ability of a manager to induce subordinates to work with confidence and zeal."

2. George R. Terry— "Leadership is the activity of influencing people to strive willingly for mutual objectives."

3. Chester I. Barnard— "Leadership is the quality of behaviour of individuals whereby they guide people on their activities in organised efforts."

4. Hemphill and Coons— "Leadership is the behaviour of an individual when he is directing the activities of a group towards a shared goal."

5. Warren Bennis— "Leadership is the capacity to translate vision into reality."

14.1.2 Features of Leadership

- Leadership is essentially an influence process. The leader influences the thoughts, the attitudes and the actions of his followers.
- It is an interpersonal relationship. It cannot exist without followers.
- It is goal-oriented. The influence of the leader is exerted towards the achievement of a particular goal.

• It implies willing followership. Leadership is, therefore, different from the use of force or compulsion.

• It is a continuous process. The leader has to keep on leading; he cannot rest on his past achievements.

• It is situational. The same person may be an effective leader in one situation and not in another.

• It implies an inequality of influence between the leader and the led, but this inequality is accepted willingly by the followers.

14.1.3 Leadership and Management—A Comparison

Although the two terms are sometimes used as if they meant the same thing, leadership and management are not exactly identical. Every manager is required to be a leader to some extent, and every formal leader has to perform certain managerial duties, but the two concepts can be distinguished as shown below:

Basis	Manager	Leader
Source of Power	Formal authority of position.	Personal qualities and influence.
Focus	Doing things right; efficiency.	Doing the right things; effectiveness and vision.
Followers	Subordinates who obey because they have to.	Followers who follow because they want to.
Time Horizon	Short-term; today's targets.	Long-term; tomorrow's possibilities.
Approach	Plans, organises and controls.	Inspires, motivates and transforms.

14.1.4 Importance of Leadership

• Leadership initiates action by translating the plans of the enterprise into actual results.

- It motivates and inspires the employees to put in their best effort.
- It provides guidance to the employees in the performance of their tasks.
- It creates confidence among the employees, both in themselves and in the management.
- It builds morale and a sense of belonging among the members of the organisation.
- It brings about coordination among the various activities and individuals.
- It facilitates change by helping the employees to understand and accept it.
- It maintains discipline by setting an example and by winning the willing acceptance of rules.
- It develops the next generation of leaders by training and grooming the subordinates.

14.2 Leadership Styles

A leadership style is the pattern of behaviour that a leader generally displays in dealing with his followers. Robert Tannenbaum and Warren Schmidt, in their well-known article "How to Choose a Leadership Pattern" published in the Harvard Business Review in 1958, suggested that leadership styles could be arranged on a continuum ranging from boss-centred to subordinate-centred. In its simplest form, three principal styles are usually identified—autocratic, democratic and laissez-faire.

14.2.1 Autocratic or Authoritarian Style

Under the autocratic style, all the authority for decision-making is concentrated in the hands of the leader. The leader decides what is to be done, how it is to be done, when it is to be done and by whom. The subordinates are expected to obey the orders without question. Communication flows mainly from the leader downwards. Three sub-types of the autocratic style may be noted:

- The strict autocrat, who relies on threats and punishment to get the work done.
- The benevolent autocrat, who is kindly and considerate but who still keeps all the decision-making powers in his own hands.

- The manipulative autocrat, who tries to make his subordinates believe that they have a say in the decisions, while in fact the decisions are taken entirely by him.

The autocratic style is suitable in emergencies, in dealing with new and untrained workers and in situations where strict discipline is essential, such as in the army or in police work. It is, however, generally disliked by educated and skilled workers, who feel resentful at being treated as mere instruments.

14.2.2 Democratic or Participative Style

Under the democratic style, the leader takes decisions in consultation with his subordinates. He invites their views, considers their suggestions and, on important matters, may even put the question to a vote. The subordinates are made to feel that they are partners in the work. Communication flows in both directions—from the leader to the subordinates and from the subordinates to the leader.

The democratic style is suitable when the subordinates are educated, experienced and willing to participate, when there is enough time for consultation and discussion, and when the matter under consideration is not so confidential that it must be kept to the leader alone. It produces higher morale, better motivation and more original ideas, but it may also slow down the process of decision-making.

14.2.3 Laissez-Faire or Free-Rein Style

The French expression "laissez-faire" means "leave alone." Under this style, the leader gives broad guidelines and then leaves his subordinates more or less free to plan and carry out their work as they think fit. He acts more as a facilitator than as a director, providing resources and information when asked but generally staying out of the way.

This style is suitable for groups of highly skilled and self-motivated professionals, such as scientists in a research laboratory, doctors in a hospital, professors in a university and creative artists in an advertising agency. It would, however, lead to chaos and confusion if applied to ordinary workers or to a group that has not yet developed the necessary discipline and self-direction.

14.2.4 Other Styles

Besides the three main styles, two more are sometimes mentioned. The paternalistic style is one in which the leader treats his subordinates as members of his family, looking after their welfare in a fatherly manner but expecting their loyalty and obedience in return. This style was common in the older Indian business houses and is still found in many family-run enterprises. The bureaucratic style is one in which the leader sticks rigidly to the rules and procedures, taking no decision that is not authorised by the book. This style is common in government departments and large public-sector enterprises.

14.3 Trait, Behavioural and Situational Theories

Researchers have, over the years, developed several theories to explain what makes a person an effective leader. These theories fall into three broad groups—the trait theories, the behavioural theories and the situational or contingency theories.

14.3.1 The Trait Theory

The trait theory, which is the oldest theory of leadership, is also known as the "Great Man" theory. It holds that leaders are born, not made, and that they possess certain inborn personal qualities or traits that distinguish them from non-leaders. The job of research, according to this theory, is to identify the traits common to all great leaders.

Studies conducted by Ralph M. Stogdill in 1948 and 1974 identified a long list of traits that were generally found in successful leaders. These included, broadly:

- physical traits such as height, weight, appearance and energy;
- mental traits such as intelligence, judgement, alertness and decisiveness;
- personality traits such as self-confidence, originality, adaptability and emotional stability;
- social traits such as sociability, tact and diplomatic skill; and
- moral traits such as honesty, integrity and a strong sense of responsibility.

The trait theory is appealing in its simplicity. It does not, however, give us a clear list of traits that are present in every leader and absent in every non-leader. Some great leaders have lacked one or more of the so-called essential traits. The theory also ignores the role of the situation and of the followers. For these reasons, the search for a universal list of leadership traits has been largely abandoned.

14.3.2 The Behavioural Theories

The behavioural theories shifted the focus from what a leader is to what a leader does. They held that effective leadership lies in particular patterns of behaviour, which can be learnt through training. Three lines of research deserve special mention here.

(a) The Ohio State Studies. Researchers at the Ohio State University, during the late 1940s and the 1950s, identified two basic dimensions of leadership behaviour—"initiating structure" (the extent to which the leader defines and organises the work, sets goals and assigns duties) and "consideration" (the extent to which the leader shows concern for the welfare and the feelings of the subordinates). Effective leaders, the studies found, scored high on both dimensions.

(b) The Michigan Studies and Likert's Systems. Rensis Likert and his colleagues at the University of Michigan distinguished between job-centred leaders and employee-centred leaders. Likert went further and identified four systems of management based on the style of leadership—System 1 (Exploitative Authoritative), System 2 (Benevolent Authoritative), System 3 (Consultative) and System 4 (Participative). His research showed that System 4 organisations performed the best in the long run.

(c) The Managerial Grid. Robert R. Blake and Jane S. Mouton, in their book The Managerial Grid (1964), arranged leadership styles on a two-dimensional grid, with concern for production along one axis and concern for people along the other. They identified five major styles: the 1,1 style (Impoverished Management—low concern for both), the 1,9 style (Country Club Management—high concern for people, low for production), the 9,1 style (Authority-Compliance—high for production, low for people), the 5,5 style (Middle-of-the-Road—moderate concern for both), and the 9,9 style (Team Management—high concern for both). They held that the 9,9 style was the best in all situations.

14.3.3 The Situational or Contingency Theories

The situational theories rejected the idea that there is one best style of leadership applicable to all situations. They held that the right style depends on the situation—the nature of the task, the maturity of the followers, the urgency of the work and the relationship between the leader and the followers. Three theories of this group deserve mention.

(a) Fiedler's Contingency Model. Fred E. Fiedler, in his book A Theory of Leadership Effectiveness (1967), held that the effectiveness of a leader depends on the match between his leadership style and the favourableness of the situation. The favourableness of the situation depends on three factors—the relations between the leader and his members, the structure of the task, and the position power of the leader. Task-oriented leaders, Fiedler found, perform better in situations that are either highly favourable or highly unfavourable, while relationship-oriented leaders perform better in moderately favourable situations.

(b) The Hersey-Blanchard Situational Theory. Paul Hersey and Kenneth Blanchard, in the 1970s, developed a theory based on the maturity of the followers. They identified four leadership styles—Telling (S1), Selling (S2), Participating (S3) and Delegating (S4)—and held that the right style depends on the maturity level of the followers. New and inexperienced followers need the Telling style; as they grow in maturity, the leader should move successively through Selling, Participating and finally Delegating.

(c) The Path-Goal Theory. Robert J. House, in his Path-Goal theory of leadership (1971), held that the function of the leader is to clear the path for the followers towards their goals. He identified four leadership styles—Directive, Supportive, Participative and Achievement-oriented—and held that the right style in any given situation depends on the personal characteristics of the followers and on the nature of the task.

14.4 Transformational and Transactional Leadership

During the 1970s and the 1980s, a new and powerful distinction was drawn between two kinds of leadership—transactional and transformational. The distinction was first proposed by James MacGregor Burns in his book Leadership (1978) and was further developed by Bernard M. Bass in his book Leadership and Performance Beyond Expectations (1985).

14.4.1 Transactional Leadership

Transactional leadership is based on an exchange or transaction between the leader and the follower. The leader offers rewards in return for good performance and punishments in return for poor performance. The relationship is based on the principle of "do this and you will get that." The leader, in this view, is essentially a manager of routine, day-to-day operations. He maintains the existing system, gets the work done within the framework of established policies and procedures, and ensures that the organisation does not deviate from its set course.

Transactional leadership is generally exercised through two mechanisms—contingent reward (the leader explains what is expected and rewards the follower when the expectation is met) and management by exception (the leader steps in only when something goes wrong, either actively by monitoring performance or passively by waiting for problems to emerge).

14.4.2 Transformational Leadership

Transformational leadership goes beyond the simple exchange of rewards. The transformational leader inspires his followers to transcend their narrow self-interest and to work for the greater good of the organisation, the community and the country. He paints a compelling vision of a better future, builds trust, develops the abilities of his followers and brings about fundamental change.

Bernard Bass identified four key components of transformational leadership, often called the four I's:

1. **Idealised Influence (Charisma)**—the leader serves as a role model and earns the admiration, respect and trust of the followers.

2. **Inspirational Motivation**—the leader articulates a compelling vision, sets high expectations and inspires the followers to rise above themselves.

3. **Intellectual Stimulation**—the leader encourages creativity and challenges the followers to think in new ways and to question old assumptions.

4. Individualised Consideration—the leader pays personal attention to each follower, understands his particular needs and helps him to grow.

Some of the greatest figures of history may be cited as examples of transformational leadership. Mahatma Gandhi transformed the Indian freedom movement and inspired millions to follow the path of non-violence. Nelson Mandela transformed South Africa from a deeply divided apartheid state into a multi-racial democracy. In the world of business, J.R.D. Tata transformed Indian industry over a period of fifty years, Verghese Kurien transformed the dairy industry through Amul, and N.R. Narayana Murthy transformed the Indian information technology industry by building Infosys on a foundation of corporate governance and middle-class values.

14.4.3 The Two Approaches—A Comparison

Basis	Transactional	Transformational
Basis of Influence	Exchange of rewards for performance.	Vision, inspiration and personal example.
Focus	Short-term goals and day-to-day operations.	Long-term goals and fundamental change.
Approach to Followers	Treats them as employees.	Develops them as future leaders.
Attitude to Status Quo	Maintains it.	Challenges and changes it.
Suitable Situation	Stable environment, routine work.	Crisis, change, growth opportunities.

14.5 Emerging Leadership Concepts

The last few decades have seen the emergence of a number of new ideas about leadership, each drawing attention to a particular aspect of the leadership role. Some of the more important of these are discussed below.

14.5.1 Charismatic Leadership

Charismatic leadership is based on the personal magnetism of the leader. The charismatic leader has the power to inspire devotion, loyalty and even self-sacrifice on the part of his followers. He has a compelling vision, the ability to communicate that vision in a stirring manner, and a personality that attracts others to him. Subhas Chandra Bose, who inspired the Indian National Army with the slogan "Tum mujhe khoon do, main tumhe azaadi doonga," was a charismatic leader. In modern business, Steve Jobs of Apple and, in India, Dhirubhai Ambani of Reliance have been cited as examples of charismatic leadership. Charismatic leadership has its dangers too, since the followers may follow the leader unquestioningly even when he is mistaken.

14.5.2 Servant Leadership

The concept of servant leadership was put forward by Robert K. Greenleaf in his essay "The Servant as Leader" published in 1970. The servant leader, according to Greenleaf, sees himself primarily as a servant of his followers, of his organisation and of his community. He places the growth, the well-being and the dignity of others above his own personal ambition. He leads not by commanding but by serving.

The Indian tradition has long been familiar with the idea of servant leadership. Mahatma Gandhi described himself simply as a sevak, a servant of the people, and his entire life was an example of leading by serving. Mother Teresa, who served the poorest of the poor on the streets of Calcutta, was another great servant leader. In modern business, leaders such as J.R.D. Tata, Azim Premji and Ratan Tata have been cited as practitioners of servant leadership.

14.5.3 Ethical Leadership

Ethical leadership is leadership based on moral principles and on a strong sense of right and wrong. The ethical leader practises what he preaches. He places honesty, integrity and the welfare of all stakeholders above the narrow pursuit of profit. He is willing to lose business rather than compromise on ethics. The growing concern about corporate scandals—the Satyam scandal of 2009 being the most striking Indian example—has placed ethical leadership at the centre of management thinking in recent years. J.R.D. Tata's famous remark that "no success or achievement in material terms is worthwhile unless it serves the needs or interests of the country and its people" captures the spirit of ethical leadership.

14.5.4 Authentic Leadership

The concept of authentic leadership, developed by Bill George in his book Authentic Leadership (2003), holds that the most effective leaders are those who are true to themselves—who know their own values, who are aware of their strengths and weaknesses, who behave consistently in all situations and who relate to others with openness and honesty. Authentic leaders do not try to imitate other successful leaders; they develop their own unique style based on who they really are.

14.5.5 Visionary Leadership

Visionary leaders are those who can see possibilities far beyond what others can see and who have the courage to act on their vision. They paint a compelling picture of the future and persuade others to share in it. Dhirubhai Ambani, who built Reliance Industries from a small textile mill into a giant in petrochemicals and telecommunications, is a striking example. M.S. Swaminathan, who led the Green Revolution in India and transformed the country from food deficiency to food sufficiency, is another. In the world of technology, the leaders of companies such as Microsoft, Apple and Google have all been visionary leaders.

14.5.6 Spiritual Leadership and the Indian Tradition

The Indian tradition has, for thousands of years, taught the principles of spiritual leadership through such texts as the Bhagavad Gita, the Ramayana, the Mahabharata and the Arthashastra of Kautilya. The Bhagavad Gita's teaching of nishkama karma, that is, performing one's duty without attachment to the fruits of action, has profound implications for leadership. The leader is seen not as someone who pursues personal glory but as a karta who carries the responsibility for the welfare of his group. The concept of dharma, or duty in accordance with moral law, provides the moral foundation of leadership. These ideas, sometimes brought together under the name "Indian Ethos in Management," have been gaining ground in business schools across the country.

14.5.7 E-Leadership

The rise of information technology, and particularly the experience of working from home during the COVID-19 pandemic, has given rise to the new field of e-leadership, that is, the leadership of teams whose members are connected mainly through electronic media. The e-leader faces special challenges—he cannot rely on personal contact to build trust, he must communicate effectively across time zones and cultures, and he must motivate team members whom he may rarely meet in person. Skills in the use of digital communication tools, sensitivity to cultural differences and the ability to give clear written instructions have become increasingly important.

Summary

Leadership is the ability of a person to influence and guide the activities of others, with their willing cooperation, towards the achievement of a common goal. It is an influence process, an interpersonal relationship, a goal-oriented and continuous activity, and a situational phenomenon. Leadership differs from management in its source of power, its focus, its time horizon and its approach to followers. Its importance lies in initiating action, motivating employees, providing guidance, building morale, facilitating change and developing future leaders.

The three principal styles of leadership are the autocratic, the democratic and the laissez-faire styles, to which the paternalistic and the bureaucratic styles are sometimes added. The theories of leadership fall into three broad groups. The trait theory, also known as the "Great Man" theory, holds that leaders are born with certain inborn qualities. The behavioural theories—represented by the Ohio State Studies, the Michigan Studies, Likert's four systems and the Managerial Grid of Blake and Mouton—hold that leadership lies in particular patterns of behaviour that can be learnt. The situational theories—represented by Fiedler's contingency model, the Hersey-Blanchard situational theory and the Path-Goal theory of House—hold that the right style depends on the situation.

A more recent distinction is between transactional leadership, which is based on the exchange of rewards for performance, and transformational leadership, which inspires followers to transcend their narrow self-interest and to work for the greater good. Bernard Bass identified four components of transformational leadership—idealised influence, inspirational motivation, intellectual stimulation and individualised consideration.

Among the emerging concepts of leadership, charismatic leadership is based on personal magnetism, servant leadership on serving others, ethical leadership on moral principles, authentic leadership on being true to oneself, visionary leadership on the power of vision, and spiritual leadership on values drawn from the Indian and other ethical traditions. The rise of remote working has also given birth to the new field of e-leadership.

Key Terms

Leadership, Influence Process, Leader vs Manager, Autocratic Style, Democratic Style, Laissez-Faire Style, Paternalistic Style, Bureaucratic Style, Tannenbaum and Schmidt, Trait Theory, Great Man Theory, Ohio State Studies, Initiating Structure, Consideration, Michigan Studies, Likert's Four Systems, Managerial Grid, Blake and Mouton, Fiedler's Contingency Model, Hersey-Blanchard Situational Theory, Path-Goal Theory, Transactional Leadership, Transformational Leadership, Four I's, Charismatic Leadership, Servant Leadership, Greenleaf, Ethical Leadership, Authentic Leadership, Visionary Leadership, Indian Ethos, Nishkama Karma, E-Leadership.

Review Questions

A. Short Answer Questions (2 marks each)

1. Define leadership.
2. Distinguish between a leader and a manager.
3. Name the three principal styles of leadership.
4. Briefly explain the trait theory of leadership.
5. What is the Managerial Grid? Who developed it?
6. Distinguish between transactional and transformational leadership.

7. State any four examples of servant leaders.

B. Long Answer Questions (10 marks each)

8. Discuss the concept, the nature and the importance of leadership in modern business.

9. Explain the autocratic, democratic and laissez-faire styles of leadership. Under what circumstances is each style most suitable?

10. Describe the major behavioural theories of leadership with special reference to the Ohio State Studies and the Managerial Grid.

11. Discuss the situational theories of leadership.

12. Explain the concept of transformational leadership and its four components, with examples from Indian business and political life.

13. Write notes on (a) servant leadership, (b) ethical leadership, and (c) visionary leadership.

C. Practical / Case-Based Questions

14. Choose any leader from Indian politics, business or social life whom you greatly admire. Analyse his or her leadership in terms of the theories and concepts discussed in this chapter.

15. You have just been appointed as the principal of a private college in Indore. Discuss the style of leadership you would adopt and explain why.

CHAPTER 15

COMMUNICATION

Learning Objectives

After studying this chapter, the reader should be able to:

- understand the meaning, the process and the importance of communication;
- describe the various types and channels of communication;
- distinguish between formal and informal communication;
- identify the major barriers to effective communication;
- apply the principles of effective communication; and
- appreciate the role of information and communication technology in modern management.

Introduction

Communication is the lifeblood of every organisation. Just as the blood circulating through the human body keeps every organ alive, the flow of information through an organisation keeps every department and every employee alive to its work. A manager may have the best of plans, the soundest of organisation structure and the most capable of subordinates, but if he fails to communicate with them effectively, none of this will produce the desired results.

The word "communication" comes from the Latin word "communis," which means "common." To communicate, then, is to establish a common understanding between two or more persons. It is a process of sharing—of information, of ideas, of feelings—so that the parties involved arrive at a common interpretation of what is being said.

Communication is something that human beings have been doing since the dawn of civilisation. In the ancient days, our ancestors communicated through gestures, signs and grunts. Later came spoken language, then writing, then printing, then the telephone, the radio, the television and now the internet. The means of communication have grown ever more powerful, but the basic purpose has remained the same—to share understanding among human beings. In the modern workplace, with its many employees, its many departments and its many locations, the volume and the variety of communication have increased enormously, and the role of communication in the work of the manager has become more important than ever before.

This chapter discusses the meaning, the process and the importance of communication, examines its various types and channels, distinguishes between formal and informal communication, identifies the major barriers to effective communication, lays down the principles of effective communication, and concludes with a discussion of the role of modern technology in transforming workplace communication.

15.1 Meaning, Process and Importance of Communication

15.1.1 Meaning and Definition

Communication may be defined as the process of sharing information, ideas, opinions and feelings between two or more persons, with a view to creating a common understanding. It is not merely the act of speaking or writing; it is the act of being understood. As Peter Drucker once observed, the most important thing in communication is to hear what is not being said.

Some well-known definitions of communication are:

1. **Koontz and O'Donnell**— "Communication is the transfer of information from one person to another, regardless of whether or not it produces confidence."

2. **Newman and Summer**— "Communication is the exchange of facts, ideas, opinions or emotions by two or more persons."

3. **Theo Haimann**— "Communication is the process of passing information and understanding from one person to another."

4. **Keith Davis**— "Communication is the process of passing information and understanding from one person to another. It is essentially a bridge of meaning between people."

5. **Louis A. Allen**— "Communication is the sum of all the things one person does when he wants to create understanding in the mind of another. It involves a systematic and continuous process of telling, listening and understanding."

15.1.2 The Communication Process

Communication is not a single act but a process consisting of several stages. The main elements of the communication process are:

1. The Sender. The person who has an idea or a piece of information that he wishes to share with another. The sender is also called the source or the encoder.

2. The Message. The idea, opinion, feeling or piece of information that the sender wishes to convey. It is the substance of the communication.

3. Encoding. The process of converting the message into words, gestures, symbols or other signs that can be transmitted. The choice of language, tone and form depends on the receiver, the situation and the medium.

4. The Channel or Medium. The means by which the message travels from the sender to the receiver. It may be a face-to-face conversation, a telephone call, a letter, an e-mail, a notice board, a video conference and so on.

5. The Receiver. The person for whom the message is intended. The receiver is also called the decoder or the destination.

6. Decoding. The process by which the receiver interprets the message and tries to extract meaning from it. The success of communication depends on whether the meaning decoded is the same as the meaning encoded.

7. Feedback. The response of the receiver back to the sender. Feedback completes the communication loop and tells the sender whether the message has been received and understood as intended.

8. Noise. Any disturbance or interference that comes in the way of clear communication. Noise may be physical (such as a loud machine in the background), semantic (use of difficult words) or psychological (preoccupation of the receiver with other matters).

15.1.3 Features of Communication

- Communication is a two-way process involving both the sending and the receiving of messages.
- It is a continuous process; it goes on all the time and at all levels

of the organisation.

- It is a pervasive activity, required in every department and at every level of management.
- It may be verbal (oral or written) or non-verbal (through gestures, expressions or body language).
- It is a process, not a one-time act.
- It is goal-oriented; it aims at producing understanding and at influencing action.
- It is not complete until the receiver has understood the message in the way the sender intended.

15.1.4 Importance of Communication

- Communication is the basis of all decision-making, since decisions depend on accurate and timely information.
- It is the means by which the manager directs his subordinates and supervises their work.
- It is essential for coordination among the various departments and individuals.
- It is the chief tool of effective leadership and motivation.
- It builds confidence and creates a feeling of belonging among the employees.
- It improves industrial relations by reducing misunderstandings and disputes.
- It enables the management to receive valuable feedback from the lower levels.
- It plays an important role in the public image of the organisation through advertising, press relations and customer service.
- It facilitates the smooth working of the entire enterprise.

15.2 Types and Channels of Communication

15.2.1 Communication on the Basis of Direction

1. Downward Communication. Flows from the higher levels of the organisation to the lower levels. It consists of orders, instructions, policies, notices, memos and feedback on the performance of the subordinates. Downward communication is the most common type of organisational communication.

2. Upward Communication. Flows from the lower levels to the higher levels. It consists of reports, suggestions, complaints, grievances and applications. Upward communication provides the management with valuable feedback from the field. The open-door policy of many modern managers and the suggestion-box system are examples of mechanisms designed to encourage upward communication.

3. Horizontal or Lateral Communication. Flows among persons at the same level of the organisation. It is necessary for coordination among different departments such as production, marketing, finance and personnel. Meetings of departmental heads, joint task forces and inter-departmental memos are examples of horizontal communication.

4. Diagonal or Crosswise Communication. Flows across different levels and different departments. It is used when an immediate exchange of information is needed and the slow process of going through the chain of command would be too time-consuming. For instance, the production manager may communicate directly with a junior officer in the finance department about an urgent payment matter.

15.2.2 Communication on the Basis of Method

1. Oral Communication. Communication through the spoken word. It takes place through face-to-face conversations, telephone calls, meetings, conferences, speeches, interviews and, in modern times, video calls. Oral communication is fast, personal and allows for immediate feedback, but it leaves no record.

2. Written Communication. Communication through the written word. It takes place through letters, memos, reports, notices, bulletins, manuals, e-mails and instant messages. Written communication provides a permanent record, is suitable for complex matters and can reach many recipients at the same time, but it is slower and lacks the personal touch of oral communication.

3. Non-Verbal Communication. Communication without the use of words. It takes place through gestures, facial expressions, posture, eye contact, tone of voice, dress and personal grooming. Non-verbal communication often reveals more about the true feelings of the sender than his words. In Indian culture, the simple act of joining the hands in a namaste, the touching of the feet of an elder or the offering of a chair to a visitor conveys a wealth of meaning without a word being spoken.

15.2.3 Oral and Written Communication—A Comparison

Basis	Oral Communication	Written Communication
Speed	Fast; immediate.	Slower; requires preparation.
Feedback	Immediate; two-way.	Delayed; often missing altogether.
Record	No permanent record.	Provides a permanent record.
Suitability	Routine and simple matters.	Important, complex or legal matters.
Cost	Lower.	Higher.
Personal Touch	High; conveys feelings.	Low; impersonal.

15.3 Formal and Informal Communication

15.3.1 Formal Communication

Formal communication is the communication that takes place through the official channels laid down by the organisation. It follows the scalar chain of authority. A subordinate communicates with his immediate superior, who communicates with his own superior, and so on up the chain. Similarly, an order flows downwards through the same chain. Formal communication is generally in writing and is recorded for future reference.

Formal communication can take several network patterns:

- The chain network, in which communication flows up and down the scalar chain.
- The wheel network, in which all communication passes through a central person, usually the leader.

- The star or all-channel network, in which every member can communicate with every other member.
- The circle network, in which each member communicates only with his two immediate neighbours.
- The Y network, which combines features of the chain and the wheel.

Each pattern has its own advantages and limitations. The wheel network is fast but places a heavy burden on the central person; the all-channel network is slower but produces higher member satisfaction.

15.3.2 Informal or Grapevine Communication

Informal communication is the communication that flows through the informal channels of the organisation, that is, through the personal relationships among the employees. Since it spreads in many directions like the branches of a grapevine, it is popularly known as the grapevine. The grapevine carries messages of all kinds—news, rumours, gossip, personal information and even confidential business matters.

Keith Davis, an American writer on organisational behaviour, identified four typical patterns of the grapevine:

1. Single-Strand Chain. The information passes from A to B, from B to C, from C to D and so on, in a straight line. This is the least common and least accurate pattern.

2. Gossip Chain. A tells the news to many persons, who pass it on to many others. This is the pattern through which interesting but unverified information spreads rapidly through the organisation.

3. Probability Chain. A passes the news on a random basis to any persons he meets, who in turn pass it on to others at random. This pattern is followed when the information is not particularly important.

4. Cluster Chain. A tells the news to a few selected persons, each of whom in turn tells it to a few more. This is the most common pattern of the grapevine, particularly for important matters.

The modern equivalent of the grapevine in many organisations is the WhatsApp group, the office canteen chat and the social media network. The wise manager does not try to suppress the informal organisation; he tries to use it for the benefit of the enterprise.

15.3.3 Formal versus Informal Communication

Basis	Formal Communication	Informal Communication
Channel	Official; through the scalar chain.	Personal; through friendships and groups.
Speed	Slower; follows defined route.	Faster; spreads quickly.
Form	Mostly written.	Mostly oral.
Record	Maintained.	No record.
Reliability	Generally accurate.	Often distorted; may carry rumours.
Authority	Carries official authority.	No official authority.

15.4 Barriers to Effective Communication

In spite of its great importance, communication in organisations is often less effective than it should be. The barriers that come in the way may be grouped under five heads.

15.4.1 Semantic Barriers

Semantic barriers relate to the language of communication—the words used, the symbols employed and the meanings attached to them. Common semantic barriers include:

- Use of badly chosen or wrongly arranged words.
- Use of words that mean different things to different persons.
- Faulty translation from one language to another.
- Unclarified assumptions that the receiver shares the sender's background and knowledge.
- Use of technical jargon or specialist's language that the receiver does not understand.
- Differences in body language across cultures.

15.4.2 Psychological or Emotional Barriers

These barriers arise from the mental and emotional state of the sender or the receiver. Common psychological barriers include:

- Premature evaluation, in which the receiver judges the message before fully hearing it.
- Inattention or lack of interest in the message.
- Loss of transmission and poor retention of the message.
- Distrust of the sender or fear of the consequences.
- Resistance to change, particularly when the message proposes new methods or new ideas.
- Emotional disturbance such as anger, anxiety or excitement that clouds judgement.

15.4.3 Organisational Barriers

These barriers arise from the structure and the policies of the organisation. Common organisational barriers include:

- Status differences between the sender and the receiver, which inhibit free communication.
- Organisational policy that discourages free communication, such as excessive secrecy or formality.
- Cumbersome rules and procedures that slow down the flow of information.
- A complex organisational structure with too many levels of management.
- A long chain of command that distorts the message as it passes from one level to another.
- Lack of proper communication facilities such as telephones, computers and meeting rooms.

15.4.4 Personal Barriers

These barriers arise from the personal attitudes and habits of the sender and the receiver. Common personal barriers include:

- An authoritarian attitude of the superior that discourages subordinates from speaking up.
- Lack of confidence on the part of the subordinate in dealing with the superior.

- Lack of incentive for upward communication.
- Fear of contradiction or punishment.
- A conservative attitude that resists any change in established methods of communication.

15.4.5 Mechanical Barriers

These barriers arise from the means by which communication is carried out. Common mechanical barriers include:

- Poor or outdated equipment, such as faulty telephones, slow internet connections or noisy meeting rooms.
- Choice of an improper medium for the message.
- Communication at an improper time.
- Information overload, in which the receiver is overwhelmed by too much information at once.
- Noise, in the literal sense or in the metaphorical sense of any disturbance.

15.5 Principles of Effective Communication

Effective communication is not an accident; it is the result of careful thought and planning. Over the years, writers on management have laid down a number of principles for effective communication. The most widely accepted of these are the so-called "Seven C's of Communication."

15.5.1 The Seven C's of Communication

1. Clarity. The message must be clear in the mind of the sender before he tries to communicate it. The language must be simple, the ideas must be well organised, and the message must be free of ambiguity.

2. Conciseness. The message must be brief and to the point. Unnecessary words, repetition and irrelevant matter should be avoided. As the saying goes, the shorter the message, the longer it lives in the memory of the receiver.

3. Concreteness. The message must be specific and concrete rather than vague and abstract. Specific figures, dates and examples are more effective than general statements.

4. Correctness. The message must be factually correct, grammatically sound and free from errors. An incorrect message destroys the credibility of the sender.

5. Completeness. The message must contain all the information that the receiver needs in order to act on it. An incomplete message leads to confusion, delays and the need for repeated clarifications.

6. Courtesy. The message must be courteous and respectful in tone, regardless of the rank or the importance of the receiver. Courtesy costs nothing but earns much.

7. Consideration. The sender must put himself in the place of the receiver and consider how the message is likely to be received. This is sometimes called the "you-attitude," as opposed to the "I-attitude."

15.5.2 Other Principles

To the seven C's, the following principles may be added:

- Principle of attention—the message must arouse and hold the attention of the receiver.
- Principle of feedback—provision must be made for the receiver to send his response back to the sender.
- Principle of strategic use of informal organisation—the manager should use the grapevine to supplement, not to bypass, the formal channels.
- Principle of effective listening—the manager must listen patiently to his subordinates, since listening is half of communication.
- Principle of right time—the message must reach the receiver at the right moment, neither too early nor too late.
- Principle of a sound communication system—the organisation must invest in good communication infrastructure and in the training of its employees in communication skills.

15.6 Role of Technology in Communication

The last few decades have witnessed an unprecedented revolution in communication technology. From the typewriter and the landline telephone of the mid-twentieth century, we have moved to a world of smartphones, the internet, video conferencing, artificial intelligence and the cloud. Modern managers have at their disposal a range of communication tools that earlier generations could not even have imagined.

15.6.1 Modern Communication Technologies

The chief communication technologies in use today include:

- Mobile telephones, which have made communication possible anywhere, anytime.
- Electronic mail (e-mail), which has largely replaced the traditional letter for both internal and external communication.
- Short Message Service (SMS) and instant messaging through applications such as WhatsApp, Telegram and Signal.
- Video-conferencing platforms such as Zoom, Microsoft Teams, Google Meet and Cisco Webex, which came into widespread use during the COVID-19 pandemic and have remained popular thereafter.
- Corporate intranets, which provide a private network for communication and information sharing within an organisation.
- Enterprise Resource Planning (ERP) systems such as SAP, Oracle and Microsoft Dynamics, which integrate the data of all departments of the company.
- Customer Relationship Management (CRM) systems, which facilitate communication with customers.
- Social media platforms such as LinkedIn (for professional networking), Twitter (or X) and Facebook (for corporate communication with the public).
- Cloud-based productivity suites such as Google Workspace and Microsoft 365, which allow many users to collaborate on the same document in real time.
- Project management and team collaboration tools such as Slack, Microsoft Teams, Asana and Trello.
- Artificial intelligence applications such as chatbots, voice assistants, automated translation and generative tools, which are being increasingly used in customer service and internal communication.

15.6.2 Advantages of Modern Communication Technology

- Speed—a message can travel from one end of the world to the other in seconds.
- Global reach—employees, customers and partners across continents can be reached instantly.

- Lower cost—electronic communication costs only a fraction of traditional postal and telephone communication.
- Permanent record—e-mails, chats and recorded video calls provide a complete record for future reference.
- Multimedia capability—text, images, audio and video can be combined in a single message.
- Round-the-clock availability—the office is, in a sense, never closed.
- Reduction in paperwork and storage costs—with documents now stored on the cloud.

15.6.3 Drawbacks of Excessive Reliance on Technology

- Information overload—the average employee today receives hundreds of e-mails and messages every day, many of them unnecessary.
- Loss of personal contact—too much electronic communication can weaken the human relationships that make for a healthy workplace.
- Risks to cyber security—hacking, data theft and ransomware attacks have become a major concern for every modern organisation.
- Privacy concerns—the line between work and personal life becomes blurred when employees are constantly available on their mobile phones.
- Technical failures—a power cut, a server breakdown or a slow internet connection can paralyse work.
- Digital divide—employees in remote areas or from less privileged backgrounds may not have equal access to modern technology.
- Health concerns—extended use of screens leads to eye strain, back pain and stress.

15.6.4 The Impact of COVID-19

The COVID-19 pandemic of 2020 was a watershed moment for workplace communication in India and across the world. With offices closed and employees confined to their homes, the entire world of work shifted online almost overnight. Video calls replaced face-to-face meetings, virtual meeting rooms replaced conference halls and e-signatures replaced handwritten signatures. Even after the pandemic has passed, many of these changes have become a permanent part of working life. Many companies in India now follow a hybrid model in which the employees come to the office only for some days of the week and work from home for the rest. The skills required of the modern manager in this hybrid world include the ability to lead virtual teams, to motivate employees whom he rarely meets in person and to manage communication across time zones and cultures.

Summary

Communication is the process of sharing information, ideas, opinions and feelings between two or more persons, with a view to creating a common understanding. It is the lifeblood of every organisation. The process of communication consists of eight elements—the sender, the message, encoding, the channel, the receiver, decoding, feedback and noise. Communication is a two-way, continuous, pervasive and goal-oriented activity.

Communication may be classified by direction (downward, upward, horizontal and diagonal), by method (oral, written and non-verbal) and by formality (formal and informal). Formal communication flows through official channels in patterns such as the chain, the wheel, the all-channel, the circle and the Y. Informal communication, popularly known as the grapevine, follows patterns identified by Keith Davis as the single-strand chain, the gossip chain, the probability chain and the cluster chain.

Effective communication is hindered by five kinds of barriers—semantic, psychological, organisational, personal and mechanical. The principles of effective communication, often summed up as the Seven C's, are clarity, conciseness, concreteness, correctness, completeness, courtesy and consideration. To these may be added the principles of attention, feedback, listening, right time and a sound communication system.

The last few decades have seen a revolution in communication technology, with the rise of mobile phones, e-mail, social media, video conferencing, ERP systems, cloud computing and artificial intelligence. These technologies have brought great benefits in terms of speed, reach and cost, but have also brought new problems such as information overload, cyber security risks and the blurring of work-life boundaries.

The COVID-19 pandemic accelerated the shift to virtual communication and has permanently changed the way managers and employees communicate.

Key Terms

Communication, Sender, Receiver, Encoding, Decoding, Feedback, Noise, Downward Communication, Upward Communication, Horizontal Communication, Diagonal Communication, Oral Communication, Written Communication, Non-Verbal Communication, Formal Communication, Informal Communication, Grapevine, Single-Strand Chain, Gossip Chain, Probability Chain, Cluster Chain, Keith Davis, Semantic Barriers, Psychological Barriers, Organisational Barriers, Mechanical Barriers, Seven C's of Communication, Email, Video Conferencing, ERP, CRM, Social Media, Cloud Computing, Hybrid Work.

Review Questions

A. Short Answer Questions (2 marks each)

1. Define communication.
2. Name the main elements of the communication process.
3. Distinguish between downward and upward communication.
4. What is meant by non-verbal communication? Give two examples.
5. What is the grapevine?
6. Name the four types of grapevine identified by Keith Davis.
7. State any four semantic barriers to communication.
8. List the Seven C's of communication.

B. Long Answer Questions (10 marks each)

9. Explain the meaning, the process and the importance of communication in business.
10. Discuss the various types and channels of communication with suitable examples.
11. Distinguish between formal and informal communication. Describe the four patterns of the grapevine.
12. What are the major barriers to effective communication? How

can they be overcome?

13. Explain the principles of effective communication.
14. Discuss the role of modern technology in workplace communication. What are its advantages and drawbacks?

CHAPTER 16

CONTROLLING

Learning Objectives

After studying this chapter, the reader should be able to:

- understand the meaning, nature and importance of controlling;
- describe the various steps in the process of control;
- distinguish between feedforward, concurrent and feedback control;
- explain the budgetary and non-budgetary techniques of control;
- appreciate the close relationship between planning and controlling; and
- identify the essentials of an effective control system.

Introduction

Controlling is the last of the five basic functions of management. It is the function by which a manager ensures that the actual performance of the enterprise is in line with the planned performance, and takes corrective action wherever it is not. Without control, even the most carefully prepared plans, the soundest of organisational structures and the most effective of directing techniques cannot guarantee that the goals of the enterprise will be achieved.

Control is found in every walk of life. The driver of a car constantly compares the actual speed with the desired speed and adjusts the accelerator and the brake. The student preparing for an examination keeps a watch on the chapters covered and the time still left. The cook checks the taste of the dish and adds a pinch more salt if needed. In each of these cases, the basic process is the same—compare the actual with the planned, identify the deviation, and take corrective action.

In a business enterprise, the function of control is performed by the manager on a much larger scale. He compares the actual sales with the planned sales, the actual costs with the planned costs, the actual quality with the planned quality, and so on. Wherever the actual figures fall short of the plan, he takes the necessary corrective action. As Koontz and O'Donnell have observed, planning and controlling are the Siamese twins of management—inseparable companions in every act of managing.

This chapter discusses the meaning, the nature and the importance of controlling, describes the steps in the process of control, distinguishes between the three types of control on the basis of time, presents the budgetary and non-budgetary techniques used by modern managers, examines the close relationship between planning and controlling, and concludes with the essentials of an effective control system.

16.1 Meaning, Nature and Importance of Controlling

16.1.1 Meaning and Definition

Controlling may be defined as the function of management which ensures that the actual activities of the enterprise conform to the planned activities. It involves setting standards, measuring actual performance, comparing the two, identifying any deviations and taking corrective action wherever necessary.

Some well-known definitions of controlling are:

1. Henri Fayol— "Control consists of verifying whether everything occurs in conformity with the plan adopted, the instructions issued and the principles established. Its object is to point out weaknesses and errors in order to rectify them and to prevent their recurrence."

2. Koontz and O'Donnell— "The managerial function of controlling is the measurement and correction of the performance of activities of subordinates in order to make sure that the enterprise objectives and the plans devised to attain them are being accomplished."

3. George R. Terry— "Controlling is determining what is being accomplished, that is, evaluating the performance and, if necessary, applying corrective measures so that the performance takes place according to plans."

4. E.F.L. Brech— "Control is checking current performance against pre-determined standards contained in the plans, with a view to ensuring adequate progress and satisfactory performance."

5. Theo Haimann— "Control is the process of checking whether or not proper progress is being made towards the objectives and the goals, and acting if necessary to correct any deviation."

16.1.2 Nature and Characteristics of Controlling

- Controlling is a pervasive function. It is required at every level of management, from the top to the bottom, and in every functional area, including production, marketing, finance and personnel.
- It is a continuous process. The work of comparing actual performance with planned performance never ends.
- It is goal-oriented. Control is exercised with the aim of achieving the objectives of the enterprise.
- It is forward-looking. Although it deals with results that have already taken place, its purpose is to influence future performance.
- It is action-oriented. Control is meaningful only when corrective action is taken on the basis of the comparison.
- It is the function that closes the management cycle. The information generated through control feeds back into the next round of planning.
- It applies to both human and non-human resources. The manager controls the work of his subordinates as well as the use of money, materials and machinery.
- It involves both measurement and judgement. Some standards can be measured in numbers, while others require the judgement of the manager.

16.1.3 Importance of Controlling

- It ensures the achievement of the objectives of the enterprise by keeping the activities on track.
- It judges the accuracy of the standards and brings about their revision wherever necessary.
- It ensures the efficient use of resources by detecting waste, idle capacity and inefficient methods.
- It improves the motivation of the employees, who know that their performance is being watched and that good performance will be recognised.
- It maintains order and discipline in the organisation.

- It facilitates coordination among the various departments by providing a common basis of comparison.
- It helps the enterprise to adjust to changes in the external environment by drawing attention to the impact of those changes on actual performance.
- It makes possible decentralisation and delegation of authority, since the top management can be assured that the work is being properly carried out.
- It provides the basis for fixing responsibility for results and for taking decisions about rewards and punishments.

16.2 Process of Control

The process of control is essentially the same in every type of organisation and at every level. It consists of the following five steps:

16.2.1 Setting of Standards

The first step in control is the setting of the standards against which actual performance is to be measured. Standards are the targets, the limits or the goals laid down in the plan. They may be expressed in physical terms (units of output, hours of labour, tonnes of raw material), in monetary terms (cost, revenue, profit), in time terms (delivery dates, completion schedules) or in qualitative terms (customer satisfaction, employee morale).

Standards may also be classified as:

- Quantitative standards, which can be measured in numbers. Examples include sales of one crore rupees a month, production of ten thousand units a day, and an absenteeism rate of not more than three per cent.
- Qualitative standards, which cannot be reduced to numbers but must be judged. Examples include the quality of customer service, the morale of the employees and the standing of the company in the eyes of the public.

Good standards have certain qualities. They are specific, measurable, attainable, realistic and time-bound—the well-known SMART criteria. They are also clear, accepted by the people who have to meet them, and reviewed from time to time.

16.2.2 Measurement of Actual Performance

The next step is to measure the actual performance of the enterprise against the standards. This involves the collection of data on what has actually been done. Data may be collected through various means—personal observation by the manager, written reports submitted by subordinates, statistical statements, financial accounts, customer feedback and management information systems.

The measurement should be timely, accurate, complete and economical. It should be carried out at appropriate intervals, neither so frequently as to be a burden nor so rarely as to allow major deviations to remain undetected.

16.2.3 Comparison of Actual Performance with the Standards

Once the actual performance has been measured, it is compared with the standard. The comparison brings to light the deviations—the gaps between the actual and the planned. Deviations may be:

- favourable, when the actual performance is better than the standard, or
- unfavourable, when the actual performance is worse than the standard.

Not every deviation calls for the manager's attention. Minor deviations within acceptable limits can be ignored, while only significant deviations need to be brought to the notice of the higher management. This is the basis of the well-known principle of management by exception, propounded by F.W. Taylor as long ago as the early 1900s.

16.2.4 Analysing the Deviations

Where significant deviations are detected, the manager must analyse them to find out their causes. The causes may be:

- faulty standards;
- changes in the external environment;
- inefficiency of the workers or the equipment;
- inadequate resources;
- poor planning or direction; or
- uncontrollable factors such as natural calamities or sudden changes in government policy.

Different causes call for different remedies, and the manager must be careful to identify the real cause rather than the apparent one.

16.2.5 Taking Corrective Action

The last and the most important step in the control process is the taking of corrective action. The action may take various forms—improving the working methods, training the workers, replacing faulty equipment, revising the standards, changing the assignments, or even modifying the original plan. The corrective action should be taken promptly so that the same deviation does not occur again, and should be followed up to ensure that it has produced the desired result. The information generated through corrective action also feeds back into the next round of planning, completing the cycle of management.

16.3 Types of Control

Modern writers on management classify control into three main types on the basis of the stage at which it is exercised—feedforward control, concurrent control and feedback control.

16.3.1 Feedforward Control

Feedforward control, also known as preventive or pre-action control, is the type of control exercised before the activity begins. Its purpose is to prevent problems from arising in the first place rather than to correct them after they have arisen. Feedforward control involves looking ahead, anticipating the problems that may occur and taking steps to prevent them.

Examples of feedforward control include the careful screening of raw materials before they enter the production process, the training of new employees before they begin work, the preparation of budgets before the financial year begins, and the pre-flight inspection of an aircraft before take-off. Feedforward control is the most desirable form of control, since it prevents the problem rather than merely treating its symptoms.

16.3.2 Concurrent Control

Concurrent control, also known as real-time or steering control, is the type of control exercised while the activity is in progress. The manager watches the performance as it unfolds and makes corrections immediately if anything appears to be going wrong. The pilot watches the cockpit instruments throughout the flight and adjusts the controls as needed. The foreman in a factory watches the workers as they perform their tasks and corrects any wrong method on the spot. The supervisor in a customer service centre listens in on calls and provides immediate feedback to the agents.

Concurrent control is particularly useful where errors can be quickly detected and corrected, where the cost of waiting until the end of the activity would be high, and where direct supervision is feasible.

16.3.3 Feedback Control

Feedback control, also known as post-action or corrective control, is the type of control exercised after the activity has been completed. The actual results are compared with the planned results, the deviations are analysed and corrective action is taken to prevent the same problem from recurring in future. Examples of feedback control include the annual financial statements, the periodic performance appraisal of employees, customer feedback received after the sale, and the post-mortem of a completed project.

Although feedback control is the most common form of control, it has the obvious drawback that the damage has already been done before the corrective action is taken. Its real value lies in providing learnings for the future.

16.3.4 Other Classifications of Control

Control may also be classified in other ways:

- On the basis of source—internal control (self-control exercised by the employees themselves) and external control (control exercised by the superiors).
- On the basis of focus—strategic control (exercised by the top management over the long-term direction of the enterprise) and operational control (exercised at the lower levels over the day-to-day activities).
- On the basis of organisation level—operational, tactical and strategic control.

16.4 Budgetary and Non-Budgetary Control Techniques

Over the years, managers have developed a wide variety of

techniques to help them in exercising control. These techniques may be divided into two broad groups—budgetary techniques and non-budgetary techniques.

16.4.1 Budgetary Control

Budgetary control is one of the oldest and the most widely used techniques of control. A budget is a quantitative expression of a plan, prepared in advance for a definite period of time. It serves both as a plan and as a basis for measuring actual performance. Budgetary control, then, is the process of preparing budgets and of comparing the actual results with the budgeted figures, identifying the deviations and taking corrective action.

Brown and Howard defined budgetary control as "the system of controlling costs which includes the preparation of budgets, coordinating the departments and establishing responsibilities, comparing actual performance with the budgeted and acting upon results to achieve maximum profitability."

The main types of budgets used in business are:

- Sales budget, forecasting expected sales in terms of units and revenue.
- Production budget, planning the quantity of goods to be produced.
- Cash budget, estimating expected receipts and payments of cash.
- Capital budget, planning expenditure on long-term assets.
- Operating budget, covering the day-to-day expenses of the various departments.
- Master budget, which brings together all the individual budgets into a single overall budget for the enterprise.
- Flexible budget, which is adjusted for different levels of activity.
- Zero-based budget, in which every item of expenditure has to be justified afresh each year, regardless of past spending.

Advantages. Budgetary control forces the management to plan ahead. It promotes coordination among the various departments. It improves communication, motivates the employees, fixes responsibility for results and provides a clear basis for performance evaluation.

Limitations. Budgets are based on forecasts, which may go wrong.

The process of preparing a detailed budget can be time-consuming and expensive. Budgets may also create rigidity, particularly in a fast-changing environment. Excessive reliance on the budget may discourage initiative, since employees may stick to the letter of the budget even when a deviation would be in the interest of the enterprise.

16.4.2 Non-Budgetary Control Techniques

Apart from budgetary control, several other techniques are used by managers. The chief non-budgetary techniques are listed below:

1. Personal Observation. The oldest and the simplest technique. The manager goes around personally, observes the work in progress and makes on-the-spot corrections wherever needed.

2. Statistical Reports. Reports prepared on the basis of statistical data, such as production reports, sales reports and quality-control reports. They provide useful information for control.

3. Break-Even Analysis. A technique that shows the level of sales at which the total revenue equals the total cost. By comparing the actual sales with the break-even point, the manager can assess the financial health of the enterprise.

4. Ratio Analysis. The analysis of the relationships between various figures in the financial statements. Important ratios include liquidity ratios (such as the current ratio and the quick ratio), profitability ratios (such as gross profit margin and return on capital employed), activity ratios (such as inventory turnover and debtor turnover) and solvency ratios (such as the debt-equity ratio).

5. Internal Audit. A continuous review of the operations of the enterprise by its own internal audit department, with the aim of detecting errors, frauds and inefficiencies.

6. External Audit. An independent examination of the books of account of the company by an external auditor, generally a chartered accountant. The annual statutory audit required under the Companies Act is the chief example.

7. Standard Costing. A technique under which standard costs are established for each operation in advance, and the actual costs are compared with the standards. The deviations are analysed to find their causes and to take corrective action.

8. PERT and CPM. Network techniques for the planning and control of large projects. The Programme Evaluation and Review Technique (PERT) and the Critical Path Method (CPM) help in identifying the most time-critical activities and in controlling the project schedule.

9. Management by Exception. A technique under which only significant deviations from the standard are brought to the attention of the higher management. Routine matters are handled at the lower levels.

10. Management by Objectives (MBO). As discussed in Chapter 4, MBO is a system in which superior and subordinate jointly set goals, and the achievement of these goals provides the basis for control.

11. Management Audit. A systematic and independent examination of the overall functioning of the management of the enterprise, with a view to identifying its strengths and weaknesses.

12. Return on Investment (ROI). A measure of the profitability of the enterprise in relation to the capital invested. ROI is widely used as a key indicator of overall performance, particularly by holding companies in evaluating their various business units.

16.4.3 Modern Techniques of Control

The last few decades have seen the rise of several new techniques of control:

- The Balanced Scorecard, developed by Robert Kaplan and David Norton in the 1990s, which evaluates the performance of an enterprise on four dimensions—financial, customer, internal process, and learning and growth.
- Six Sigma, a quality-control technique developed by Motorola and made famous by General Electric, which aims at reducing defects to a level of fewer than 3.4 per million opportunities.
- Total Quality Management (TQM), an approach that places quality at the centre of the management of the enterprise.
- Activity-Based Costing (ABC), which assigns costs to products on the basis of the activities involved in their production rather than on a simple volume basis.
- Benchmarking, the process of comparing the performance of one's

own company with that of the best in the industry.

- Economic Value Added (EVA), a measure of the value created by the enterprise for its shareholders, popularised by the consulting firm Stern Stewart.
- Key Performance Indicators (KPIs), specific measures used to track the performance of the enterprise on its critical success factors.
- Management Information Systems (MIS), which provide the manager with timely and accurate information for control.

16.5 Relationship between Planning and Controlling

Of all the functions of management, none are as closely related as planning and controlling. Koontz and O'Donnell have described them as the Siamese twins of management. Planning lays down the targets to be achieved; controlling makes sure that the targets are in fact achieved. Without planning, control is impossible, since there are no standards against which actual performance can be measured. Without control, planning loses much of its meaning, since there is no way of knowing whether the plans have been carried out.

16.5.1 How Planning and Controlling are Related

- Planning is the basis of controlling. The plans of the enterprise lay down the standards which the control system uses for comparison.
- Controlling provides the basis for future planning. The information generated through control reveals the strengths and weaknesses of the existing plans and feeds into the preparation of the next round of plans.
- Both have a common objective—the achievement of the goals of the enterprise.
- Both involve a comparison—planning compares the present with the desired future, while controlling compares the actual present with the planned present.
- Planning is looking ahead, while controlling is looking back; but, taken together, they form a continuous cycle of looking ahead, acting, looking back, and looking ahead again.

16.5.2 Differences between Planning and Controlling

In spite of their close relationship, planning and controlling are not the same function. The chief differences between them are summarised below:

Basis	Planning	Controlling
Sequence	First function of management.	Last function of management.
Time Orientation	Concerned with the future.	Concerned mainly with the past, looking back to find deviations.
Nature	Thinking function; deciding what to do.	Doing function; checking whether plans are being carried out.
Activity	Forecasting, goal-setting, deciding alternatives.	Measuring, comparing, correcting.
Type of Process	Intellectual and creative.	Analytical and corrective.

16.6 Essentials of an Effective Control System

Not every control system works well. An effective control system has certain essential features, which are described below:

1. Suited to the Organisation. The control system should be designed to suit the size, the structure, the nature of the business and the type of employees of the particular enterprise. A control system that works well in a large multinational company may be quite unsuitable for a small family-run business in Indore.

2. Reflects the Plans and Objectives. The control system should be based on the plans and the objectives of the enterprise. If the plans are weak or unclear, the control system too will be weak.

3. Simple and Understandable. The system should be simple enough to be understood and operated by those who have to use it. A control system that the employees do not understand will fail to achieve its purpose.

4. Forward-Looking. While dealing with past performance, the system should provide information that helps the manager in taking decisions about the future.

5. Economical. The benefits of the control system must exceed its cost. An elaborate control system that consumes more resources than it saves is not worth having.

6. Flexible. The system should be flexible enough to be adjusted to changes in the environment, in the plans and in the conditions of the enterprise.

7. Focused on Key Result Areas. The system should concentrate on the most important areas of the work—those which have the greatest impact on the success of the enterprise. Trying to control everything equally leads to wastage of effort.

8. Prompt in Reporting. Deviations should be reported as quickly as possible so that corrective action can be taken in time. A control report that comes too late is of little value.

9. Suggests Corrective Action. A good control system not only points out the deviations but also suggests possible corrective action.

10. Accurate and Reliable. The information provided by the control system must be accurate, reliable and based on sound data. Incorrect information leads to wrong decisions.

11. Strategic and Exception-Based. The system should focus on strategic points and should bring only significant deviations to the notice of the higher management. This is the application of the principle of management by exception.

12. Acceptable to the Employees. The control system must be acceptable to the employees on whose work it operates. A system that is regarded by the employees as unfair, oppressive or threatening will not produce the desired results.

13. Provides Feedback at the Right Time. Both positive and negative feedback should reach the concerned employees at the right time, so that good performance is reinforced and poor performance is corrected.

14. Subject to Regular Review. The control system itself must be reviewed from time to time, to ensure that it continues to serve its purpose in the light of changing conditions.

Summary

Controlling is the function of management which ensures that the actual activities of the enterprise conform to the planned activities. It involves setting standards, measuring actual performance, comparing the two, analysing the deviations and taking corrective action. Controlling is a pervasive, continuous, goal-oriented and forward-looking function. It is the function that closes the management cycle and feeds back into the next round of planning.

The process of control consists of five steps—setting standards, measuring actual performance, comparing the two, analysing the deviations and taking corrective action. Standards may be quantitative or qualitative, and should meet the SMART criteria. On the basis of the time at which it is exercised, control may be classified into feedforward control (before the activity), concurrent control (during the activity) and feedback control (after the activity). Of these, feedforward control is the most desirable, since it prevents the problem rather than treating its symptoms.

The techniques of control are of two main types—budgetary and non-budgetary. Budgetary control involves the preparation of budgets such as the sales budget, the production budget, the cash budget, the capital budget, the master budget and the flexible budget, and the comparison of the actual figures with the budgeted figures. The non-budgetary techniques include personal observation, statistical reports, break-even analysis, ratio analysis, internal and external audit, standard costing, PERT and CPM, management by exception, MBO, management audit and ROI. Modern techniques such as the Balanced Scorecard, Six Sigma, TQM, ABC, Benchmarking, EVA and KPIs have greatly enriched the practice of control.

Planning and controlling are closely related and have been described as the Siamese twins of management. Planning lays down the standards; controlling makes sure that the standards are met; and the information generated through control feeds back into future planning. An effective control system is suited to the organisation, reflects its plans and objectives, is simple, forward-looking, economical, flexible, focused on key result areas, prompt in reporting, accurate, exception-based and acceptable to the employees.

Key Terms

Controlling, Standards, Quantitative Standards, Qualitative Standards, SMART, Measurement, Deviation, Management by Exception, Corrective Action, Feedforward Control, Concurrent Control, Feedback Control, Internal Control, External Control, Strategic Control, Operational Control, Budgetary Control, Budget, Sales Budget, Cash Budget, Master Budget, Flexible Budget, Zero-Based Budget, Personal Observation, Break-Even Analysis, Ratio Analysis, Standard Costing, PERT, CPM, MBO, Management Audit, ROI, Balanced Scorecard, Six Sigma, TQM, ABC, Benchmarking, EVA, KPI, MIS, Siamese Twins.

Review Questions

A. Short Answer Questions (2 marks each)

1. Define controlling.
2. State any four characteristics of controlling.
3. What are the five steps in the process of control?
4. Distinguish between feedforward and feedback control.
5. What is meant by management by exception?
6. Name any four types of budgets used in business.
7. Expand the abbreviation EVA and explain it in brief.
8. Why are planning and controlling called the "Siamese twins of management"?

B. Long Answer Questions (10 marks each)

9. Discuss the meaning, nature and importance of controlling.
10. Describe the various steps involved in the process of control.
11. Explain feedforward, concurrent and feedback control with suitable examples.

12. What is budgetary control? Discuss its advantages and limitations along with the major types of budgets.

13. Explain the non-budgetary techniques of control.

14. "Planning and controlling are inseparable." Discuss this statement, bringing out both the relationship and the differences between the two functions.

15. State the essentials of an effective control system.

C. Practical / Case-Based Questions

16. You have been appointed as the General Manager of a small textile mill in Indore. Suggest a suitable control system for the enterprise, indicating the standards, the measurement methods and the techniques you would use.

17. Identify any well-known Indian company that has been in the news for its control failures (for example, the Satyam scandal of 2009 or any banking fraud). Discuss what went wrong and what kind of control system could have prevented it.

CHAPTER 17

BUSINESS ETHICS AND CORPORATE SOCIAL RESPONSIBILITY

Learning Objectives

After studying this chapter, the reader should be able to:

- understand the concept, the nature and the importance of business ethics;
- identify the major ethical issues that arise in modern management;
- explain the principles and the practices of corporate governance;
- describe the concept and the scope of Corporate Social Responsibility (CSR);
- understand the CSR provisions under the Companies Act, 2013; and
- appreciate the meaning of sustainability and the Triple Bottom Line.

Introduction

A business enterprise does not exist in a vacuum. It is a part of the larger society and draws upon its resources—its land, its capital, its workforce, its customers and its government. In return, it has certain obligations to the society. These obligations go beyond the simple legal duty of paying taxes and obeying the law. They extend to the moral duty of dealing honestly with all those whom the business touches—its shareholders, its employees, its customers, its suppliers, the local community, the country and the natural environment.

In the last two or three decades, the question of how business should behave has come to the centre of public attention. A series of scandals—the Enron and the WorldCom collapses in the United States in 2001–2002, the Satyam fraud in India in 2009, the global financial crisis of 2008, the IL&FS and PNB scams in India in more recent years—have shaken public confidence in business. At the same time, growing concerns about climate change, pollution, inequality and the welfare of workers have placed new demands on the business community. Words such as ethics, corporate governance, corporate social responsibility, sustainability and the triple bottom line, which were once confined to academic discussions, are now part of everyday business vocabulary.

This chapter discusses the concept and the importance of business ethics, examines the major ethical issues faced by modern managers, explains the principles and the practices of corporate governance, describes the concept and the scope of corporate social responsibility, outlines the CSR provisions under the Companies Act, 2013, and concludes with a discussion of sustainability and the triple bottom line.

17.1 Concept and Importance of Business Ethics

17.1.1 Meaning and Definition

Business ethics may be defined as the application of moral principles to the conduct of business. It deals with what is right and what is wrong in the various activities of an enterprise. Business ethics goes beyond mere compliance with the law; it is concerned with the spirit of the law and with the broader question of what is morally acceptable.

Some well-known definitions of business ethics are:

1. Wheeler— "Business ethics is the art and discipline of applying ethical principles to examine and solve complex moral dilemmas in business."

2. Andrew Crane— "Business ethics is the study of business situations, activities and decisions where issues of right and wrong are addressed."

3. Raymond C. Baumhart— "The ethics of business is the ethics of responsibility. The businessman must promise that he will not harm the interest of others knowingly."

4. Edwin Epstein— "Business ethics is the systematic and reflective consideration of the moral consequences of the decisions of business managers."

17.1.2 Features of Business Ethics

- It is a code of conduct that lays down what is right and what is wrong in business.

- It is based on moral and ethical values rather than on legal rules alone.
- It is largely voluntary; no one can be forced to behave ethically.
- It goes beyond legal compliance and is concerned with the spirit of the law.
- It applies to every function and every level of management.
- It is influenced by religion, culture, family upbringing and the values of the larger society.
- Its standards may vary from culture to culture and from time to time.

17.1.3 Types of Ethics in Business

Ethics in business may be classified in several ways:

- Personal ethics—the moral principles followed by a particular individual.
- Professional ethics—the code of conduct followed by members of a particular profession, such as doctors, lawyers, chartered accountants and engineers.
- Business ethics in general—the ethical principles applicable to all business activity.
- Functional ethics—ethical issues in particular functional areas such as marketing, finance, human resources and production.

17.1.4 Importance of Business Ethics

- Ethical conduct builds the long-term reputation and goodwill of the enterprise.
- It wins the trust of customers, employees, suppliers and investors.
- It boosts the morale and the loyalty of the employees, who feel proud to work for an ethical company.
- It provides a competitive advantage in a market where consumers are increasingly conscious of corporate behaviour.
- It reduces the risk of legal disputes, regulatory penalties and adverse publicity.
- It attracts investors, particularly the growing number of socially responsible investment funds.

- It paves the way for sustainable growth, in contrast to the short-term gains that may follow from cutting ethical corners.
- It contributes to the welfare of the society and to the development of a healthy business environment.

17.1.5 Sources of Ethical Standards

Ethical standards in business come from many sources—the religious traditions of the society (the teachings of the Bhagavad Gita, the Bible, the Quran, the Buddhist scriptures and others), the philosophical traditions, the cultural values of the country, the family upbringing of the individual, the codes of professional bodies, the laws of the land and the international standards set by bodies such as the United Nations.

17.2 Ethical Issues in Management

Ethical issues arise in every function of business. The chief areas in which they appear are described below.

17.2.1 Ethical Issues in Marketing

- False or misleading advertising, in which the product is claimed to do things it cannot do.
- Unfair pricing practices, such as price-fixing, predatory pricing and price discrimination.
- Targeting children and other vulnerable groups with unhealthy or harmful products, such as junk food, tobacco or addictive games.
- Misuse of customer data, particularly in the digital age.
- Aggressive sales tactics that pressure customers into buying things they do not need.

17.2.2 Ethical Issues in Finance and Accounting

- Window-dressing of accounts to show a healthier financial position than the reality.
- Insider trading, in which company officials misuse confidential information to trade in the shares of the company.
- Tax evasion as distinguished from legitimate tax planning.
- Bribery and kickbacks in obtaining contracts, licences and clearances.
- Financial frauds, such as those at the centre of the Satyam scandal of 2009 and the Punjab National Bank case involving Nirav Modi in

2018.

17.2.3 Ethical Issues in Human Resource Management

- Discrimination on grounds of caste, religion, region, gender, age, disability or sexual orientation.
- Sexual harassment at the workplace.
- Unfair termination or denial of due benefits.
- Unsafe working conditions and the exploitation of contract labour.
- Invasion of the privacy of employees, particularly through electronic monitoring.

17.2.4 Ethical Issues in Production

- Production and sale of substandard or unsafe products.
- Cutting corners on quality to save costs.
- Pollution of air, water and soil through industrial waste.
- Use of child labour or forced labour, often through suppliers in less regulated countries.
- Sale of counterfeit or duplicate goods.

17.2.5 Other Ethical Issues

- Conflict of interest, in which a manager's personal interests come into conflict with those of the company.
- Whistleblowing—the duty of an employee to report wrongdoing, and the protection of whistleblowers from victimisation.
- Bribery and corruption in dealings with government officials, particularly in countries where these are widespread.
- Corporate spying and theft of trade secrets.

17.2.6 Major Indian Cases

The recent history of Indian business has thrown up several major cases of ethical failure. The Satyam Computer Services fraud of 2009, in which the chairman B. Ramalinga Raju admitted to inflating the company's accounts by over seven thousand crore rupees, was one of the largest accounting scandals in Indian corporate history. The crisis at IL&FS in 2018 revealed serious lapses in governance at one of India's largest infrastructure finance companies. The Nirav Modi-PNB scam of the same year exposed the misuse of bank guarantees worth over thirteen thousand crore rupees. Similar lapses came to light at Yes Bank, DHFL and several other companies. Each of these cases has highlighted the importance of strong ethical foundations and effective corporate governance.

17.3 Corporate Governance

17.3.1 Meaning and Definition

Corporate governance refers to the system by which a company is directed, managed and controlled. It is the framework of rules, relationships, systems and processes within which the affairs of the company are conducted. Corporate governance is concerned with the relationships among the various stakeholders of the company—the shareholders, the Board of Directors, the management, the employees, the creditors, the customers, the suppliers, the government and the community at large.

Some well-known definitions of corporate governance are:

1. The Cadbury Committee Report (1992)— "Corporate governance is the system by which companies are directed and controlled."

2. The Organisation for Economic Cooperation and Development (OECD)— "Corporate governance involves a set of relationships between a company's management, its board, its shareholders and other stakeholders. It also provides the structure through which the objectives of the company are set, and the means of attaining those objectives and monitoring performance are determined."

3. The N.R. Narayana Murthy Committee on Corporate Governance (2003)— "Corporate governance is the acceptance by management of the inalienable rights of shareholders as the true owners of the corporation and of their own role as trustees on behalf of the shareholders."

17.3.2 Need for Corporate Governance

- The separation of ownership and control in the modern company requires a clear framework for the protection of the interests of the shareholders.
- Globalisation of business and the rise of multinational corporations have increased the need for common standards of

governance across countries.

- Major corporate scandals—Enron, WorldCom, Parmalat and Satyam, among others—have shaken public confidence in business.
- Investors, both domestic and foreign, demand high standards of governance before placing their money.
- Strong corporate governance is in the public interest, since the failure of a major company can have severe effects on the economy.

17.3.3 Principles of Corporate Governance

- Transparency—disclosure of all material information to the stakeholders.
- Accountability—a clear allocation of responsibility for results, with consequences for failure.
- Fairness—equitable treatment of all shareholders, including minority and foreign shareholders.
- Responsibility—recognition by the Board and the management of their responsibilities towards all the stakeholders.
- Independence—the presence of independent directors and the freedom of the Board from the dominance of any particular interest group.
- Integrity—honesty in all dealings.
- Disclosure—timely and accurate reporting of the affairs of the company to the regulators and to the public.

17.3.4 Corporate Governance in India

India has built up a fairly elaborate framework of corporate governance in the last two decades. A number of committees have made important contributions to this framework:

- The Confederation of Indian Industry (CII) Code, prepared in 1998.
- The Kumar Mangalam Birla Committee Report (1999), which formed the basis of Clause 49 of the Listing Agreement of stock exchanges.
- The N.R. Narayana Murthy Committee on Corporate Governance (2003).
- The Naresh Chandra Committee on Corporate Audit and

Governance (2002).

• The J.J. Irani Committee on Company Law (2005), whose recommendations led to the Companies Act, 2013.

• The Uday Kotak Committee on Corporate Governance (2017), set up by the Securities and Exchange Board of India (SEBI).

The Companies Act, 2013 has brought in several major provisions to strengthen corporate governance. These include the requirement of independent directors on the Board, mandatory audit committees, nomination and remuneration committees, the rotation of auditors, the right of shareholders to file class action suits, the mandatory vigil mechanism for whistleblowers, and the disclosure of related-party transactions. SEBI's Listing Obligations and Disclosure Requirements (LODR) Regulations, 2015, lay down further requirements for listed companies. The Insider Trading Regulations seek to prevent the misuse of unpublished price-sensitive information.

17.4 Concept and Scope of CSR

17.4.1 Meaning and Definition

Corporate Social Responsibility, or CSR, refers to the voluntary contribution that a business makes to the welfare of the society of which it is a part. It is the recognition by the business that it has obligations beyond those to its shareholders—obligations to its employees, its customers, its suppliers, the local community, the country and the natural environment.

Some well-known definitions of CSR are:

1. Howard R. Bowen, often regarded as the father of CSR, defined it in his 1953 book Social Responsibilities of the Businessman as "the obligations of businessmen to pursue those policies, to make those decisions, or to follow those lines of action which are desirable in terms of the objectives and the values of our society."

2. Keith Davis— "CSR refers to the businessman's decisions and actions taken for reasons at least partially beyond the firm's direct economic or technical interest."

3. The World Business Council for Sustainable Development— "CSR is the continuing commitment by business to behave ethically and to contribute to economic development while improving the quality of life of the workforce and their families, as well as of the local community and the society at large."

17.4.2 Carroll's Pyramid of CSR

Archie B. Carroll, an American writer on management, proposed in 1991 a four-level pyramid to represent the responsibilities of a business:

- At the base are the economic responsibilities—the duty to be profitable so that the business can survive and continue to provide goods and services.
- Above these are the legal responsibilities—the duty to obey the laws of the land.
- Higher still are the ethical responsibilities—the duty to do what is right, even when not required by law.
- At the top are the philanthropic responsibilities—the duty to contribute to the welfare of the community, to support education, health, art and culture, and to be a good corporate citizen.

Carroll's pyramid has been widely accepted as a useful way of thinking about the various responsibilities of business.

17.4.3 Arguments For and Against CSR

Arguments for CSR. (i) The long-term interest of the business itself is served, since a healthy society creates a healthy market. (ii) CSR earns the goodwill of the public, the trust of customers and the loyalty of employees. (iii) CSR helps the company to attract and retain the best talent. (iv) Many activities of CSR pay back the company indirectly through reduced regulatory pressure, improved reputation and better risk management. (v) Business uses the resources of society and, therefore, has an obligation to give something back.

Arguments against CSR. (i) The primary duty of business is to make profits for its shareholders; CSR diverts attention from this duty (the famous view of Milton Friedman). (ii) CSR involves costs that ultimately fall on the shareholders, the customers or the employees. (iii) Many CSR activities are not within the core competence of the business and are better left to the government and to specialised non-profit organisations. (iv) CSR may be used as a public relations exercise rather than as a genuine contribution.

17.4.4 Scope and Areas of CSR

The scope of CSR is very wide. The main areas in which Indian companies have undertaken CSR activities include:

- Education—support to schools, colleges, scholarships, digital learning programmes.
- Health—hospitals, clinics, maternal and child health, sanitation, COVID-19 relief during the pandemic.
- Environment—afforestation, water conservation, pollution control, promotion of renewable energy.
- Rural development—livelihood support, agricultural extension, drinking water, rural infrastructure.
- Women empowerment and gender equality—skill training, self-help groups, anti-trafficking programmes.
- Skill development—vocational training, support to industrial training institutes.
- Hunger and poverty alleviation—food security, mid-day meal programmes.
- Sports and culture—support to sports persons, preservation of heritage sites.
- Disaster relief and rehabilitation—as seen during floods, cyclones, earthquakes and the COVID-19 pandemic.

17.4.5 Indian Companies Known for CSR

Indian business has a long tradition of voluntary contribution to society. The Tata Group, through Tata Trusts, has been a pioneer in this field for more than a century, having built institutions such as the Indian Institute of Science, the Tata Memorial Hospital and the Tata Institute of Fundamental Research. The Aditya Birla Centre for Community Initiatives and Rural Development carries out extensive work in rural areas. The Reliance Foundation focuses on health, education, rural transformation and sports. The Infosys Foundation, led for many years by Sudha Murthy, has supported education, healthcare and the welfare of women. Wipro, the Mahindra Group, ITC, Hindustan Unilever, Bharti Foundation and many other Indian companies have made substantial contributions in their chosen areas.

17.5 CSR Provisions under the Companies Act, 2013

India was the first country in the world to make CSR a statutory obligation for large companies. Section 135 of the Companies Act, 2013, which came into force on 1 April 2014, lays down detailed provisions in this regard.

17.5.1 Applicability

The provisions of Section 135 apply to every company that meets any one of the following criteria in the immediately preceding financial year:

- a net worth of five hundred crore rupees or more; or
- a turnover of one thousand crore rupees or more; or
- a net profit of five crore rupees or more.

17.5.2 Key Provisions

1. CSR Committee. Every company covered by Section 135 must constitute a CSR Committee of the Board, consisting of at least three directors, of which at least one must be an independent director.

2. CSR Policy. The CSR Committee must formulate a CSR Policy for the company, which is then approved by the Board. The policy lays down the activities to be undertaken and the manner of carrying them out.

3. CSR Spending. The company must spend, in every financial year, at least two per cent of the average net profits made during the three immediately preceding financial years on CSR activities. The activities must be those specified in Schedule VII of the Act.

4. Unspent Amount. Following the 2019 amendment, any amount remaining unspent at the end of the financial year must, except in certain cases of ongoing projects, be transferred within six months to one of the funds specified in Schedule VII, such as the Prime Minister's National Relief Fund.

5. Reporting. The Board's Report of the company must include a detailed report on the CSR activities of the year, including the policy, the projects undertaken, the amount spent and the reasons for any underspending.

17.5.3 Schedule VII Activities

Schedule VII of the Act lists the activities that qualify as CSR. These include, among others:

- eradicating hunger, poverty and malnutrition;
- promoting education, including special education and employment-enhancing vocational skills;
- promoting gender equality and empowering women;
- reducing child mortality and improving maternal health;
- ensuring environmental sustainability and the conservation of natural resources;
- protecting national heritage, art and culture;
- measures for the benefit of armed forces veterans, war widows and their dependants;
- training to promote rural sports, nationally recognised sports, Paralympic and Olympic sports;
- contribution to the Prime Minister's National Relief Fund or to the PM CARES Fund or to any other government fund set up for the welfare of weaker sections;
- contributions to incubators and to research projects in central or state universities;
- rural development projects, slum area development, and disaster management including relief, rehabilitation and reconstruction.

17.6 Sustainability and the Triple Bottom Line

17.6.1 Concept of Sustainability

Sustainability has become one of the central concerns of business in the twenty-first century. The classic definition was given by the Brundtland Commission in its 1987 report Our Common Future: "Sustainable development is development that meets the needs of the present without compromising the ability of future generations to meet their own needs."

Sustainability rests on three pillars—the economic, the social and the environmental. Economic sustainability means that the business must be financially viable and must continue to generate jobs, income and wealth. Social sustainability means that the business must respect human rights, treat its workers fairly and contribute to the welfare of the community. Environmental sustainability means that the business must use natural resources responsibly and must not harm the environment in ways that endanger the life of future generations.

17.6.2 The Triple Bottom Line

The phrase "Triple Bottom Line" was coined by John Elkington in 1994 to express the idea that a business should be judged not by its financial performance alone but by its performance in three areas, often called the three P's—People, Planet and Profit.

People (Social Bottom Line). The business must look after the welfare of its employees, treat its customers fairly, respect its suppliers and contribute to the development of the local community. Issues such as workplace safety, fair wages, diversity, inclusion and human rights fall under this head.

Planet (Environmental Bottom Line). The business must minimise its harmful impact on the natural environment. It must control air, water and noise pollution, manage its waste responsibly, conserve water and energy, reduce its carbon footprint, and increasingly turn to renewable sources of energy and to circular economy practices.

Profit (Economic Bottom Line). The business must, of course, continue to be profitable, since profit is the source of investment, employment, taxes and economic value. But profit is not the only measure of performance, and it must be earned in ways that are consistent with the other two bottom lines.

17.6.3 ESG—Environment, Social and Governance

In recent years, the closely related concept of ESG—Environment, Social and Governance—has gained great importance. ESG provides a framework for investors to evaluate companies on these three dimensions. A growing number of investment funds now use ESG ratings to decide where to invest. The Securities and Exchange Board of India has, since the financial year 2022–23, made it mandatory for the top one thousand listed companies to publish a Business Responsibility and Sustainability Report (BRSR), which captures their ESG performance.

17.6.4 The UN Sustainable Development Goals

In 2015, the United Nations General Assembly adopted the 2030

Agenda for Sustainable Development, with seventeen Sustainable Development Goals (SDGs) covering everything from the eradication of poverty and hunger to climate action, gender equality, quality education, clean water, decent work, sustainable cities and partnerships for development. Business has been recognised as an important partner in the achievement of these goals.

17.6.5 Indian Initiatives

India has taken several important steps in the direction of sustainability. The National Voluntary Guidelines on Social, Environmental and Economic Responsibilities of Business were issued in 2011 by the Ministry of Corporate Affairs. The Business Responsibility Report was made mandatory for the top one hundred listed companies in 2012 and was extended in stages. At the Glasgow Climate Conference (COP26) in 2021, India announced its commitment to achieve net zero emissions by the year 2070. The Mission LiFE (Lifestyle for Environment), launched in 2022, calls on every individual to live in a way that is in harmony with nature. The Indian tradition itself, with its deep respect for nature and its philosophy of seeing the divine in all living things, has much to contribute to the global conversation on sustainability.

Summary

Business ethics is the application of moral principles to the conduct of business. It is largely voluntary, based on values that go beyond mere legal compliance. Ethical issues arise in every function of business—marketing, finance, human resources, production and information technology. The Indian corporate world has witnessed several major cases of ethical failure, including the Satyam scandal of 2009, the IL&FS crisis of 2018 and the PNB-Nirav Modi fraud of the same year.

Corporate governance is the system by which a company is directed and controlled. It is based on the principles of transparency, accountability, fairness, responsibility, independence, integrity and disclosure. India has built a strong framework of corporate governance through committees such as the Kumar Mangalam Birla Committee, the N.R. Narayana Murthy Committee and the Uday Kotak Committee, and through the provisions of the Companies Act, 2013 and the SEBI Listing Regulations.

Corporate Social Responsibility is the voluntary contribution that a business makes to the welfare of society. Carroll's Pyramid identifies four levels of responsibility—economic, legal, ethical and philanthropic. India became the first country in the world to make CSR a statutory obligation when Section 135 of the Companies Act, 2013 came into force in 2014. Qualifying companies are required to spend at least two per cent of their average net profits on the activities listed in Schedule VII, which cover education, health, environment, rural development, women empowerment and many other areas. Indian companies such as the Tata Group, the Aditya Birla Group, Reliance, Infosys and Mahindra are well known for their CSR contributions.

Sustainability, as defined by the Brundtland Commission, is development that meets the needs of the present without compromising the ability of future generations to meet their own needs. The Triple Bottom Line, coined by John Elkington, expresses the idea that business should be judged on its performance in three areas—People, Planet and Profit. The closely related concept of ESG and the UN Sustainable Development Goals provide modern frameworks for sustainable business. India has taken important steps in this direction, including the BRSR requirement, the COP26 commitment to net zero by 2070 and the Mission LiFE initiative.

Key Terms

Business Ethics, Code of Conduct, Personal Ethics, Professional Ethics, Insider Trading, Whistleblowing, Satyam Scandal, IL&FS, PNB-Nirav Modi Case, Corporate Governance, Cadbury Committee, OECD, N.R. Narayana Murthy Committee, Kumar Mangalam Birla Committee, Uday Kotak Committee, Independent Director, Audit Committee, LODR, Corporate Social Responsibility, Howard Bowen, Carroll's Pyramid, Section 135, Companies Act 2013, Schedule VII, CSR Committee, Two Per Cent Rule, Sustainability, Brundtland Commission, Triple Bottom Line, John Elkington, People-Planet-Profit, ESG, BRSR, UN Sustainable Development Goals, Net Zero, Mission LiFE.

Review Questions

A. Short Answer Questions (2 marks each)

1. Define business ethics.
2. State any four features of business ethics.
3. Name any four major ethical issues in marketing.
4. What is corporate governance?
5. State any four principles of corporate governance.
6. Who is regarded as the father of CSR?
7. Briefly explain Carroll's Pyramid of CSR.
8. To which companies do the CSR provisions of Section 135 apply?
9. What is the Triple Bottom Line?
10. Expand the term ESG.

B. Long Answer Questions (10 marks each)

11. Discuss the concept, the features and the importance of business ethics.

12. Examine the major ethical issues that arise in modern management, with suitable Indian examples.

13. What is corporate governance? Discuss its principles and the framework of corporate governance in India.

14. Define corporate social responsibility. Discuss its scope, with examples from leading Indian companies.

15. Discuss the CSR provisions under the Companies Act, 2013.

16. Explain the concept of sustainability and the Triple Bottom Line.

C. Practical / Case-Based Questions

17. Take any one well-known case of ethical failure in Indian business (such as Satyam, PNB-Nirav Modi or IL&FS). Analyse what went wrong and what lessons it offers for the future.

18. Visit the website of any large Indian company and study its CSR report for the latest year. Identify the areas in which it has spent its CSR funds and comment on the suitability of its activities.

CHAPTER 18

MANAGEMENT OF CHANGE AND CONFLICT

Learning Objectives

After studying this chapter, the reader should be able to:

- understand the nature and the causes of organisational change;
- describe the change models given by Kurt Lewin and John Kotter;
- identify the causes of resistance to change and the ways of overcoming it;
- understand the concept and the various types of organisational conflict; and
- explain the strategies used by managers to handle conflict.

Introduction

Change and conflict are two facts of life that no manager can escape. The world in which a modern business operates is in a state of constant change. New technologies, new competitors, new customer preferences, new laws and new social attitudes are all reshaping the business environment from year to year. The economic reforms of 1991, the rise of the internet, the spread of mobile telephones, the COVID-19 pandemic of 2020 and the arrival of artificial intelligence are some of the great changes that have transformed Indian business in our own lifetime. Conflict, too, is unavoidable in any organisation in which human beings work together. Differences of opinion, of interest, of personality and of style are bound to give rise to friction from time to time.

The successful manager is one who can manage both change and conflict—who can lead his organisation through change without losing the loyalty of his employees, and who can deal with conflict without allowing it to damage the working of the enterprise. As Heraclitus, the ancient Greek philosopher, observed long ago, the only thing that is constant is change. The Indian philosopher Adi Shankaracharya too taught that the world is in a state of constant flux. In the modern age, the pace of change has only accelerated, and the management of change has become one of the most important responsibilities of every manager.

This chapter discusses the nature and the causes of organisational change, the well-known change models given by Kurt Lewin and John Kotter, the causes of resistance to change and the ways of overcoming it, the concept and the various types of conflict in organisations, and the strategies used by managers to handle conflict.

18.1 Nature and Causes of Organisational Change

18.1.1 Meaning and Definition

Organisational change refers to any modification in the existing way of working of an enterprise. It may involve a change in the goals, in the strategy, in the structure, in the people, in the technology, in the products or in the processes. Change may be small and incremental, such as the introduction of a new piece of software, or it may be large and transformational, such as the merger of two companies or the entry of the company into a completely new line of business.

Some well-known definitions of organisational change are:

1. R.M. Hodgetts— "Organisational change refers to any alteration that occurs in the overall work environment of the organisation."

2. Newstrom and Davis— "Change is any alteration occurring in the work environment that affects the way in which the employees must act."

3. Wendell French— "Change refers to the adaptations made by the organisation to maintain or improve its performance in the face of an evolving environment."

18.1.2 Features of Organisational Change

- Change is universal—no organisation can escape it.
- It is continuous; one change is followed by another, and so on.
- It affects all parts of the organisation, even when it appears to be confined to one department or one process.
- It may be planned and deliberate, or unplanned and forced by external events.
- It may be incremental (small steps over time) or transformational (radical and far-reaching).

- It is multidirectional—changes in one area trigger changes in many others.

18.1.3 Types of Change

- Planned versus unplanned change.
- Incremental versus transformational change.
- Reactive (in response to events) versus proactive (anticipating the future) change.
- Strategic (long-term direction) versus operational (day-to-day) change.
- Structural change (changes in organisation design), technological change, people-related change and process change.

18.1.4 Causes of Organisational Change

The causes of organisational change may be divided into two broad groups—external forces and internal forces.

(a) External Forces

1. Economic Forces. The economic environment is one of the most powerful forces of change. The economic reforms of 1991 in India opened up the country to foreign investment and competition and forced every Indian company to change its way of working. Recessions, inflation, interest rate changes and currency fluctuations also force companies to adapt.

2. Technological Forces. Technological change has become the most powerful driver of business transformation. The rise of the internet, mobile telephones, digital payments, artificial intelligence, automation, robotics, the Internet of Things and 5G networks have changed almost every industry. Companies that fail to adopt new technology quickly fall behind.

3. Political and Legal Forces. Changes in government policy, laws and regulations force companies to adjust. The introduction of the Goods and Services Tax (GST) in 2017, the new Companies Act of 2013, the new labour codes and the various policies for "Make in India" have all required Indian companies to make significant changes.

4. Social and Cultural Forces. Changes in customer preferences, lifestyles and values force companies to change their products and their methods. The growing demand for healthy food, organic products, electric vehicles and sustainable fashion are examples of social changes affecting business.

5. Competition. The entry of new competitors—whether foreign multinationals or new domestic players—forces existing companies to improve their performance. The arrival of Reliance Jio in 2016 forced every other Indian telecom operator to rethink its strategy.

6. Globalisation. Indian companies today must compete with the best in the world, both at home and abroad. Globalisation has also opened up new opportunities, with Indian firms in information technology, pharmaceuticals and engineering services becoming major global players.

7. Natural and Health Crises. The COVID-19 pandemic of 2020 was a powerful reminder that natural and health crises can force sudden and radical change. Climate change is another long-term force that is reshaping the business environment.

(b) Internal Forces

- Changes in the objectives, mission or vision of the enterprise.
- Changes at the top management, such as a new Managing Director or a new Chairman.
- Mergers, acquisitions and restructuring.
- Changes in the expectations and attitudes of the employees, particularly the younger generation.
- Quality problems, customer complaints and falling profits, which force the management to look for new ways.
- Introduction of new products, services or business models.

18.2 Lewin's and Kotter's Change Models

18.2.1 Kurt Lewin's Three-Step Model

Kurt Lewin (1890–1947), a German-American social psychologist, is often regarded as the founder of modern change management. In a famous paper published in 1947, he proposed a simple but powerful three-step model of planned change—Unfreezing, Changing and Refreezing.

1. Unfreezing. The first step is to prepare the organisation for change by breaking down the existing way of working. The management must convince the employees that change is necessary, that the existing methods are no longer adequate, and that the new direction will benefit the enterprise as well as themselves. This stage involves creating dissatisfaction with the status quo, communicating the need for change and overcoming resistance.

2. Changing or Moving. The second step is the actual implementation of the change. New ways of working are introduced, new technology is installed, new structures are set up, new procedures are followed. Employees are trained in the new methods, supported through the transition and given the resources they need to succeed. This is generally the most difficult and the longest stage of the change process.

3. Refreezing. The third step is to make the change permanent. The new ways of working are reinforced through training, rewards, recognition and the building of new habits. The change becomes the new normal, and the organisation reaches a new state of equilibrium.

18.2.2 Lewin's Force-Field Analysis

Closely related to his three-step model is Lewin's concept of force-field analysis. According to Lewin, any situation is the result of a balance between two sets of forces—driving forces, which push for change, and restraining forces, which resist change. So long as the two are balanced, the situation remains in equilibrium. Change happens when the driving forces are strengthened or the restraining forces are weakened. The manager who wishes to bring about change must, therefore, identify both sets of forces and act on them deliberately.

18.2.3 John P. Kotter's Eight-Step Model

Building on the work of Lewin, the Harvard professor John P. Kotter proposed a more detailed eight-step model of leading change in his book Leading Change, published in 1996. Kotter's model has become one of the most widely used frameworks for managing change in the corporate world. The eight steps are:

1. Create a Sense of Urgency. The leader must make the organisation aware of the threats and opportunities that demand change, and must build a strong sense that something must be done immediately.

2. Form a Powerful Guiding Coalition. A team of leaders with the necessary authority, expertise and credibility must be brought together to lead the change.

3. Develop a Vision and a Strategy. A clear and inspiring vision of the future state is developed, together with a strategy for achieving it.

4. Communicate the Change Vision. The vision is communicated repeatedly and through every available channel, so that every employee understands and accepts it.

5. Empower Employees to Act on the Vision. Barriers to change—whether in the form of resistant managers, restrictive systems or inadequate skills—are removed, and employees are given the authority and the means to act.

6. Generate Short-Term Wins. Early successes are planned, celebrated and used to build momentum and to win over the doubters.

7. Consolidate Gains and Produce More Change. Building on the early successes, the change is extended to more areas, deeper levels and harder problems.

8. Anchor the New Approaches in the Culture. The new ways of working are embedded in the culture of the organisation through training, leadership development and the building of new habits.

18.2.4 Other Models

Several other models of change deserve a brief mention:

- The ADKAR Model, developed by Prosci, which focuses on five stages experienced by the individual undergoing change—Awareness, Desire, Knowledge, Ability and Reinforcement.
- The McKinsey 7-S Framework, which emphasises that change must address seven interrelated elements—Strategy, Structure, Systems, Style, Staff, Skills and Shared Values.
- The Bridges Transition Model, given by William Bridges, which focuses on the emotional transition of the people through three stages—Endings, Neutral Zone and New Beginnings.

18.3 Resistance to Change and How to Overcome It

In spite of the obvious need for change, employees often resist it. Some level of resistance is, in fact, the rule rather than the exception. The wise manager understands the causes of resistance and uses suitable techniques to overcome them.

18.3.1 Causes of Individual Resistance

- Fear of the unknown. People feel comfortable with what they know; the new and the unfamiliar make them anxious.
- Fear of loss. Employees may fear the loss of their jobs, of their status, of their authority, of their familiar relationships or of their accustomed routines.
- Habit. Existing ways of working become so deeply ingrained that even simple changes feel difficult.
- Insecurity. Employees who are not confident of their ability to learn new skills may resist the introduction of new technology or new methods.
- Lack of trust in the management. If past changes have ended in retrenchment or in unfair treatment, employees will be wary of new proposals.
- Misunderstanding. Resistance often springs from a wrong understanding of what the change involves and of how it will affect particular individuals.
- Different perceptions. The same change may look good to the management and bad to the workers.

18.3.2 Causes of Organisational Resistance

- Structural inertia. Established structures, processes and reporting relationships develop a momentum of their own and resist disturbance.
- Group inertia. Even when individuals are willing to change, the norms of the group may hold them back.
- Threat to existing power relationships. Change may shift power from one group to another, and the losing group will resist.
- Threat to specialised expertise. Long-time specialists may find their skills becoming obsolete and resist the new methods.
- Threat to established resource allocations. Departments that fear losing budgets, staff or status may oppose the change.

18.3.3 Overcoming Resistance to Change

John P. Kotter and Leonard A. Schlesinger, in a well-known article published in the Harvard Business Review in 1979, identified six methods for dealing with resistance to change. These are:

1. Education and Communication. Explain the reasons for the change, the expected benefits and the consequences of not changing. Open and honest communication is the most powerful way of overcoming resistance based on misunderstanding.

2. Participation and Involvement. Involve the employees in planning and implementing the change. People are far less likely to resist something they have helped to design.

3. Facilitation and Support. Provide training, counselling and emotional support to those who are finding the change difficult. The fear of inability to cope is often the real cause of resistance.

4. Negotiation and Agreement. Where some groups are clearly going to lose out from the change, offer them something in return for their acceptance. This may take the form of compensation packages, voluntary retirement schemes or special transition arrangements.

5. Manipulation and Co-optation. In rare cases, the management may resort to covert influence—selective release of information or the giving of important roles to potential resisters. This method should be used very sparingly, as it can damage trust if discovered.

6. Explicit and Implicit Coercion. As a last resort, the management may use the threat of dismissal, transfer or loss of promotion to push through the change. This method is fast but leaves behind anger and resentment.

In addition to these techniques, the change effort is greatly helped by visible leadership commitment, regular communication, training and skill-building, pilot programmes that demonstrate success in a small area before scaling up, the celebration of early wins, and the steady building of trust between the management and the employees.

18.4 Concept and Types of Conflict

18.4.1 Meaning and Definition

Conflict may be defined as a state of opposition, disagreement or incompatibility between two or more persons or groups in an organisation. It arises whenever the interests, the goals, the values or the perceptions of the parties involved come into clash with one another.

Some well-known definitions of conflict are:

1. Stephen P. Robbins— "Conflict is a process that begins when one party perceives that another party has negatively affected, or is about to negatively affect, something that the first party cares about."

2. L.R. Pondy— "Conflict consists of the perceived divergence of interest, or a belief that the parties' current aspirations cannot be achieved simultaneously."

3. Joe Kelly— "Conflict is a struggle between incompatible or opposing needs, wishes, ideas, interests or people. It arises whenever a choice has to be made."

18.4.2 Three Views of Conflict

(a) The Traditional View, popular in the 1930s and 1940s, regarded conflict as bad and as something to be avoided at all costs. Conflict was seen as a sign of poor management.

(b) The Human Relations View, popular from the late 1940s to the 1970s, regarded conflict as natural and unavoidable in human organisations. Conflict was to be accepted and managed, not eliminated.

(c) The Interactionist View, popular today, holds that some level of conflict is actually necessary for the health of an organisation. A completely conflict-free organisation may be a stagnant one, in which no new ideas are challenged and no improvements are made. The task of the manager is not to suppress all conflict but to keep it at a level that stimulates fresh thinking without harming the organisation.

18.4.3 Functional and Dysfunctional Conflict

From this point of view, conflict may be of two kinds:

- Functional conflict, which contributes to the goals of the organisation and improves its performance. It stimulates new ideas, surfaces problems, sharpens decisions and prevents complacency.
- Dysfunctional conflict, which hinders the performance of the organisation. It damages relationships, lowers morale, wastes time and reduces productivity.

The skill of the manager lies in encouraging functional conflict while controlling dysfunctional conflict.

18.4.4 Types of Conflict

Conflict in an organisation may take several forms:

1. Intrapersonal Conflict. Conflict within the mind of a single individual—for instance, when a manager is torn between an attractive job offer from another company and his loyalty to his current employer.

2. Interpersonal Conflict. Conflict between two individuals, such as between a manager and his subordinate or between two colleagues at the same level.

3. Intragroup Conflict. Conflict within a group, such as differences of opinion in a project team about how to proceed.

4. Intergroup Conflict. Conflict between two or more groups within the organisation, such as the well-known rivalry between the sales department and the production department, or between the head office and the regional offices.

5. Inter-Organisational Conflict. Conflict between two or more organisations, such as that between a company and its supplier, its trade union or its competitor.

Other classifications include vertical conflict (between different levels) and horizontal conflict (across departments at the same level); task conflict (about what is to be done), process conflict (about how it is to be done) and relationship conflict (about personal issues). L.R. Pondy further distinguished between latent conflict (where the underlying conditions exist but no one has noticed), perceived conflict (where the parties are aware of the disagreement), felt conflict (where emotions become involved), manifest conflict (where the conflict shows itself in behaviour) and conflict aftermath (the residue left after the conflict has been resolved or suppressed).

18.4.5 Causes of Conflict

- Incompatible goals between individuals or departments.
- Competition for limited resources, such as budget, manpower and equipment.
- Communication barriers and misunderstandings.
- Differences of personality, values and working style.
- Role ambiguity and overlap of responsibilities.

- Power struggles and the desire for control.
- Cultural and demographic differences in a diverse workforce.
- Unfair distribution of work, rewards or recognition.

18.5 Conflict Management Strategies

18.5.1 The Thomas-Kilmann Model of Conflict-Handling Styles

Kenneth W. Thomas and Ralph H. Kilmann, in the 1970s, developed a widely used model of conflict-handling styles, based on two dimensions—assertiveness, which is the extent to which the person tries to satisfy his own concerns, and cooperativeness, which is the extent to which he tries to satisfy the concerns of the other party. The combination of these two dimensions gives rise to five conflict-handling styles.

1. Avoiding (Low Assertive, Low Cooperative). The person withdraws from the conflict or refuses to engage with it. This style may be suitable for trivial issues, when the cost of confrontation exceeds the benefits, or when more important matters are pressing.

2. Accommodating (Low Assertive, High Cooperative). The person yields to the wishes of the other party. This style is suitable when one realises that one is wrong, when the issue is far more important to the other party, or when preserving the relationship is more important than winning the point.

3. Competing (High Assertive, Low Cooperative). The person presses for his own viewpoint at the expense of the other party. This style produces a win-lose outcome and is suitable for emergencies, for the enforcement of unpopular decisions and for situations in which one is clearly right.

4. Compromising (Moderate Assertive, Moderate Cooperative). The two parties agree to give up something in order to reach a middle-ground solution. Each side gets part of what it wanted. This style is practical when the parties have equal power, when time is short and when a temporary settlement is enough.

5. Collaborating (High Assertive, High Cooperative). The two parties work together to find a solution that fully satisfies both. This is the win-win style, and is the most desirable when the issue is important, when both parties' concerns are too important to be compromised, and when there is time for full discussion.

18.5.2 Stages of Conflict

L.R. Pondy, in his well-known model of conflict, identified five stages through which a conflict typically passes:

- the latent stage, in which the underlying conditions for conflict already exist;
- the perceived stage, in which one or both parties become aware of the disagreement;
- the felt stage, in which emotions of frustration, anger or anxiety become involved;
- the manifest stage, in which the conflict comes out into the open through arguments, fights or other observable behaviour; and
- the aftermath stage, in which the conflict has been resolved or suppressed, and the parties live with its consequences—whether bitterness, satisfaction or improved relationships.

18.5.3 Techniques for Resolving Conflict

Apart from the five conflict-handling styles, managers use a variety of techniques to resolve specific conflicts:

1. Negotiation. The parties to the conflict come together, present their positions and try to reach a settlement through give-and-take.

2. Mediation. A neutral third party helps the disputing parties to communicate, to understand each other and to reach a voluntary settlement. The mediator does not impose a decision.

3. Arbitration. A neutral third party listens to both sides and gives a decision that is binding on the parties. Many commercial disputes in India are now settled through arbitration under the Arbitration and Conciliation Act, 1996.

4. Conciliation. A milder form of mediation, often used in industrial disputes, in which the conciliator tries to bring the parties to an agreement through informal discussion.

5. Problem-Solving Approach. The parties define the problem jointly, gather information, generate alternatives, evaluate them and choose the one that best meets the concerns of both. This is the collaborative approach in action.

6. Authoritative Command. The senior manager simply decides the issue and orders the parties to accept the decision. This is fast but may breed resentment.

7. Smoothing. The manager plays down the differences and emphasises the common interests of the parties. This may bring temporary peace but does not address the underlying issues.

8. Avoidance and Withdrawal. Sometimes the best course is simply to keep the parties apart and allow tempers to cool before any attempt is made to resolve the issue.

18.5.4 Techniques for Stimulating Functional Conflict

Where conflict is too low and the organisation has become complacent, the manager may need to stimulate a healthy level of disagreement. The techniques used for this purpose include:

- Bringing in outsiders with different backgrounds and viewpoints to challenge the existing thinking.
- Appointing a devil's advocate whose role is to argue against any major proposal so that its weaknesses are exposed.
- Restructuring the organisation in ways that disturb settled patterns and create new working relationships.
- Encouraging open debate and the questioning of long-standing assumptions.
- Using techniques such as brainstorming and the nominal group technique to bring out different ideas.

Summary

Organisational change refers to any modification in the existing way of working of an enterprise. It is universal, continuous and multidirectional, and may be planned or unplanned, incremental or transformational. The causes of change are both external—economic, technological, political, social, competitive, global and natural—and internal—changes in objectives, leadership, structure and employee expectations.

Kurt Lewin's three-step model of unfreezing, changing and refreezing, supported by his concept of force-field analysis, remains the foundation of modern change management. John P. Kotter built on this with his eight-step model of leading change, which covers the entire journey from creating urgency to anchoring the change in the culture. Other useful models include the ADKAR Model, the McKinsey 7-S Framework and the Bridges Transition Model.

Resistance to change is the rule rather than the exception, and may arise from individual factors such as fear of the unknown, fear of loss, habit and lack of trust, as well as from organisational factors such as structural inertia, group inertia and threats to established power. Kotter and Schlesinger identified six approaches to overcoming resistance—education and communication, participation and involvement, facilitation and support, negotiation and agreement, manipulation and co-optation, and coercion.

Conflict is a state of opposition, disagreement or incompatibility between two or more persons or groups. The modern interactionist view treats some level of conflict as necessary for organisational health. Conflict may be functional or dysfunctional, intrapersonal, interpersonal, intragroup, intergroup or inter-organisational. The Thomas-Kilmann model identifies five conflict-handling styles—avoiding, accommodating, competing, compromising and collaborating—based on the two dimensions of assertiveness and cooperativeness. Conflict-resolution techniques include negotiation, mediation, arbitration, conciliation, problem-solving, authoritative command and smoothing. Where conflict is too low, the manager may use techniques such as devil's advocacy and the bringing in of fresh perspectives to stimulate healthy disagreement.

Key Terms

Organisational Change, Planned Change, Transformational Change, External Forces, Internal Forces, Kurt Lewin, Unfreezing, Changing, Refreezing, Force-Field Analysis, John Kotter, Eight-Step Model, ADKAR Model, McKinsey 7-S, Bridges Transition Model, Resistance to Change, Structural Inertia, Kotter-Schlesinger, Education and Communication, Participation, Facilitation, Negotiation, Co-optation, Coercion, Conflict, Functional Conflict, Dysfunctional Conflict, Intrapersonal, Interpersonal, Intragroup, Intergroup, L.R. Pondy, Latent

Conflict, Manifest Conflict, Thomas-Kilmann Model, Avoiding, Accommodating, Competing, Compromising, Collaborating, Negotiation, Mediation, Arbitration, Conciliation, Devil's Advocate.

Review Questions

A. Short Answer Questions (2 marks each)

9. Define organisational change.

10. State any four external forces of change.

11. Name the three steps of Kurt Lewin's model of change.

12. What is meant by force-field analysis?

13. Name any four steps of Kotter's eight-step model.

14. State any four causes of resistance to change.

15. Distinguish between functional and dysfunctional conflict.

16. Name the five conflict-handling styles given by Thomas and Kilmann.

B. Long Answer Questions (10 marks each)

17. Discuss the nature and the major causes of organisational change.

18. Explain Kurt Lewin's three-step model of change. How does it differ from Kotter's eight-step model?

19. Discuss the major causes of resistance to change and the techniques for overcoming it.

20. Explain the concept of conflict and discuss its various types.

21. Describe the Thomas-Kilmann model of conflict-handling styles.

22. Discuss the various techniques for resolving conflict in an organisation.

C. Practical / Case-Based Questions

23. Recall any major change that you have witnessed in any organisation—your school, college or workplace. Analyse the change in terms of Kotter's eight-step model.

24. Suppose you are the head of a department in which two senior

members of your team are constantly at odds with each other and the conflict is affecting the work of the entire group. Outline the steps you would take to resolve the conflict.

CHAPTER 19

TOTAL QUALITY MANAGEMENT AND PRODUCTIVITY

Learning Objectives

After studying this chapter, the reader should be able to:

- understand the concept and the importance of Total Quality Management (TQM);
- explain the contributions of the leading quality gurus—Deming, Juran and Crosby;
- describe the popular tools and techniques of TQM such as Six Sigma, Kaizen and 5S;
- understand the working of Quality Circles and the technique of Benchmarking; and
- discuss the concept of productivity and the various ways of improving it.

Introduction

In the modern world of intense global competition, quality and productivity have become two of the most important sources of competitive advantage. The remarkable rise of Japan as a global economic power after the Second World War—and the rise of Korean companies such as Samsung and Hyundai in more recent decades—has been built largely on the foundations of quality and productivity. Indian companies, too, have made great strides in these areas. Companies such as Maruti Suzuki, Tata Steel, Tata Motors, Mahindra & Mahindra, TVS Motor Company, Hero MotoCorp, Bajaj Auto, Sundaram-Clayton and Asian Paints have won the prestigious Deming Prize for quality, while several Indian firms have won the Malcolm Baldrige and JUSE awards as well.

Quality and productivity are closely related. A company that improves its quality almost always improves its productivity as well, since less waste, less rework and fewer defects mean more output from the same inputs. Conversely, a company that focuses only on cutting costs without paying attention to quality often finds its productivity falling, since customers turn away and rework eats up the savings. Modern management, therefore, treats quality and productivity as two sides of the same coin.

This chapter discusses the concept and the importance of Total Quality Management, the contributions of the great quality thinkers—W. Edwards Deming, Joseph M. Juran and Philip B. Crosby—the popular tools and techniques of TQM such as Six Sigma, Kaizen and 5S, the role of Quality Circles and Benchmarking, and finally the concept of productivity and the various ways of measuring and improving it.

19.1 Concept and Importance of TQM

19.1.1 Concept of Quality

Quality may be defined as the fitness of a product or a service for the purpose for which it is intended, as judged by the customer. The International Organisation for Standardisation (ISO) defines quality as "the degree to which a set of inherent characteristics fulfils requirements." Joseph M. Juran defined quality as "fitness for use." Philip B. Crosby defined it as "conformance to requirements." Each of these definitions, in its own way, emphasises that quality is ultimately determined by the customer, not by the producer.

19.1.2 Concept of TQM

Total Quality Management, or TQM, is a comprehensive approach to managing an organisation in which every employee, every process and every aspect of the business is focused on quality and on continuous improvement. The word "total" indicates that everyone in the organisation is involved; "quality" indicates the focus on meeting customer expectations; and "management" indicates that this is a deliberate, planned, system-wide effort.

Joseph Jablonski defined TQM as "a cooperative form of doing business that relies on the talents and capabilities of both labour and management to continually improve quality and productivity using teams." John Oakland defined it as "an approach to improving the effectiveness and flexibility of business as a whole. It is essentially a way of organising and involving the whole organisation: every department, every activity, every single person at every level."

19.1.3 Evolution of Quality Management

The journey of modern quality management has passed through several stages:

- The inspection era of the early twentieth century, in which quality was sought to be ensured by inspecting the finished product and rejecting the defective ones.
- The statistical quality control era of the 1930s and 1940s, pioneered by Walter A. Shewhart of Bell Laboratories, in which statistical techniques were applied to monitor production processes.
- The quality assurance era of the 1950s and 1960s, in which the emphasis shifted from detection of defects to their prevention.
- The era of Total Quality Management, which began in Japan in the 1950s under the influence of Deming and Juran and spread to the West from the 1980s onwards. TQM treats quality as the responsibility of the entire organisation rather than of a separate quality control department.

19.1.4 Features of TQM

- Customer focus—the customer, internal or external, is at the centre of every decision.
- Total involvement—every employee, from the chief executive to the shop floor worker, is responsible for quality.
- Process orientation—quality is built into the process, not inspected into the product.
- Continuous improvement—known by the Japanese word kaizen, the unending search for small improvements.
- Fact-based decision-making, supported by data and statistical analysis.
- Long-term commitment by the top management.
- Empowerment of employees to take decisions about quality in their own areas of work.
- Strong partnership with suppliers and customers.

19.1.5 Importance of TQM

• TQM increases customer satisfaction and loyalty, the most precious assets of any business.

• It reduces the cost of quality—the cost of defects, rework, scrap, warranty claims and lost customers.

• It improves productivity, since waste is reduced and processes are streamlined.

• It raises the morale of employees, who feel a sense of pride in producing high-quality work.

• It strengthens the competitive position of the company, both in the domestic and in the international markets.

• It enhances the brand image and the reputation of the company.

• It reduces the risk of liability for defective products.

19.2 Principles and Philosophies—Deming, Juran and Crosby

19.2.1 W. Edwards Deming (1900–1993)

Dr. W. Edwards Deming, an American statistician, is often regarded as the father of the modern quality movement. Although his ideas were largely ignored in his own country in the early years, he was invited to Japan in 1950 by the Japanese Union of Scientists and Engineers (JUSE) to lecture on quality. His ideas had a profound influence on the recovery of Japanese industry after the Second World War. In recognition of his contribution, JUSE instituted the Deming Prize in 1951, which has since become the most prestigious quality award in the world.

Deming's 14 Points. Deming's philosophy is best captured in his famous Fourteen Points for the transformation of management. These include: creating constancy of purpose for the improvement of products and services; adopting the new philosophy of quality; ceasing dependence on inspection to achieve quality; ending the practice of awarding business on the basis of price alone; improving constantly the system of production and service; instituting training on the job; instituting leadership; driving out fear so that everyone may work effectively; breaking down barriers between departments; eliminating slogans, exhortations and numerical targets for the workforce; eliminating numerical quotas; removing barriers that rob workers of their pride of workmanship; instituting a vigorous programme of education and self-improvement; and putting everybody to work to accomplish the transformation.

The PDCA Cycle. Deming popularised the PDCA cycle, also known as the Deming cycle or the Shewhart cycle—Plan, Do, Check, Act. The manager plans an improvement, carries it out on a small scale, checks the results, and acts on the findings—either standardising the improvement or trying again. This simple four-step cycle of continuous improvement is at the heart of the TQM philosophy.

19.2.2 Joseph M. Juran (1904–2008)

Dr. Joseph M. Juran, a Romanian-born American engineer, was another major figure in the quality movement. Like Deming, he was invited to Japan in the 1950s, where he too had a great impact. Juran is best known for his Quality Trilogy, his application of the Pareto principle to quality problems and his work on the cost of quality.

The Juran Trilogy. According to Juran, the management of quality consists of three closely related processes:

- Quality Planning—identifying the customers and their needs, and designing products and processes that meet those needs.
- Quality Control—measuring actual performance, comparing it with the standards and taking action on the deviations.
- Quality Improvement—continually raising the level of quality through breakthrough projects.

The Pareto Principle. Juran applied to quality problems the Pareto principle, also known as the 80/20 rule, originally formulated by the Italian economist Vilfredo Pareto. According to this principle, about eighty per cent of the consequences flow from about twenty per cent of the causes. In quality terms, this means that a small number of "vital few" causes are responsible for most of the defects, while the rest are merely the "trivial many." Juran taught managers to focus on the vital few.

Cost of Quality. Juran was also a pioneer in measuring the cost of quality—the prevention costs, the appraisal costs, the internal failure costs (such as scrap and rework) and the external failure costs (such as warranty claims and lost customers). He showed that the cost of poor quality in a typical company can be as high as twenty to thirty per cent of sales—a hidden goldmine waiting to be tapped.

19.2.3 Philip B. Crosby (1926–2001)

Philip B. Crosby, an American businessman who worked for many years at ITT, became famous for his book Quality is Free, published in 1979. Crosby argued that the cost of not having quality is so high that quality more than pays for itself. He is also known for the slogan "Zero Defects."

Crosby's Four Absolutes of Quality.

1. Quality is defined as conformance to requirements.
2. The system of quality is prevention, not inspection.
3. The performance standard for quality is zero defects, not "that's close enough."
4. Quality is measured by the price of non-conformance (PONC), not by indexes.

Crosby's message to managers was simple and powerful—do it right the first time, and quality becomes free.

19.2.4 Other Quality Gurus

Besides Deming, Juran and Crosby, several other thinkers deserve mention:

- Kaoru Ishikawa (1915–1989) of Japan, who developed the cause-and-effect diagram (the fishbone or Ishikawa diagram) and the company-wide quality control movement.
- Genichi Taguchi, also of Japan, who developed the Taguchi methods of robust design and the loss function.
- Shigeo Shingo, the inventor of poka-yoke, the technique of mistake-proofing the production process.
- Masaaki Imai, who popularised the concept of kaizen in the West through his book Kaizen: The Key to Japan's Competitive Success (1986).
- Armand V. Feigenbaum, who introduced the concept of Total Quality Control in his book of the same name in 1961.

19.3 Tools and Techniques of TQM

19.3.1 Six Sigma

Six Sigma is a disciplined, data-driven approach to eliminating defects in any process. The word "sigma" is the Greek letter used in statistics to denote the standard deviation. "Six sigma" level of quality means that there are fewer than 3.4 defects per million opportunities—a near-perfect level of performance. The methodology was developed at Motorola in 1986 and was famously adopted at General Electric by Jack Welch, who claimed that Six Sigma saved GE billions of dollars.

The standard Six Sigma project follows the DMAIC framework:

- Define the problem and the customer requirements.
- Measure the current performance of the process.
- Analyse the data to find the root causes of the defects.
- Improve the process by eliminating the root causes.
- Control the improved process so that the gains are sustained over time.

Six Sigma practitioners are organised into a hierarchy modelled on the martial arts—Yellow Belt, Green Belt, Black Belt and Master Black Belt. Many Indian companies, including Wipro, TCS, ICICI Bank and Tata Steel, have implemented Six Sigma programmes with great success.

19.3.2 Kaizen

Kaizen is the Japanese word for "change for the better" or "continuous improvement." The philosophy of kaizen, popularised by Masaaki Imai, is that improvement should be the responsibility of every employee, every day, in every aspect of the work. It is the spirit of continuous, small-step improvement rather than of occasional, large-scale change.

The kaizen approach is supported by several specific practices, including suggestion schemes, in which every employee is encouraged to submit ideas for improvement; quality circles, in which small groups meet regularly to discuss and solve work-related problems; and just-in-time inventory systems, in which materials arrive exactly when they are needed. Toyota Motor Company is perhaps the most famous practitioner of kaizen, and the Toyota Production System has inspired companies all over the world. In India, companies such as Maruti Suzuki, TVS Motors, Tata Motors and Sundaram Fasteners have adopted kaizen with excellent results.

19.3.3 The 5S System

The 5S system is a workplace organisation technique originally developed in Japan. Its name comes from five Japanese words, each beginning with the letter "S":

1. Seiri (Sort). Sort out the items in the workplace. Keep what is needed; remove or dispose of what is not needed.

2. Seiton (Set in Order). Arrange the needed items so that they can be easily found and used. "A place for everything and everything in its place."

3. Seiso (Shine). Clean the workplace and the equipment thoroughly. A clean workplace is the basis of safety and quality.

4. Seiketsu (Standardise). Standardise the practices of Sort, Set in Order and Shine so that they are followed consistently by all.

5. Shitsuke (Sustain). Build the discipline to maintain the 5S system over time. This calls for ongoing training, audits and management commitment.

The 5S system, simple though it sounds, has a powerful effect on workplace efficiency, safety, employee morale and the quality of output.

19.3.4 The Seven Basic Quality Tools

Kaoru Ishikawa identified seven basic quality control tools, often called the "Magnificent Seven," which together can solve most quality problems on the shop floor. These tools are:

- the cause-and-effect (fishbone or Ishikawa) diagram, which traces the various possible causes of a problem;
- the check sheet, used to collect and organise data;
- the control chart, used to monitor a process over time;
- the histogram, which shows the distribution of a variable;
- the Pareto chart, which displays the most important causes in order of frequency;
- the scatter diagram, which shows the relationship between two variables; and
- the flowchart, which depicts the steps of a process.

19.3.5 Other Quality Tools

Besides the techniques discussed above, the modern manager has many other tools at his disposal:

- The ISO 9000 family of international quality management standards, used by lakhs of companies in India and across the world.
- Just-in-Time (JIT), a Japanese system of producing only what is needed, only when it is needed.
- Lean manufacturing, which extends the JIT principle to eliminate every kind of waste.
- Total Productive Maintenance (TPM), which involves every employee in the maintenance of equipment.
- Poka-Yoke (mistake-proofing), the technique of designing processes so that errors cannot occur.
- Statistical Process Control (SPC), the use of statistical methods to monitor and control a process.
- The Failure Mode and Effects Analysis (FMEA), a systematic study of possible failures and their consequences.

19.4 Quality Circles and Benchmarking

19.4.1 Quality Circles—Concept and Origin

A quality circle is a small group of employees from the same work area who voluntarily meet regularly to identify, analyse and solve work-related problems. The concept originated in Japan in 1962, under the leadership of Kaoru Ishikawa and the Japanese Union of Scientists and Engineers (JUSE). Within two decades, it had spread to almost every industrial country in the world.

19.4.2 Features of Quality Circles

- Voluntary participation by the members.
- Small size, generally six to twelve members.
- Members are drawn from the same work area, so that they understand the problems of that area.
- Regular meetings, usually once a week, often during working hours.
- Members are trained in problem-solving techniques such as brainstorming and the seven basic quality tools.
- Problems are identified by the members themselves, not imposed

by the management.

- Solutions are presented to the management for approval and implementation.

19.4.3 Process of a Quality Circle

5. Identification of problems by the members of the circle.
6. Selection of the most important problem for study.
7. Analysis of the problem using tools such as the fishbone diagram and the Pareto chart.
8. Development of possible solutions.
9. Selection of the best solution.
10. Presentation of the solution to the management.
11. Implementation, follow-up and review.

19.4.4 Benefits of Quality Circles

- Improvement in the quality of products and services.
- Reduction in waste, rework and cost.
- Better employee involvement and a sense of belonging.
- Development of leadership and problem-solving skills among workers.
- Improved communication between the workers and the management.
- Higher morale, lower absenteeism and reduced labour turnover.

19.4.5 Quality Circles in India

Quality circles were introduced in India in the early 1980s and have been widely adopted by leading companies. The Quality Circle Forum of India (QCFI), set up in 1982 with its headquarters at Secunderabad, has been the main body for the promotion of quality circles in the country. It organises an annual National Convention on Quality Circles and an International Convention every year, in which thousands of workers participate. Companies such as Bharat Heavy Electricals Limited (BHEL), Tata Steel, Bharat Petroleum, Oil and Natural Gas Corporation, Indian Oil Corporation, Maruti Suzuki and a number of public-sector banks have implemented quality circles with notable success.

19.4.6 Benchmarking—Concept and Origin

Benchmarking is the process of comparing the products, services and practices of one's own company with those of the best in the industry, and using the findings to improve one's own performance. The technique was pioneered by Xerox Corporation in the late 1970s and early 1980s, when the company found itself losing market share to Japanese rivals and decided to study them systematically.

Robert C. Camp, who developed the methodology at Xerox, defined benchmarking as "the search for industry best practices that will lead to superior performance."

19.4.7 Types of Benchmarking

- Internal Benchmarking, in which the performance of different units of the same company is compared.
- Competitive Benchmarking, in which the company compares itself with its direct competitors.
- Functional Benchmarking, in which a particular function of the company is compared with the same function in any company known to excel in it, regardless of industry.
- Generic Benchmarking, in which the basic processes of the company are compared with the best processes in any field.

19.4.8 Process of Benchmarking

12. Plan—identify what is to be benchmarked and who is to be benchmarked against.
13. Search—find the best practices in the chosen area.
14. Observe and study—understand how the best performers achieve their results.
15. Analyse—compare the findings with one's own performance and identify the gaps.
16. Adapt and implement—apply the learnings to one's own organisation.

Indian companies such as Maruti Suzuki, Infosys, ICICI Bank and the Tata Group have used benchmarking extensively, often comparing themselves not only with Indian competitors but with the best in the world.

19.5 Productivity Management

19.5.1 Concept and Definition of Productivity

Productivity is the ratio of output to input. It measures how efficiently the resources of the enterprise—labour, capital, materials, energy—are converted into goods and services. The formula is simple:

Productivity = Output / Input

The International Labour Organisation (ILO) defines productivity as "the ratio between the output of goods and services and the input of resources used to produce them." Peter F. Drucker described it as "the balance between all factors of production that will give the greatest output for the smallest effort."

19.5.2 Productivity Distinguished from Production

Productivity is sometimes confused with production, but the two are quite different. Production refers to the absolute volume of output, that is, the total number of units produced. Productivity refers to the ratio of output to input. A factory that doubles its output by doubling its workforce has increased production but not productivity. A factory that doubles its output with the same workforce has increased both production and productivity.

19.5.3 Types of Productivity

- Labour productivity—the ratio of output to labour input, usually measured in terms of output per worker or per worker-hour.
- Capital productivity—the ratio of output to capital input.
- Material productivity—the ratio of output to material input.
- Energy productivity—the ratio of output to energy consumed.
- Total factor productivity—the ratio of total output to the total input of all factors taken together.

19.5.4 Importance of Productivity

- Higher productivity leads to higher profits for the enterprise.
- It enables the enterprise to pay better wages to its workers.
- It reduces the cost of production and the price to the consumer.
- It strengthens the competitive position of the enterprise in the market.
- It raises the standard of living of the people, since more goods and

services become available at lower cost.

- It contributes to the economic development of the country.

19.5.5 Factors Affecting Productivity

- Human factors—the skill, training, motivation and health of the workforce.
- Technological factors—the level of technology, the use of automation and the investment in research and development.
- Material factors—the quality and availability of raw materials and the efficiency of inventory management.
- Managerial factors—the quality of planning, organisation, leadership and control.
- Capital factors—the availability of finance and the efficiency of its use.
- Environmental factors—government policies, labour laws, the state of infrastructure and the macroeconomic environment.

19.5.6 Techniques for Improving Productivity

Managers use a wide variety of techniques to improve productivity:

1. Work Study. Work study, which includes method study and time study, is one of the oldest techniques. Method study aims at finding the best way of doing a job. Time study aims at finding the standard time required to do it.

2. Job Design and Ergonomics. Designing jobs so that they make full use of the abilities of the worker, and designing the workplace so that it is comfortable and safe, both raise productivity.

3. Training and Development. A well-trained workforce is a productive workforce. Investment in training is one of the best investments any enterprise can make.

4. Motivation and Incentives. Motivated workers produce more and produce better. Financial incentives such as productivity-linked wages and non-financial incentives such as recognition and participation play a key role.

5. Automation and Modern Technology. The use of modern machinery, computers, robotics and artificial intelligence can dramatically increase productivity, particularly in repetitive and standardised work.

6. Process Improvement. Continuous improvement of processes through TQM, Six Sigma, lean manufacturing and similar approaches steadily raises productivity over time.

7. Material Management. Effective inventory control, efficient purchasing, just-in-time delivery and the reduction of waste all improve material productivity.

8. Energy Management. With rising energy costs and growing environmental concerns, energy productivity has become an important focus. Energy audits, efficient equipment and the use of renewable energy all help.

9. Sound Industrial Relations. Productivity cannot be raised without the willing cooperation of the workforce. A peaceful workplace, fair dealings and good communication are essential.

19.5.7 Productivity in India

The level of productivity in India has historically been lower than in the developed countries. This was largely the result of small scale of operations, outdated technology, poor infrastructure, restrictive labour laws and limited investment in education and skills. The economic reforms of 1991 and the various initiatives taken in subsequent years—such as the Make in India programme, the Skill India mission and the Production-Linked Incentive (PLI) schemes—have aimed at raising the productivity of Indian industry. The National Productivity Council (NPC), set up in 1958 under the Ministry of Industry, has been the chief national body for the promotion of productivity. It observes National Productivity Week every year from 12 to 18 February to spread productivity awareness across the country.

Summary

Total Quality Management is a comprehensive approach to managing an organisation in which every employee, every process and every aspect of the business is focused on quality and on continuous improvement. Its main features are customer focus, total involvement, process orientation, continuous improvement, fact-based decisions, long-term commitment and employee empowerment. TQM has evolved through the stages of inspection, statistical quality control, quality assurance and total quality management.

Three thinkers stand out as the great pioneers of the quality movement. W. Edwards Deming gave the Fourteen Points for management, the PDCA cycle and the inspiration behind the Japanese quality miracle. Joseph M. Juran gave the Quality Trilogy of planning, control and improvement, applied the Pareto principle to quality problems and pioneered the measurement of the cost of quality. Philip B. Crosby gave the slogan "Quality is Free," the standard of "Zero Defects" and the Four Absolutes of Quality. Other important contributors include Ishikawa, Taguchi, Shingo, Imai and Feigenbaum.

The popular tools and techniques of TQM include Six Sigma, with its DMAIC framework and its goal of fewer than 3.4 defects per million opportunities; Kaizen, the philosophy of continuous small-step improvement; the 5S system of workplace organisation; the seven basic quality tools developed by Ishikawa; and other techniques such as ISO 9000, JIT, lean manufacturing, TPM, poka-yoke and FMEA. Quality circles are small voluntary groups of workers who meet regularly to identify and solve work-related problems; they have been widely used by Indian companies, with the Quality Circle Forum of India as the main promoting body. Benchmarking is the systematic comparison of one's own performance with the best in the industry, pioneered by Xerox and now used by Indian companies such as Maruti Suzuki, Infosys and the Tata Group.

Productivity is the ratio of output to input. It is a measure of efficiency, not of absolute volume. Productivity may be calculated for labour, for capital, for materials, for energy or for all factors taken together. It is affected by human, technological, material, managerial, capital and environmental factors. Techniques for improving productivity include work study, job design, training, motivation, automation, process improvement, material management, energy management and sound industrial relations. India has, in recent decades, taken many steps to raise the productivity of its industry, including the economic reforms of 1991, the Make in India programme and the

Production-Linked Incentive schemes. The National Productivity Council, set up in 1958, has been the main national body for the promotion of productivity.

Key Terms

Quality, TQM, Customer Focus, Continuous Improvement, Kaizen, Deming, PDCA Cycle, Deming Prize, Fourteen Points, Juran, Quality Trilogy, Pareto Principle, 80/20 Rule, Cost of Quality, Crosby, Quality is Free, Zero Defects, Four Absolutes, Ishikawa Diagram, Taguchi Methods, Poka-Yoke, Feigenbaum, Six Sigma, DMAIC, Yellow Belt, Green Belt, Black Belt, Master Black Belt, Motorola, Jack Welch, Toyota Production System, 5S System, Seven Basic Quality Tools, ISO 9000, Just-in-Time, Lean Manufacturing, TPM, FMEA, Quality Circles, Quality Circle Forum of India, Benchmarking, Robert Camp, Xerox, Internal Benchmarking, Competitive Benchmarking, Functional Benchmarking, Generic Benchmarking, Productivity, Production, Labour Productivity, Capital Productivity, Total Factor Productivity, Work Study, Method Study, Time Study, National Productivity Council, Make in India, PLI Scheme.

Review Questions

A. Short Answer Questions (2 marks each)

17. Define quality.
18. What is meant by Total Quality Management?
19. State any four features of TQM.
20. What is the PDCA cycle?
21. State the four absolutes of quality given by Philip Crosby.
22. What is Six Sigma? Name its five steps.
23. What does the term 5S stand for?
24. Define a quality circle.
25. What is benchmarking?
26. Distinguish between production and productivity.

B. Long Answer Questions (10 marks each)

27. Discuss the concept, the features and the importance of Total

Quality Management.

28. Compare and contrast the contributions of Deming, Juran and Crosby to the quality movement.

29. Explain Six Sigma and the DMAIC framework. How does it differ from the kaizen approach?

30. What is a quality circle? Describe its features, working and benefits, with examples from Indian companies.

31. Explain the concept of benchmarking. Describe its types and process.

32. Define productivity. Discuss the factors that affect productivity and the techniques for improving it.

C. Practical / Case-Based Questions

33. Take any successful Indian manufacturing company (such as Maruti Suzuki, Tata Motors or Hero MotoCorp) and discuss how it has applied the principles of TQM to gain a competitive edge.

CHAPTER 20

CONTEMPORARY ISSUES AND EMERGING TRENDS IN MANAGEMENT

Learning Objectives

After studying this chapter, the reader should be able to:

- understand the meaning and the implications of globalisation for the modern manager;
- appreciate the role of knowledge and information in the new economy;
- explain the concepts of diversity and cross-cultural management;
- describe the key technologies driving the digital transformation of business;
- understand the concept of green management and sustainable business; and
- identify the major trends that are shaping the future of management.

Introduction

Throughout the previous nineteen chapters of this book, we have studied the principles and the practices of management as they have evolved over the past hundred and twenty-five years or so. We have travelled from the scientific management of F.W. Taylor to the administrative theory of Henri Fayol, from the human relations school of Elton Mayo to the modern theories of motivation and leadership, from the time-honoured functions of planning, organising, staffing, directing and controlling to the modern concerns of ethics, social responsibility, change, conflict, quality and productivity.

Yet the journey of management thought is far from over. The world of business is changing more rapidly today than at any time in the past, and the manager of the next decade will face challenges and opportunities that his predecessors could not have imagined. Globalisation has linked the economies of the world together as never before. The digital revolution—artificial intelligence, big data, cloud computing, the Internet of Things—is transforming every industry. Climate change has placed sustainability at the centre of every boardroom discussion. The COVID-19 pandemic of 2020 has permanently changed the way we work. New generations of workers, with new values and new expectations, are entering the workforce. New business models are being born, and old ones are being disrupted, every day.

In this concluding chapter, we look at the contemporary issues and the emerging trends that are shaping the future of management. We examine globalisation and international management, knowledge and information management, diversity and cross-cultural management, the digital transformation of business, green management and sustainable business, and finally cast a glance at what the future of management is likely to look like. India, with its young population, its vibrant economy and its ancient tradition of wisdom, is uniquely placed to make important contributions to this future.

20.1 Globalisation and International Management

20.1.1 Concept of Globalisation

Globalisation refers to the process by which the economies, the societies and the cultures of the world have become increasingly integrated through cross-border flows of goods, services, capital, technology, people and ideas. Although globalisation in some form is as old as international trade itself, the modern phase of globalisation began after the Second World War with the setting up of the Bretton Woods institutions (the International Monetary Fund and the World Bank) in 1944 and the General Agreement on Tariffs and Trade (GATT) in 1947, later succeeded by the World Trade Organisation (WTO) in 1995.

For India, the great turning point came with the economic reforms of 1991, when the country opened its doors to foreign investment, reduced tariffs and freed many industries from the licence-permit raj. The reforms transformed Indian business beyond recognition and brought it into the mainstream of the global economy.

20.1.2 Features and Drivers of Globalisation

- Free or freer flow of goods and services across national boundaries.
- Free flow of capital, with foreign direct investment and portfolio investment crossing borders in trillions of dollars.
- Free flow of technology and knowledge, made possible by the internet.
- Greater movement of people, including managers, professionals, students and tourists.
- The rise of multinational corporations operating across many countries.
- The emergence of global supply chains, in which a single product may be designed in one country, financed in a second, manufactured from parts made in a third and sold in a fourth.
- The growing influence of international institutions such as the WTO, the IMF and the World Bank.

20.1.3 International Management

International management refers to the management of business operations in more than one country. A company that operates internationally faces problems that a purely domestic company does not—different languages, different cultures, different legal systems, different currencies, different consumer tastes and different competitive conditions. International management has, therefore, become a specialised field of study.

Companies can enter international markets through several modes, ranging from the simple to the complex:

- Exporting goods produced in the home country.
- Licensing, in which a foreign company is allowed to use one's brand, technology or process for a fee.
- Franchising, common in fast-food chains, hotels and retail.
- Joint ventures with a partner in the foreign country.
- Wholly owned subsidiaries set up in the foreign country.
- Cross-border mergers and acquisitions, in which one company

buys another in a foreign country.

20.1.4 Indian Companies on the Global Stage

Since the reforms of 1991, Indian companies have made remarkable strides on the global stage. Infosys, Tata Consultancy Services, Wipro, HCL and Tech Mahindra have become major players in the global information technology industry, serving customers across more than a hundred countries. The Tata Group has acquired iconic foreign companies such as Jaguar Land Rover, Tetley Tea and Corus Steel. Reliance Industries has built world-class facilities in petrochemicals and telecommunications. Bharti Airtel has expanded into Africa. Indian pharmaceutical companies such as Sun Pharma, Cipla, Dr. Reddy's Laboratories and Lupin have become major suppliers of generic medicines to the world, earning India the title of "the pharmacy of the world." The Mahindra Group, the Aditya Birla Group, Larsen & Toubro and many others have built sizable international operations. A new generation of start-ups—Flipkart, Zomato, Byju's, Ola, Paytm and many others—has put India firmly on the global digital map.

20.2 Knowledge and Information Management

20.2.1 The Rise of the Knowledge Economy

Peter F. Drucker, in his book Post-Capitalist Society (1993), declared that we had entered the age of the knowledge society. Land, labour and capital, he argued, were no longer the primary resources of the modern economy; the primary resource was knowledge. The workers of this new economy, whom he called knowledge workers, used their brains rather than their hands and earned their living through the application of knowledge.

India's information technology industry, which now employs over five million people and exports services worth more than two hundred billion dollars a year, is the most striking example of the knowledge economy at work. Pharmaceuticals, research, education, financial services, engineering services and the media are all knowledge-intensive industries that have grown rapidly in India over the last three decades.

20.2.2 Types of Knowledge

In an enterprise, knowledge exists in two distinct forms:

- Explicit knowledge, which can be written down, codified and stored—such as company manuals, technical drawings, patents, databases and research reports.
- Tacit knowledge, which exists in the heads of the employees in the form of experience, skill, intuition and judgement, and which is much harder to capture.

The Japanese scholars Ikujiro Nonaka and Hirotaka Takeuchi, in their well-known book The Knowledge-Creating Company (1995), argued that the success of Japanese firms lay in their ability to convert tacit knowledge into explicit knowledge and back again, in a continuous cycle of knowledge creation.

20.2.3 Knowledge Management

Knowledge management refers to the systematic process by which an organisation creates, captures, stores, shares and applies knowledge to achieve its objectives. The basic activities of knowledge management are:

- Knowledge creation, through research, learning and innovation.
- Knowledge capture, through documentation and interviews with experts.
- Knowledge storage, in databases, manuals, intranets and document repositories.
- Knowledge sharing, through training programmes, communities of practice and collaborative tools.
- Knowledge application, that is, the actual use of knowledge in solving problems and making decisions.

20.2.4 Information Management

Information management deals with the systematic handling of information in an organisation. The traditional hierarchy of data, information, knowledge and wisdom—often called the DIKW pyramid—helps in understanding the concept. Raw data become information when they are organised and presented in a meaningful way. Information becomes knowledge when it is understood and integrated with existing knowledge. Knowledge becomes wisdom when it is applied with judgement and ethics.

Modern enterprises rely on several types of information systems: Management Information Systems (MIS), Decision Support Systems (DSS), Executive Information Systems (EIS), Enterprise Resource Planning (ERP) and Customer Relationship Management (CRM). The rise of big data—characterised by the so-called "three Vs" of Volume, Velocity and Variety, to which Veracity and Value are often added—has opened up entirely new possibilities for the management of information.

20.3 Diversity and Cross-Cultural Management

20.3.1 Workforce Diversity

The workforce of the modern enterprise is far more diverse than ever before. Men and women, young and old, persons of different castes, religions, regions, languages and backgrounds work side by side in the same office or factory. With the rise of multinational corporations, the workforce is also becoming increasingly multinational, with persons of different nationalities working together.

Workforce diversity may be of several kinds:

- Demographic diversity—age, gender, ethnicity, religion, region, language.
- Cognitive diversity—different thinking styles, problem-solving approaches, perspectives.
- Experiential diversity—different educational backgrounds, work experiences, life experiences.
- Functional diversity—persons from different disciplines and departments.

20.3.2 Managing Diversity

A diverse workforce is a great asset, but it also poses certain challenges. Different people may have different communication styles, different expectations and different cultural sensitivities. Managing diversity, therefore, has become an important task for the modern manager. The chief practices in this area include:

- Building a culture of inclusion in which every employee feels valued and respected.
- Anti-discrimination policies and equal opportunity practices.
- Diversity and sensitivity training for managers and employees.

• Mentoring programmes for women and members of underrepresented groups.

• Flexible work arrangements that accommodate different family situations.

• Affirmative action and reservation policies where required by law.

20.3.3 Hofstede's Cultural Dimensions

The Dutch social psychologist Geert Hofstede, on the basis of his pioneering study of IBM employees in over fifty countries during the 1970s, identified six dimensions along which national cultures differ:

1. Power Distance—the extent to which less powerful members of society accept that power is distributed unequally. India scores high on this dimension.

2. Individualism versus Collectivism—whether people see themselves primarily as individuals or as members of a group. India is largely collectivist, in contrast to the individualist United States.

3. Masculinity versus Femininity—the extent to which a society values assertiveness and achievement (masculine) or care and quality of life (feminine). India is moderately masculine.

4. Uncertainty Avoidance—the extent to which a society feels threatened by uncertainty and tries to avoid it. India is moderately tolerant of uncertainty.

5. Long-Term versus Short-Term Orientation—the extent to which a society values future rewards over present gains. India tends towards long-term orientation.

6. Indulgence versus Restraint—the extent to which a society allows the free gratification of natural human desires.

20.3.4 Cross-Cultural Management

Cross-cultural management refers to the management of business activities across different cultures. The Indian manager working with American, European, Japanese, Chinese or African colleagues and customers must understand and respect their cultural differences. Communication styles, negotiation styles, decision-making patterns, attitudes to time, hierarchy, gender roles and personal space all vary from culture to culture. Successful international managers develop what is now called cultural intelligence (CQ)—the ability to function effectively in culturally diverse settings.

20.4 Digital Transformation—AI, Automation and Big Data

The most powerful force shaping the future of management is the digital transformation of business. Driven by the rapid development of new technologies, this transformation is reshaping every industry and is forcing managers to rethink the way they do business.

20.4.1 Artificial Intelligence

Artificial intelligence (AI) refers to the development of computer systems that can perform tasks that normally require human intelligence—understanding language, recognising images, taking decisions, learning from experience and even creating new content. Machine learning, deep learning, natural language processing and computer vision are the major branches of AI. The release of generative AI tools such as ChatGPT in 2022 was a watershed moment, bringing AI into the daily life of millions of users.

AI is being applied in business in numerous ways: customer service chatbots, recommendation engines on e-commerce sites, fraud detection in banks, predictive maintenance in factories, automated translation, medical diagnosis, autonomous vehicles and many others. At the same time, AI raises serious questions about the future of work, the ethics of machine decisions and the safety of AI systems—questions that will occupy managers, governments and society for years to come.

20.4.2 Big Data and Analytics

Big data refers to the very large, fast-moving and varied data sets that are generated every minute through the internet, social media, e-commerce, sensors, mobile phones and other sources. The analysis of such data, through techniques known as data analytics, can reveal hidden patterns, predict future events and support better decisions. Companies such as Amazon, Google, Netflix and, in India, Flipkart and Zomato have built their competitive advantage on big-data analytics.

20.4.3 Internet of Things

The Internet of Things (IoT) refers to the network of physical objects—machines, vehicles, household appliances, sensors—that are connected to the internet and that can send and receive data. In a factory, IoT sensors can monitor the condition of equipment in real time and predict when maintenance will be needed. In agriculture, sensors can monitor soil moisture and weather conditions to guide irrigation. The combination of IoT, big data and AI is often called Industry 4.0—the fourth industrial revolution.

20.4.4 Cloud Computing

Cloud computing refers to the delivery of computing services—storage, software, processing power—over the internet rather than from local computers. Services are typically offered in three forms—Infrastructure as a Service (IaaS), Platform as a Service (PaaS) and Software as a Service (SaaS). Amazon Web Services, Microsoft Azure and Google Cloud are the major global providers. Cloud computing has enabled even small companies to access world-class technology without large capital investments.

20.4.5 Blockchain and Other Technologies

Blockchain is a distributed digital ledger that records transactions in a way that is secure, transparent and tamper-proof. Its best-known application is in cryptocurrencies such as Bitcoin and Ethereum, but the technology is also being applied to supply chain management, land records, voting systems and smart contracts. Other emerging technologies include robotics and Robotic Process Automation (RPA), 3D printing, augmented and virtual reality (AR and VR), 5G mobile networks and, on the horizon, quantum computing.

20.4.6 India's Digital Journey

India has emerged as one of the most exciting digital markets in the world. The Digital India programme, launched in 2015, has aimed at making the country a digitally empowered society. The Aadhaar identification system covers over 1.3 billion people. The Unified Payments Interface (UPI), launched in 2016, has revolutionised digital payments and now handles more transactions than any other system in the world. The Open Network for Digital Commerce (ONDC) is creating an open public network for e-commerce. The e-NAM (National Agriculture Market) connects mandis across the country. DigiLocker provides secure storage of important documents. Government services from passport applications to tax returns have moved largely online. India's start-up ecosystem has produced over one hundred unicorns and is now the third largest in the world.

20.5 Green Management and Sustainable Business

20.5.1 The Concept of Green Management

Green management, also known as environmental management or eco-management, is the management of business in a way that minimises the harmful impact of its activities on the natural environment. It is a response to the growing concerns about climate change, pollution, deforestation, the depletion of natural resources and the loss of biodiversity. What was once seen as a moral or regulatory issue is now seen as a strategic imperative for survival in the long term.

20.5.2 The Need for Green Management

- Climate change is now widely accepted as the most serious long-term challenge facing humanity.
- Pollution of air, water and soil is causing serious health and economic damage.
- Natural resources, particularly water, are becoming scarce.
- Governments are tightening environmental regulations across the world.
- Consumers, particularly younger ones, increasingly prefer products and brands that are environmentally friendly.
- Investors are channelling funds towards companies with strong ESG performance.
- Employees, particularly the younger generation, prefer to work for companies that take their environmental responsibilities seriously.

20.5.3 Areas of Green Management

- Green products—designed to minimise environmental impact throughout their life cycle.
- Green processes—manufacturing processes that consume less energy, water and materials, and produce less waste and pollution.
- Green supply chain management, which extends green practices to suppliers and customers.

• Green marketing, in which environmentally friendly attributes are highlighted in promoting the product.

• Green human resource management, including training, motivation and rewards related to environmental performance.

• Green finance, including green bonds, sustainable investment and impact investing.

20.5.4 The Concept of a Circular Economy

Traditional industrial economies are described as linear—"take, make, dispose." The circular economy aims to replace this model with a cyclical one, in which materials are kept in use for as long as possible through reuse, repair, refurbishment and recycling, and waste is minimised at every stage. The circular economy is now seen as essential for a sustainable future.

20.5.5 India's Commitment to Sustainability

India has played an increasingly important role in the global efforts towards sustainability:

• India was an early signatory to the Paris Climate Agreement of 2015 (COP21).

• At the Glasgow Climate Conference (COP26) in 2021, India announced its commitment to achieve net zero emissions by the year 2070.

• The International Solar Alliance, launched by India and France in 2015, now has over a hundred member countries and aims at the rapid expansion of solar energy in tropical countries.

• Mission LiFE (Lifestyle for Environment), launched in 2022, calls on every individual to live in harmony with nature.

• The Swachh Bharat (Clean India) Mission, the Ujjwala Yojana for clean cooking fuel and the Jal Jeevan Mission for piped water supply are among the major government initiatives.

• The One Sun, One World, One Grid (OSOWOG) initiative aims at creating a global solar power grid.

20.5.6 Indian Companies and Sustainability

A growing number of Indian companies have placed sustainability at the centre of their business. ITC has become the world's only large corporation to be water positive, carbon positive and solid-waste recycling positive simultaneously. The Mahindra Group has emerged as a leader in electric vehicles and renewable energy. The Tata Group, through its companies Tata Power and Tata Power Renewable Energy, is a major player in clean energy. ReNew Power and Adani Green Energy have become among the largest renewable energy companies in the world. Hindustan Unilever has set ambitious sustainability targets across its product portfolio. Even smaller and mid-sized companies are increasingly adopting sustainable practices, partly in response to customer demand and partly as a matter of conviction.

20.6 The Future of Management

What will the management of the future look like? Although no one can predict the future with certainty, the following trends are likely to shape it powerfully.

20.6.1 Emerging Trends in Management

1. Hybrid and Flexible Work. The COVID-19 pandemic of 2020 has permanently changed the way we work. Hybrid models, in which employees work partly from the office and partly from home, are likely to remain the norm in many industries.

2. AI and Automation. Artificial intelligence and automation will continue to change the nature of work. Routine and repetitive tasks will be increasingly automated, while creative, analytical and emotional tasks will remain with humans. The skills required of managers and employees will, therefore, keep evolving.

3. Reskilling and Lifelong Learning. With knowledge becoming outdated faster than ever, employees and managers will have to keep learning throughout their working lives. Companies will invest heavily in reskilling and upskilling their workforce.

4. The Gig Economy. Traditional long-term employment is giving way to short-term contracts, freelance work and platform-based gig work. India already has tens of millions of gig workers in transport, delivery, content creation and other fields. Managing this fluid workforce will be a new challenge.

5. Mental Health and Employee Well-being. Stress, anxiety and burnout have become serious problems in the modern workplace. Forward-looking companies are giving high priority to mental health, work-life balance and employee well-being.

6. ESG and Stakeholder Capitalism. The narrow focus on shareholder value is giving way to a broader concept of stakeholder capitalism, in which the interests of customers, employees, suppliers, the community and the environment are also taken into account.

7. Data-Driven Decisions. Decisions in every area of business—marketing, finance, operations, human resources—are increasingly being made on the basis of data analytics rather than gut feeling alone.

8. Diversity, Equity and Inclusion. Diversity is no longer seen as a matter of compliance but as a source of strength. Companies are working to build truly inclusive workplaces where every employee, regardless of background, can give his or her best.

9. Sustainable Business Models. Environmental sustainability is moving from the margins to the mainstream of business strategy. New business models such as the circular economy, the sharing economy and impact business are gaining ground.

10. Personalised Customer Experience. Aided by data and AI, companies are moving from mass marketing to one-to-one personalisation, treating each customer as a unique individual.

11. Cyber Security and Data Privacy. As businesses become more digital, the risks of cyber attacks and data breaches grow. The Digital Personal Data Protection Act of 2023 has placed new responsibilities on Indian companies in this area.

12. Innovation as a Core Capability. In a fast-changing world, the ability to innovate continuously has become essential for survival. Companies that fail to innovate quickly find themselves overtaken by more agile competitors.

20.6.2 Skills for the Future Manager

The manager of the future will need a new set of skills:

- Digital literacy and the ability to work with new technologies such as AI, big data and the cloud.
- Strong analytical and critical thinking skills.

- Emotional intelligence and the ability to manage one's own emotions and to understand those of others.
- Cultural intelligence for working in a globalised, multicultural world.
- Adaptability and resilience in the face of constant change.
- Strong ethical foundations and a sense of responsibility to all stakeholders.
- Systems thinking, that is, the ability to see the connections among the various parts of a complex situation.
- Creativity and the ability to innovate.
- A spirit of collaboration and the ability to work in diverse teams.
- A commitment to lifelong learning.

20.6.3 The Indian Ethos and the Future of Management

As management evolves to meet the challenges of the twenty-first century, the ancient wisdom of India has much to offer. The Bhagavad Gita's teaching of nishkama karma—performing one's duty without attachment to the fruits of action—speaks directly to the modern problem of stress and burnout. The concept of dharma provides a moral foundation for ethical leadership. The principle of trusteeship taught by Mahatma Gandhi anticipates the modern idea of stakeholder capitalism. The yogic disciplines of mind and body offer practical tools for managing stress and improving well-being. The Indian tradition of seeing the divine in all living things provides a deep spiritual basis for sustainability. The growing field of "Indian Ethos in Management" is bringing together this ancient wisdom with modern management thinking, and is one of the exciting frontiers of management research in our country.

20.6.4 Conclusion

As we come to the end of this long journey through the principles and practices of management, three thoughts may be left with the reader. First, management is a living, growing discipline; it has come a long way in the past hundred and twenty-five years, and it will continue to evolve in the years to come. Secondly, the future manager will need to be both a master of new technologies and a person of strong human values;

technology without values can be dangerous, while values without competence are powerless. Thirdly, India is uniquely placed to make important contributions to the future of management, drawing on both its modern professional skills and its ancient spiritual wisdom. The young men and women who study this book today will be the managers of the India of tomorrow—the India that will, within the lifetime of many of them, become one of the largest economies in the world. The future is theirs to shape, and good management will be central to whatever they create.

Summary

This chapter has surveyed the major contemporary issues and emerging trends that are shaping the future of management. Globalisation has linked the economies of the world together as never before, and Indian companies have become major players on the global stage in fields such as information technology, pharmaceuticals, telecommunications and automobiles. The knowledge economy has made knowledge the primary resource of business, and knowledge management has emerged as a vital function. Diversity and cross-cultural management have become essential skills for the modern manager, with frameworks such as Hofstede's cultural dimensions providing useful guidance.

The digital transformation of business is being driven by powerful new technologies—artificial intelligence, big data, the Internet of Things, cloud computing, blockchain, robotics and 5G. India's digital journey, with initiatives such as Digital India, Aadhaar, UPI, ONDC, DigiLocker and a thriving start-up ecosystem, has placed the country at the forefront of the global digital revolution. Green management and sustainable business have moved from the margins to the mainstream, with concerns about climate change, pollution, resource depletion and biodiversity loss reshaping business strategy. India's commitment to net zero by 2070, its leadership of the International Solar Alliance and its Mission LiFE initiative are important contributions to the global effort.

The future of management will be shaped by trends such as hybrid work, AI and automation, lifelong learning, the gig economy, mental health, ESG and stakeholder capitalism, data-driven decisions, diversity and inclusion, sustainable business models, personalised customer experiences, cyber security and innovation. The manager of the future will need a new combination of skills—digital literacy, analytical thinking, emotional intelligence, cultural intelligence, adaptability, ethics, systems thinking, creativity and a spirit of collaboration. The ancient wisdom of India, with its teachings of nishkama karma, dharma and trusteeship, has much to contribute to this evolving field.

Key Terms

Globalisation, WTO, International Management, Multinational Corporation, Modes of Entry, Joint Venture, Knowledge Economy, Knowledge Worker, Explicit Knowledge, Tacit Knowledge, Knowledge Management, DIKW Pyramid, MIS, ERP, CRM, Big Data, Workforce Diversity, Cross-Cultural Management, Hofstede's Dimensions, Power Distance, Cultural Intelligence, Digital Transformation, Artificial Intelligence, Machine Learning, Generative AI, ChatGPT, Big Data Analytics, Internet of Things, Industry 4.0, Cloud Computing, IaaS, PaaS, SaaS, Blockchain, Robotic Process Automation, 5G, Digital India, UPI, Aadhaar, ONDC, DigiLocker, e-NAM, Start-up Ecosystem, Unicorns, Green Management, Sustainable Business, Circular Economy, COP21, COP26, Net Zero 2070, International Solar Alliance, Mission LiFE, OSOWOG, ITC, Tata Power, Adani Green, Hybrid Work, Gig Economy, ESG, Stakeholder Capitalism, Reskilling, Cyber Security, Indian Ethos.

Review Questions

A. Short Answer Questions (2 marks each)

1. Define globalisation.
2. Distinguish between explicit and tacit knowledge.
3. Name any four dimensions of culture given by Hofstede.
4. Expand DMAIC, UPI and ONDC.
5. What is meant by Industry 4.0?
6. Define the circular economy.
7. What is India's commitment regarding net zero emissions?

8. Name any four skills required by the manager of the future.

B. Long Answer Questions (10 marks each)

9. Discuss the meaning, the drivers and the implications of globalisation. How have Indian companies adapted to the global economy?

10. Explain the concepts of knowledge management and information management. Why are they important in the modern economy?

11. Discuss the meaning and the importance of workforce diversity and cross-cultural management. Describe Hofstede's cultural dimensions.

12. Discuss the major technologies driving the digital transformation of business. How is India placed in this digital revolution?

13. Explain the concept of green management. Discuss India's major initiatives towards a sustainable future.

14. Discuss the major trends shaping the future of management and the skills required by the manager of the future.

C. Practical / Case-Based Questions

15. Choose any well-known Indian company that has successfully gone global (such as Infosys, Tata Motors, Sun Pharma or Bharti Airtel) and analyse its journey in terms of the various modes of international entry, the challenges it has faced and the lessons it offers.

16. Imagine that you have to set up a new business in Indore. Discuss how you would incorporate the principles of digital transformation and green management from the very beginning of your enterprise.

— End of the Book —

